PRAISE FOR *KILLER STORY*

"Whenever I would hear about a mysterious murder that had just taken place in Texas, my first thought was always, 'I wonder if Claire is already on the story.' And yes, there she was, hanging out in the offices of the attorneys who were involved in the case, arranging interviews with witnesses, and usually getting an exclusive interview with the murder suspect himself. She was so polite, and yet she had a backbone of steel, leaving the rest of her fellow reporters in the dust. Reading her memoir made me, once again, shake my head in admiration."

–Skip Hollandsworth, *New York Times* bestselling author of *The Midnight Assassin* and executive editor of *Texas Monthly*

"Claire deftly takes readers through the often unbelievable, heart-pounding moments of chasing a competitive true crime story. But just as important as relaying the boots-on-the-ground experiences, with both humility and humanity, Claire gives even deeper insight into the personal challenge of covering these kinds of traumatic cases, the choices journalists—especially women—are often forced to make in order to be considered successful."

–Maureen Maher, award-winning investigative journalist and former *48 Hours* correspondent

"The stories of why and how some people choose to murder other people have captivated humanity for centuries. In *Killer Story*, Claire St. Amant takes us into the inner workings of prime-time true crime television, the most powerful—and profitable—industry telling those stories. From the blood-stained bedrooms to the tension-filled courtrooms to ego-driven newsrooms, Claire weaves a fascinating tale of her journey behind the scenes at one of the world's highest profile true crime broadcasts. Fans of *48 Hours*, *Dateline*, *20/20*, or any number of other popular shows and podcasts will absolutely luxuriate in the details and discoveries she makes along the way."

–Michael J. Mooney, *New York Times* bestselling author of *The Life and Legend of Chris Kyle*

"A bold and candid memoir from a seasoned true crime insider, *Killer Story* is essential reading for aspiring journalists and true crime enthusiasts alike."

–Amanda M. Fairbanks, author of *The Lost Boys of Montauk* and award-winning journalist

"A take-no-prisoners, name-naming inside look at the world of crime television from a veteran producer on the front lines."

–Alec Sirken, Emmy Award–winning producer at CBS News
and former correspondent for NBC News

KILLER
STORY

KILLER
STORY

A Memoir

KILLER STORY

THE TRUTH BEHIND TRUE CRIME TELEVISION

CLAIRE ST. AMANT

BenBella Books, Inc.
Dallas, TX

BenBella Books, Inc.
8080 N. Central Expressway
Suite 1700
Dallas, TX 75206
benbellabooks.com
Send feedback to feedback@benbellabooks.com

BenBella is a federally registered trademark.

Printed in the United States of America
10 9 8 7 6 5 4 3 2 1

Library of Congress Control Number: 2024034197
ISBN 9781637746059 (hardcover)
ISBN 9781637746066 (electronic)

Editing by Rick Chillot
Copyediting by Scott Calamar
Proofreading by Sarah Vostok and Cheryl Beacham
Text design and composition by Aaron Edmiston
Cover design by Faceout Studio, Amanda Hudson
Cover image © Shutterstock / Andrey Sedoy (remote) and Kirill P (knife)
Printed by Lake Book Manufacturing

To Riley, who makes all my dreams possible.
To our son, who is life's greatest gift.

CONTENTS

1

HIDING IN PLAIN SIGHT

I'm standing in front of a judge, in a courtroom deep in the bowels of the Harris County Jail in Houston. My head is down, and my feet are absolutely motionless. Which as a runner, I always find to be a challenge.

I force myself to stare a hole in my shoes rather than look up, where the action is unfolding. I'm not the one on trial. But it feels like that could be the next logical step, given the current predicament.

Although I've never been charged with a crime, I've gotten swept up in investigations a time or two. This is one of those times. Usually I'm excellent at this tightrope walk: I've nearly perfected the balancing act of staying just close enough to a case to understand it intimately, but far enough away not to fall headfirst into legal trouble.

I'm a producer for the true crime television show *48 Hours*, and I've been brought into this closed-door jailhouse hearing by a defense attorney in a capital case: a kidnapping and murder-for-hire conspiracy that made headlines the world over.

The allegations were right out of a Hollywood script: two doctors turned lovers paid a hit man ten thousand dollars to off their exes, so they could avoid child support payments and the rest of the unpleasantness that comes from divorce. They didn't realize their hit man was an undercover Houston Police Department officer, but they should have. What self-respecting hit man would arrange a meeting at an Olive Garden? Or drink a hard lemonade? All the signs of a setup were there, but that's easy for me to say. Hindsight is 20/20, and I got to review the entire discovery in the case ahead of the trial, including all the parties' cell phone dumps. And they were doozies.

I still can't believe sexting is a thing. Don't people realize nothing is private in the digital age?

At this moment in the Harris County Jail, neither the judge nor the prosecution has any idea that a member of the media is present, and I'm not about to volunteer that information. One of the ethical boundaries for US journalists is that you have to identify yourself as such if someone directly asks who you are, but otherwise you're free to observe and report anonymously. I can always distinguish the local media from the national outlets out in the wild by who's wearing a press lanyard. Only the locals make that mistake. Network producers are too smart to give up their camouflage that easily. CBS News standards dictate that I can't lie, but I also don't have to offer up my role unless asked. See what I mean about the tightrope walk?

"And just how did the discovery in this case end up on national television, before trial?" the judge asks sternly.

I study the gray pattern on the jailhouse floor until it blurs, and my hair slips over my face.

He doesn't see me. No one knows who I am. I am invisible.

I squeeze my eyes shut and take a deep breath.

The crazy thing is multiple people in that courtroom *do* know exactly who I am, and that I am responsible for the pre-trial sneak peek. Because the defense attorney, for reasons I still don't understand, is the one who sneaked me into jail in the first place.

Defense attorney George Parnham is a legal legend in Houston. Although his reputation looms large, he's a slight man, with a head of thick white hair and a close beard that covers most of his face. Bespectacled and usually smirking, he speaks with a charming Southern drawl. But don't let his grand-fatherly appearance fool you. Parnham is a talented and shrewd attorney.

He's represented every high-profile murder defendant in Harris County, Texas, for the last twenty-five years. His specialty is crafting convoluted case theories presented with an "aw shucks" believability, somehow making his clients sympathetic in the face of horrendous charges.

Parnham famously represented Andrea Yates, the mother of five who con-fessed to systematically drowning each of her children in the family bath-tub. She was found not guilty by reason of insanity. Then there was Clara Harris, a dentist who admitted to running over her cheating husband in her Mercedes-Benz, twice, in a hotel parking lot. She was facing life in prison but got only twenty years, which is like a speeding ticket in the world of cold-blooded murder.

Early this morning, Parnham himself had ushered me through security, waving away the jailer and calling out, "She's with me!" as he rounded up the actual members of his law firm and hustled me along beside them.

The wheels were set in motion the day before, when I asked Parnham about the next hearing on the docket. It had appeared with an unusual acro-nym beside it, one that I wasn't familiar with yet. After all the time I'd spent in courthouses, I know just enough legal jargon to be dangerous. Sit through three or four criminal trials every year, gavel to gavel, and you pick up a lot by osmosis.

While there are incredibly interesting days in court, including opening arguments and any time the defendant takes the stand, most trial days are mind-numbingly boring. Laying the predicate, establishing expertise, and proving chain of custody for evidence are key parts of any criminal case, but they don't make for good television. To stay awake, I try to guess the objec-tions before the attorneys call them out, or I look for verbal tics and keep a tally. You wouldn't believe how often some people clear their throats when they're nervous, or repeat phrases like "as a matter of course."

Despite my courtroom education, I was at a loss when I looked up the lat-est docket entry for the hit man case on the Harris County website. So I dialed up Parnham's cell and asked him to explain it to me. I think the exact words I used were: "Can you help me solve a mystery?" He was all too happy to decipher the code for me. "It means the hearing is being held in a courtroom inside the jail," he told me.

"Ah," I said. "Mystery solved." Then, just for kicks, I asked if I could come observe. I didn't actually expect him to say yes. About 90 percent of the requests I make to police officers, attorneys, defendants, and witnesses get shot down. But it's the outliers that count and bring me into clandestine courtrooms.

I've learned the best way to blend in when I'm in court is to dress like an attorney. Dark suit, sensible shoes, understated jewelry, and no makeup. No one looks twice at me. I'm one of them. On this day, I blend in so well that the prosecutors a few feet away don't even recognize me, which is particularly amusing as I just interviewed them the week before. But they aren't looking for me here, at an arraignment hearing inside the jail that's not open to the public. They don't expect to see me, and so they don't.

"I need an answer, Counselors," the judge insists, growing impatient. "You are the only two people who should have access to this discovery, and somehow it got to the media."

If I close my eyes, I can still see the evidence he's referring to, laid out on the conference table in Parnham's office. The files are all neatly categorized into folders, a treasure trove hiding in each one.

"I'm going to leave the room now," Parnham told me. "Take as long as you need."

When Parnham politely excused himself with the evidence still on the table, I couldn't believe it was finally happening.

Over the past few months, I'd certainly gotten quite cozy with Parnham. Taking him out to dinner, stopping by his office with coffee, and sending congratulatory messages about his courtroom victories had become routine. In short, I'd been investing considerable effort in our relationship. While I never explicitly asked for favors, I'd hoped my gestures might lead to some reciprocity.

I'd camped out in his lobby for hours that day, patiently waiting for a chance to discuss my repeated request to review the evidence. Half the day had passed with no sign he was giving in. I'd forced myself to appear relaxed, at ease even, with the unknown timeline. Stamina has never been a problem for me. I might not be the first to arrive, but I'll be the last to give up. I found an abandoned newspaper and read it page by page as I reclined on the lobby sofa that day. By the time I finished, Parnham's secretary was standing in front of me. "He'll see you now," she said brightly.

And soon after, I was alone with the files in a glass-lined conference room. I used a spare hard drive and made digital copies of everything, from the body cam footage to the cell phone dumps. I let myself peek at a few choice files just to make sure it was all really there.

I'd pulled off some impressive pre-trial feats in the past, but this was on a whole other level.

Winning over key players in high-profile cases, before they ever went to trial, was becoming something of my specialty. There are months, sometimes years, that go by before a major murder case ever makes it to a jury. And most media play nice and wait for the case to wind through the legal system and get all tied up in a bow at trial. But where's the fun in that?

After years of being corralled like cattle alongside producers from ABC's *20/20* and NBC's *Dateline*, I got wise and changed the game. Now, I went after the attorneys early, before there was even an inkling of a trial date. I'd wine and dine them and be on a first-name basis with their spouses and kids before the competition had looked up the case number.

It didn't always work out perfectly, and many times I'd strike out on my initial strategy and get stuck playing by the same rules as everyone else. But those exceptions that did break my way kept me swinging for the fences. If I played it just right, by the time the case got to trial, I'd already won. And ABC and NBC were left to fight over second place.

The best-case scenario was that I'd score such huge pre-trial interviews that the judge would issue a gag order after our episode aired. That was a real trump card, because I already had my statements on the record. Sealing it just secured my victory in a column no one else could touch.

So in the high-stakes world of true crime television, I often found myself weighing the risks of unbelievable success or epic failure. Time would tell which side of the line I would end up on for this story.

Our pre-trial episode for this case, "Operation Murder," had aired the week before, and the ratings were through the roof. It wasn't every day you got to see police body cam footage of a murder-for-hire sting operation. The midnight arrest in a Houston high-rise apartment was the culmination of weeks' worth of subterfuge, and the video included the defendants kissing each other while in handcuffs.

Thanks to all the cops involved, we got to watch the whole thing play out from seven different angles. And as if that wasn't enough of a coup, I'd actually infiltrated the original investigation and gotten the whistleblower to give us an exclusive interview by flying him and his brother to New York City, all expenses paid.

It was admittedly some of my finest work. But right now, I don't want any credit for it. You couldn't pay me enough to claim it as my own. I just want to get out of this jailhouse courtroom unscathed, with my anonymity intact.

It's true what they say about jail: easy to get in, hard to get out. So I wait, biding my time as the prosecution and defense each try to convince the judge they weren't the leak to the media. One of them is being honest; the other one could be held in contempt of court.

Despite the very real trouble I would face if the judge realized who I am, I can't help but start to enjoy myself just a little bit. I'm running the show, and they think I'm an extra. I really do love my job.

I'm not the kind of person who typically lands a position with the national media in my twenties. I didn't go to an Ivy League school. I'm not even from the East Coast. I'm a Texan, born and raised. My hometown had an outlet mall, a movie theater, Friday night lights, and not much else.

The first time I came to New York alone was for a screening of one of my *48 Hours* episodes. I was so freaked out at the idea of being by myself in the Big Apple that I booked the closest hotel to the CBS Broadcast Center. No one told me it was a shithole next to a methadone clinic. Welcome to New York.

Just a few years into my journalism career, I couldn't have imagined I'd become a producer for CBS News, flying across the country on a moment's notice, with a one-way ticket to the latest national calamity. In 2010, I'd started out on the bottom rung of the journalism ladder as a local newspaper reporter in Dallas. It wasn't a paper you would have actually heard of either. Despite my repeated efforts, the *Dallas Morning News* had declined to hire me. The nickname for the *News*, chiseled into the stone of the building right out front, was "The Rock of Truth." Maybe they could tell I wasn't their type. Don't get me wrong: while I'm unflinchingly honest with my readers and in my reporting, I'm not above a lie of omission here and there to get the story.

And I found my first opportunity to do just that when I got a job at People Newspapers, a chain of weeklies serving the Dallas suburbs. I was a general assignment reporter, and I quickly learned that no good stories are ever handed to you. If I didn't go out and find my own leads, I'd be stuck covering something lame with a press release. A fate worse than death.

My big break in local news was covering a sexual assault case against a prestigious private school in civil court.[1] Somehow, all the reporters at the Rock of Truth missed the memo, and for opening arguments, I was the sole journalist in the courtroom. I've always known a good story when I hear it, and the details coming out in this one were more sensational by the minute. I could hardly keep up with my paper and pen.

I had planned to write my story at the lunch recess, but as I looked around and saw everyone typing away on their phones, I figured, why wait? I whipped out my first-generation iPhone, logged into our CMS, and started filing my story as a live blog entry on our newspaper's fledgling website. I kept my head down and took copious notes, quoting verbatim where I could and paraphrasing the rest.

At lunch, I inhaled a sandwich and called my boss. It was an interesting conversation for several reasons, not the least of which was because he had told me point-blank that I wasn't assigned to the trial. As I braced for a reprimand, he surprised me by talking about how great the traffic had been on our website.

"It's way more than we usually get, like, for the whole month," he told me enthusiastically. "I know I said you couldn't go to the trial, but now I'm telling you that you can't leave that courtroom."

"Yes, sir," I responded. You can get away with a lot if you're polite enough about it.

I raced back into the courthouse and found my seat as the din of legal wrangling played out in the background. I was still logging into the blog when I heard the gavel pound.

---

1 Claire St. Amant, "The ESD Sex Scandal," *D Magazine*, October 2011, https://www.dmagazine.com/publications/d-magazine/2011/october/episcopal-school-of-dallas-sex-scandal/.

"Excuse me, ladies and gentlemen," Judge D'Metria Benson said. "I've just been informed that someone is live blogging these proceedings. And I need that person to stand up and identify themselves immediately."

Everyone looked around for the culprit and blood rushed to my face as I realized it was me. I hesitated for a moment, trying to think of a way out of this public nightmare.

Finding none, and sensing my delay would only make things worse, I stood up and raised my hand.

"Uh, Your Honor, that would be me. Hi there," I said, and immediately regretted the last part.

She waved me forward. "Come on up here, young lady. The rest of you can go. We are now in recess."

I walked up the center aisle as everyone else in the gallery filed out. The way courtrooms are designed, the judge's bench is raised up on a pedestal. They literally look down on you, the people, in judgment. It has the desired effect of being very intimidating.

"Who are you, and what made you think you could live blog my court-room?" she asked me pointedly.

Although it might not look like it, I hadn't come into this trial blindly unprepared. That's not how I operate. I'm a troublemaker, sure, but I'm not haphazard about it. The day before, I had called the court coordinator to introduce myself and ask about any rules for the media covering the trial. Unimpressed, she had told me bluntly, "It's a public courtroom. You can come in and observe just like anybody else. There are no special rules for the media."

Thankfully, I had jotted this down, along with her name, in my reporter's notebook. I flipped back to the page. Then I took a deep breath and responded to the judge, who was still glaring down at me from her perch high on the bench.

"Hi, Your Honor, I'm a reporter for People Newspapers. I'm so sorry if I broke a rule in your courtroom by live blogging. I had no idea it wasn't allowed, because when I called on Friday and talked to Jessica, she told me that this was a public courtroom and there were no special rules for the media. I thought I was allowed to use my phone to do my job, just like I saw everyone else doing."

The judge narrowed her gaze and sized me up. "I thought you were a law firm intern playing *Angry Birds*, not a journalist taking down quotes and putting them on the internet."

"Well, Judge, sorry to disappoint you, but I'm not much of a gamer," I quipped without even thinking.

The attorneys behind me guffawed. I was threatened with contempt of court, but I'd like to think that even the judge realized she didn't really have a case against me. My phone was confiscated, and a new sign appeared at the entrance to the courtroom: "No cell phone use allowed except by attorneys."

That live blogging incident was my first time in front of a judge as a journalist, and I never got comfortable with the feeling.

As counterintuitive as it might seem, anonymity is your friend as a journalist— if you're smart enough to know how to use it.

And back in this jailhouse courtroom in Houston, my secret identity is my only lifeline. I can't believe I'm standing right there as they discuss the "media leak" and how to track it down to the source. Parnham is playing dumb, assuring the judge he has no idea how the evidence ended up on national television. I gotta hand it to him; he's a good actor.

I study scuff marks on my flats while I tick through possible scenarios of being outed. Who would be the most likely culprit for my demise? Surely Parnham wouldn't risk his own skin by revealing who I was, but he did have that whole crazy-like-a-fox thing going on, and I didn't feel like I could rule out the possibility. If there was an opportunity for him to get ahead by throwing me under the bus, I knew he wouldn't hesitate to give me a push.

The prosecution would probably jump at the chance to point out that a member of the media was standing shoulder to shoulder with the defense team, but if they hadn't noticed me by now, it seemed they never would.

My eyes land on the worn-out tennis shoes a few tiles away from me. The ones with the shackles around them. They belong to the defendant, a real piece of work and straight-up psychopath. It was hard to believe that before he was arrested for conspiracy to commit capital murder, he'd been on his way to becoming a transplant surgeon. His phone dump revealed the double life he'd been living. Photos of his kids playing at the park, sprinkled in with lurid texts describing how he wanted his ex-girlfriend kidnapped and tortured.

Dr. Leon Jacob was handsome and came from the kind of privilege that made him believe he could buy his way out of any problem. In other words, he was a total wild card. Without meaning to, I look up at him. He's staring right back at me with a devilish grin. *He's enjoying this.* I watch him chew a contraband piece of gum like a schoolboy. I guess we're all playing fast and loose with the rules on this side of the courtroom.

The first time I met Dr. Jacob, he was just as excited to see me as he appeared to be today, and both times he was behind bars. What was with this guy? Didn't he know he was facing life in prison on rock-solid evidence? But his confidence knew no bounds, and instead of acting contrite and apologetic, Dr. Jacob was positively giddy to have a television producer visiting him in jail.

The day I met him, it was a hundred degrees and dripping humidity in Houston, so I'd broken my cardinal rule about dressing like an attorney. Instead of my usual business suit, I was in a wrinkle-free dress that I'd shoved in my carry-on luggage as I ran out the door to the airport. Dr. Jacob's eyes went straight to my V neckline, and I instinctively put my hand under my chin to block his view.

Despite what you've seen depicted about journalists in TV and movies, I never slept with any of my sources or got anywhere close to something resembling a romantic relationship. I don't know anyone who operated like that. In addition to being morally bankrupt, it's a great way to get fired and never work in the industry again. But why let the truth get in the way of a classic male fantasy of power and seduction? It's a played-out stereotype, and personally, I think the facts are pretty entertaining on their own.

Back in the visitor's room at the jail, Dr. Jacob picked up the black telephone wired to the wall and placed it to his ear. "Claire?" he inquired. "Leon," I replied warmly. "Nice to finally meet you."

We'd already exchanged letters and talked on the phone a half-dozen times before this. I'd taken his jailhouse calls while giving my son a bath, in waiting rooms for appointments, and in the midst of running errands. Jail schedules aren't very conducive to the real world, and the calls only go one way: from the inside out. If you miss the call, it might be days before you get another one. On those always ill-timed calls, I'd act totally unbothered by him interrupting my day, excited even at the privilege of talking to an accused, would-be murderer, as though his collect calls from jail were a delightful addition to my suburban life.

After some small talk, I'd move into the real purpose of the call and pitch him about doing a pre-trial interview for our show. Every letter, conversation, and even this visit was simply a dress rehearsal for the moment I hoped would come one day soon, when he'd actually go on camera.

It doesn't always work out, but my batting average for getting defendants "in the chair," as we TV types call it, was pretty close to perfect. And I'd been on a hot streak lately, scoring two jailhouse interviews in a row leading up to the good doctor. Could I extend my run to three?

It had taken months, but I finally got face-to-face with him, which really is half the battle. I'm so much better in the room than on the phone. We had an hour for our visit, so I spent the first thirty minutes just shooting the shit with him, laughing at all his jokes, and acting generally impressed with whatever drivel came out of his murderous mouth. He ate up the attention. He asked me if I'd ever watched *Orange Is the New Black* on Netflix, and then he waved his hands in protest as I started to tell him about the latest episodes.

"No spoilers!" he said with a laugh.

My God, I thought, *he really thinks he's getting out of here. That's some high-level delusion.*

But as the clock ticked past the halfway point of our visit, I knew I had to get down to business. I sized him up; what particular pitch would appeal to this brand of rich-kid megalomaniac?

Should I make him my white knight, rescuing me from getting fired by missing out on a key interview? Or should I go for the classic "Everyone's talking but you, and I'd hate to see you get left out of the show when you have such an important story to tell."

Decisions, decisions. As it turned out, I didn't have to sell him on the idea at all. By the end of the visit, he had booked himself.

"So when are you coming back for my interview, with the cameras and stuff?" he asked me. "I want to tell my side of the story."

I smiled back at him. "What are you doing later this week?"

I made the interview arrangements through the Harris County Jail and got permission to bring in a dress shirt so Dr. Jacob would look presentable.

Despite the catchy title of the Netflix series, no one looks good in an orange jumpsuit.

A few days later it was lights, camera, action. And once you have the defendant in the chair, the rest of the interviews fall into place. The prosecution was all too happy to play ball when they found out the defense was talking. The way they saw it, we were doing their pre-trial homework for them. It was a win-win situation.

Peter Van Sant interviews Leon Jacob, a coup for *48 Hours* that put me in some hot water.

That is, until the judge saw the episode and feared the trial would turn into a media circus. And, well, he wasn't wrong.

So, fast-forward, I'm in the jail courtroom, with a front-row seat to the attorney acrobatics. And while it's been entertaining, I'm ready for the curtain to fall.

The longer this discussion goes on, the more concerned I'm getting that the judge is going to ask all the parties to identify themselves for the record. That's usually a perfunctory item on the hearing agenda, just something to make the court reporter's life easier. But in this case, it would be a bombshell. I wouldn't be able to hide my identity if directly asked by the judge. I would have to out myself and face the consequences.

I feel my heart racing, and I worry that my pounding chest is visible to the naked eye. I start counting my breaths like I'm running hills. I lull myself into a sense of tranquility as I wait for what feels like the inevitable instruction to identify myself.

But mercifully, it never comes. I am so deep into my own head that I don't even hear the judge adjourn the hearing. I just see everyone gathering up their belongings and shuffling out of the courtroom. I quickly get in step behind them and begin plotting my escape.

I scan the concrete walls for the bright red EXIT letters that spell my freedom. As I catch sight of them around the corner, I have to stop myself from breaking into a jog. Looking back at Parnham, I call out, "I'll catch up to you outside," trying to make the words come out as casually as possible. Then I dart down the hallway.

The jailer smiles as he buzzes me through the iron bars.

"Anxious to get outta here, huh?" he says playfully. "You must be a new attorney."

I smile back at him and remain silent as I walk out of the Harris County Jail, a free woman once again.

2
FIRST KILL

Four years earlier

I'm sitting in the lobby of the Keller Police Department, nervously fiddling with a personal check for $112. It's three times the approved budget for a story at the start-up news website where I now work, CultureMap Dallas, and I'm not sure it'll all get reimbursed.

From the looks of it, the Keller Police Department doesn't get much action. The floors are gleaming, the windows are spotless, and there are four rows of perfectly straight blue chairs, all empty, save for mine. At this point in my young career, I haven't been in many police departments yet. But even to a rookie crime reporter, the cleanliness of the facility sticks out.

As I'm guessing how long I'll have to wait for someone to respond to the buzzer I rang, a woman slides open a partition to speak to me. "How can I help you, ma'am?"

I tell her my name and that I'm here to pick up the records I'd requested in the Michele Williams case. Then I hand her my check, where I'd written out the case number in the memo line. She looks it over and smiles back at me.

"I'll have this right out," she says.

I return to my seat and wonder if it can really be this simple. The records in question are part of an open criminal case, a murder charge that was knocked down to something called "deadly conduct" in a plea deal. I had read about the unusual charges in a scant story that ran in the *Dallas Morning News* a few weeks earlier.[2]

According to the article, Michele Williams, forty-four, was pleading guilty to shooting her husband, Greg, while he was lying in bed in 2011. In exchange for her cooperation, Michele was being sentenced to eighteen years for charges of evidence tampering and "deadly conduct." The crime had originally been investigated as a home invasion, and Michele herself had been the one to call 911. Now she was admitting she was the one behind the trigger, and for some reason she was being given leniency. The October article stated that the sentencing wouldn't take place until April, for reasons that were not explained. It was all so bizarre. I just stared at the article and wondered how someone at the Rock of Truth could publish a story with so many unanswered questions.

As the managing editor for CultureMap Dallas, a big part of my job is staying on top of the news cycle in one of the biggest cities in the country. I start my day by scanning the front pages of both major papers, the *Dallas Morning News* and the *Fort Worth Star-Telegram*. And I listen to the local public radio station on my sunrise run. By 8 AM I'm at my desk, fully read into the day and planning out our editorial coverage.

There are the big stories that everyone will cover, and I make sure we aren't left out of the conversation. But my favorite thing to do is find the story that had slipped off everyone's radar and to put it on ours. The story of Michele Williams jumped out at me as just such an opportunity.

The details of the case were tantalizing, and I was left with three key questions: Who gets a plea deal for murder in Texas? Why is her prison sentence being delayed by seven months? And what in the world is "deadly conduct"?

Apparently I was the only one asking these questions. Because when I did a little digging, there was very little additional reporting on the mysterious death of Greg Williams, who I learned was a wealthy tech entrepreneur.

2   Matt Peterson, "Keller woman faces 18 years for shooting husband, trying to cover up crime," *Dallas Morning News*, October 9, 2013, https://www.dallasnews.com/news/crime/2013/10/09/keller-woman-faces-18-years-for-shooting-husband-trying-to-cover-up-crime/.

According to the district attorney's office, Michele was pregnant with twins, and that's why the state had agreed to delay her prison sentence. My curiosity was now at a fever pitch.

When I had taken the position as managing editor at CultureMap, I had carved out space for investigative reporting in my job responsibilities. After seeing my reporting on the private school sex scandal and the complicated civil trial, the founders of CultureMap had approached me about joining the team and shaping the brand of the new Dallas site.

I had been happy enough at People Newspapers, and my risk-taking coverage had led to a local magazine cover story and a promotion at the paper. Did I really want to leave the newsroom that had rewarded my hard work? But in the end, the lure of a new challenge and the opportunity to run a nimble news site was too tempting to pass up. As managing editor, I was in charge of three staff writers, a small army of freelance writers, and I still got to select and report my own daily stories.

A news website runs on a steady stream of fresh content, and we always had to feed the beast. But I knew that truly original reporting, the kind that makes an impact and changes the conversation, is worth doing. And so I'd made a point of keeping space on my calendar for long-range, investigative pieces. Sometimes that space was on nights and weekends, but I didn't let it slip off my schedule. I knew that if I did, I'd end up spending years just churning out a bunch of nothingburger stories and listicles; you know, those "articles" that are really lists written in paragraph form.

You could fill a journalism career with that kind of reporting and pay the bills. But I wanted to do more than just chase the news cycle and cash my check. As I read and reread that summary of the Michele Williams case, I had the sneaking feeling that there was so much more to the story than two hundred words. I cracked my knuckles and got to work.

First, I found out that "deadly conduct" was a rare felony charge that existed only in Texas and Louisiana. It was basically created for the reckless handling of a firearm that accidentally resulted in death. The most common example I found was cleaning a gun in the presence of another person—and being negligent enough to kill someone in the process.

That didn't seem at all to fit the circumstances of Greg Williams's death or the alleged behavior of his wife, Michele. She was accused of shooting him with his own gun, staging the scene to look like a home invasion, dousing the gun in bleach, and then calling 911. At no point did any of Michele's behavior sound like an accident.

Just who was this woman? I needed some concrete records to find out. I went online and searched for the marriage license for Greg and Michele Williams to get Michele's maiden name. When I ran a new search, I learned that wasn't her maiden name after all. She'd been married three times in total. This was really getting good. Where were these former husbands? And would they talk to me?

It took a couple days to find contact information for them, and even then, all I could track down was a mailing address for her second husband. I dropped a letter in the mail with my cell phone number and hoped for the best.

Meanwhile, I learned from Greg's obituary that he'd also been married before, and he had a teenage daughter from a previous relationship. I followed the trail to Greg's ex-wife, Kathy Williams, who had an active social media presence. I messaged her on Facebook and got a near-immediate response.

The stories she told me were jaw-dropping. Michele had apparently concocted elaborate schemes for years, faking pregnancies and lying about her own children's paternity. There were also allegations that she'd been unfaithful to Greg with multiple men. But could this just be the words of a jealous ex-wife? How could I corroborate Kathy's claims?

I wouldn't have to question the accuracy of Kathy's statements for long. Just twenty-four hours after mailing a letter to Michele's (second) ex-husband, my cell phone rang. The man on the other end of the line described a chaotic relationship dating back to their childhood and asked that I not use his real name.

According to him, when they got married, Michele had lied about nearly everything, from her job to the fact that she was still married to her first husband. He said that Michele seemed to have a special power over men. He called her "a professional manipulator."

He told stories of Michele growing up in the small town of Hurst, Texas. He said her father would jump in front of cars and attempt to collect insurance payments, and he believed that was where she'd first learned the art of the con. It was just one of many schemes Michele's family was accused of running over the years. But even though he knew she was no good, husband number two fell head over heels for Michele's charms and her three adorable children.

It was an instant family, but the marriage wouldn't last. The beginning of the end was when a neighbor tipped the man off to frequent visitors at the house when he was at work. Suspicious, he set up an audio recorder and hid it in their bedroom. He said it captured evidence of Michele having two affairs in a single afternoon. Soon after that, he demanded a divorce.

In the days that followed, Michele's ex-husband said, she went into a rage, pouring Comet in his expensive saltwater fish tank and drugging his dalmatian before convincing a local vet to put it down. I was shocked at these allegations, but her ex-husband wasn't. He actually seemed amused as he told me that I hadn't even scratched the surface of how diabolical Michele was.

While most of these allegations were impossible to fact-check, I knew there were some key details I needed to pin down before running with the story. After I got off the phone with him, I went to the Hurst Public Library and found yearbooks with Michele and her first husband smiling back at me. That was the moment that I knew I had my first killer story, and I wasn't going to stop until I told the whole thing.

The next few weeks were a blur. I was meeting sources in parking lots, submitting open records requests, and spending all my free time writing the twisted story of Michele Williams.

Through Greg's first wife, Kathy, I learned that Michele had been the one behind Greg's cremation, which had been performed almost immediately after the body was released from the coroner. And perhaps even more disturbing, I learned of a second man in Michele's orbit who had died of a single gunshot wound to the head just ten months earlier. He was also promptly cremated at her direction.

In December 2010, Brynn Fletcher, who was both married to Greg's sister and an integral part of Greg's computer company, died from what appeared to be a self-inflicted gunshot wound to the head. His body was discovered in a company truck, parked just off the shoulder in a no-man's-land south of Dallas. The location, though seemingly random, was en route to a prepro-grammed GPS destination in Waco; Michele Williams, then the office manager of the computer company, had reportedly entered the address for Brynn.

Adding to the confusion in the case was the fact that Brynn Fletcher's wife is also named Michelle. Michelle Fletcher believed this allowed Michele Williams to slip in as the key point of contact with police in the case and assume the duties of next of kin that should have fallen to his wife, not his sister-in-law.

The nineteen-page police file on Brynn Fletcher's death offered more questions than answers about the basic facts of the case, such as the location of the gunshot wound. One report says right eye; another says mouth. The medical examiner's report says Brynn was shot in the center of his forehead.

The final police report pronouncing "case closed" says Brynn used his right hand to shoot himself in the right eye. But Brynn was left-handed.

It seems we'll never get any clarity on the actual entry of the bullet, in large part due to Michele Williams.

"She had my husband cremated so fast, the ink hadn't even dried on his autopsy report," Michelle Fletcher told me.

But very few people, including me, knew about this shocking series of events back in the fall of 2013, when I was just beginning to dig into the sordid past of Michele Williams.

As I sit waiting in the pristine lobby of the Keller Police Department, Michele's plea deal in Greg Williams's death isn't even final yet. The case against her is technically still open. It's a detail that seemed to have slipped past everyone.

A journalist has the right to request information from the police and the courts at any time. It is the responsibility of law enforcement and attorneys to know what is releasable by law, and when it is required to be handed out and kept private. In other words, it's never a crime to ask for something. And I ask a lot. The worst that can happen is to be told no. The second worst is to have your request filled and then later get slapped with a subpoena. But that's a problem for another day.

After sending in the request to the records department at the Keller Police Department, I'd followed up several times by phone and email. I was as surprised as anyone when I finally received a response telling me the records could be produced for the tidy sum of $112. It was a small price to pay to peel back the curtain on a mysterious murder, but it was also way more than I knew CultureMap would approve for a single story.

We were a start-up website that didn't always make payroll. We were allotted thirty dollars in expenses per story, including mileage. Many stories didn't require me to leave my desk. I could write them by working the phones and fact-checking details online. But those story budgets didn't carry over, so I was already pushing it and likely funding the story on my own for the foreseeable future.

A former Peace Corps Volunteer, I'd learned how to live on a shoestring budget; I was no stranger to dipping into my own pocket to finance projects that I believed in. So I didn't even consider waiting for approval. I just looked at the balance in my bank account and knew the check wouldn't bounce. That was all the permission I needed in my twenties.

I never expected to make any real money in journalism. Back then, I couldn't have dreamed of the six-figure budgets that awaited me in network television, and the seven-figure profits the execs were all pulling down. The truth is, there is a ridiculous amount of money floating around in the media. It just rarely goes to the people actually writing and producing the content.

It's all about ownership and IP (intellectual property), and most reporters sign that all away the day they take the job, without so much as a second thought as to where the money is flowing. I should know. I used to be one of them, just happy to have a somewhat steady paycheck and a place to post my byline. Editorial control was the highest premium I could imagine, and I had it in spades at CultureMap. If I could find the time to write it, they would publish it. In other words, my dream job.

Back in the lobby, I run the $112 check back and forth through my fingers, making little ocean waves and imagining the ripple effect of getting access to this report. I still feel like it could come crashing down at any moment. I give myself fifty-fifty odds that the person who returns to the window will be empty-handed and deliver a line about not being able to release records in an active investigation. "Sorry for the miscommunication," I might expect to hear, if I even get an apology at all.

In the middle of my daydream, the partition slides back open. A woman smiles at me and extends a sealed white folder with my name written in cursive on it.

I practically leap from my chair to claim it. A few forms later and I'm speed walking to the parking lot. I punch my office address into the GPS and realize it's over thirty minutes away. No chance I'm waiting that long to read this treasure trove.

Pulled over at a gas station, I rip open the envelope and thumb through over a hundred pages of written reports. There were also CDs with evidence that I'd dig into once I was back at a computer.

I start reading, captivated by the details. I'm not sure how much time I've been parked at this gas station, but when someone raps their knuckles on my window and asks if I'm "going to buy gas or what?" I know it's time to leave.

So I dog-ear my progress on the report and drive off into the dipping afternoon sun. I have a long night ahead of me, and I couldn't be happier about it if someone gave me all the money in the world.

The day my Michele Williams story hit the internet,[3] I could already see we were riding a new kind of reporting wave. Our traffic was climbing steadily, and the links were piling up. Pretty soon, the story was being picked up by our competitors and repackaged to look like they'd been on the inside track all along. Imitation is the sincerest form of flattery, and I relished being ripped off by bigger outlets. By virtue of using pseudonyms for Michele's family members, no one could figure out how to land their own interviews with the real people fast enough. They were forced to quote my reporting and link back to CultureMap if they wanted to include all the layers of the story in their initial reporting.

As the weeks ticked by, our coverage was still leading the pack. Then the calls started coming in from New York. NBC's *Dateline* was the first to find me, and I almost fell victim to a classic predatory play.

The associate producer who got me on the phone was a smooth talker, and she was laying the compliments on thick and rich. I was eating up the attention, then came the real purpose of her call. "This story is so good, it's actually unbelievable," she said, baiting me.

"Thanks," I replied, still clueless.

"The thing is, my senior producer won't let us run with it without seeing the source material to back it up. The talk is that you probably exaggerated

3   Claire St. Amant, "The Making of the Keller Black Widow," CultureMap Dallas, October 31, 2013, https://dallas .culturemap.com/news/city-life/10-31-13-keller-black-widow-michele-williams-murder-husband-greg.

the claims and won't actually have the documentation to prove it up. To go any further, we have to review the original reports ourselves."

After I'd gotten the Keller Police Department to fulfill my request, they'd been inundated with calls from the media writ large. But the thing about open records laws is that the agency has ten business days before they have to respond to a new request. At that point, they can challenge the validity of the request and restart the clock, or they can kick the request up to the attorney general of Texas for a ruling. And that takes at least thirty days.

All the news outlets from Dallas to New York were chasing my reporting and trying to source it. The Keller Police Department was not accustomed to media attention, and their response was to hit the pause button. At this point, the story was already everywhere, but the original source material was only in my hands. How much trouble could one local journalist cause? We were all about to find out together.

Having the validity of your work questioned by the national media was a new experience for me. And it hit my ego like a ton of bricks. My immediate reaction was to fire up my laptop and start digitizing the reports.

She thinks I'm a fraud? I'll show her.

I actually loaded all the attachments to an email, and was just about to hit send, when a wave of doubt washed over me. My reporter's gut instinct kicked in, and I knew what I had to do. This producer wasn't my friend. In fact, she was my worst enemy, deftly working against me while appearing to be on my side. If she had all my source documents, she wouldn't need me at all.

I almost got played for a fool.

My pulse was still racing as I deleted each attachment and then the entire body of the email.

I stared at my blank cursor and then fired off a very different missive.

"Thanks for your call today. I'm confident in my reporting. And it's proprietary. Appreciate your interest in the story that I dug up. Hope you find your own one day." Send.

I shared my experience with some more seasoned colleagues, and they all gave me the same advice: steer clear of television producers. They are sharks, I was warned, and will stop at nothing when they smell blood. The phrase "If it bleeds, it leads" never had a truer meaning.

Calls from ABC's *20/20* started coming in next, and I was in no mood to play games. I listened to their full pitch and took notes, mostly for my own edification but also because I wanted a record of the conversation. When the producer finished, I politely declined to participate in their reporting and wished them luck. There was silence on the other end of the line. "Do you realize what an opportunity you are passing up?" he asked incredulously.

"I don't trust TV journalists, especially ones from New York," I replied. "There's too much risk and no guarantee of a reward."

With that thinly veiled reference to money, they were out the door. It told me everything I needed to know about their business model and the true nature of their interest in my reporting. I suppose I couldn't blame them, but it's not my problem they couldn't land their own story.

Media giants thwarted, I continued to study Michele Williams's web of lies. Through my sources, I got word that the district attorney's office in Fort Worth was considering taking their plea deal with Michele off the table for her husband's death.

Apparently, Michele's alleged pregnancy with twins had never been medically verified. This was the reason her attorneys had given as to why she needed to be out on bond while awaiting sentencing. Now the prosecutors were questioning if she'd made it all up.

Despite a "high risk pregnancy," GPS data from her court-mandated ankle monitor showed she'd never once been at the coordinates of a doctor's office. She'd been out on bond for eight months.

While Michele wasn't getting any pregnancy checkups, she was making regular visits to other establishments: strip clubs and an aerobics studio. The evidence was right there, buried in the technical data that no one was monitoring. Michele was holding down multiple jobs that showcased her physique, which made the pregnancy even more unbelievable. I'm still not sure how she managed her wardrobe as an exotic dancer, but I know for a fact she was teaching fitness classes in bell-bottom workout pants to hide her ankle monitor.

That's because she was profiled in the *Fort Worth Star-Telegram* for owning her own business.[4] She used the name "Shelley," and no one at the

---

4 "Michele Williams teaching Kettle Bell fit classes." YouTube video, 1:04. Posted by *Fort Worth Star-Telegram*, March 7, 2014, https://www.youtube.com/watch?v=usaX15ZLp2I.

paper had realized her true identity. That is, until my story came out and they updated the headline on YouTube as clickbait.

I had just left the courthouse and popped over to McDonald's to use the free internet when my phone rang with a 212 area code. New York digits. *This should be a good one.*

A deep voice greeted me: "This is Ryan Smith with CBS News *48 Hours*; I'm trying to reach Claire St. Amant about the Michele Williams story."

I closed my eyes and laughed silently before responding. This guy was late to the party, and I was in no mood to hear another sycophantic pitch that was really an attempt to steal my reporting. I decided to cut him off before he got any further down the script.

"Look, Ryan, I get what you're trying to do. I've already been contacted by *Dateline* and *20/20*. My story is out there for everyone to read online. I don't see the benefit of doing TV."

I was about to hang up when Ryan jumped in with the magic words I didn't know I'd been waiting to hear.

"What if I could show you the benefits? Are you free for dinner this weekend?" he asked boldly.

"I'm a married woman," I said in disbelief.

"Great, bring your husband. What's your favorite restaurant in Dallas?" Ryan said without missing a beat.

Like many couples, my husband, Riley, and I are a true case of opposites attract. To borrow a true crime cliché, I'm the extrovert who never met a stranger. And he's the introvert who would rather not meet anyone at all. I was drawn to his quiet confidence and enigmatic personality from the moment we bumped into each other in an upper-level writing class at Baylor University. His apparent aloofness toward me was irresistible, and his intelligence was immediately obvious. Piercing blue eyes and a deep stare that tells you he isn't missing a thing by not speaking up.

We were paired together in a group project based on alphabetic groupings of our last names, and we exchanged cell phone numbers. Fate stepped in and gave us a lame duck third group member who never showed up to any of our late-night study sessions. My friends think Riley paid him off to stay away, and I wouldn't put it past him. When I mention it to this day, he just smiles back at me, happy to leave the mystery intact. We really are two different sides of the same coin.

The first two years I knew Riley, we were always dating other people. We kept up the "just friends" charade even though we both felt something more was brewing. The summer before my senior year at Baylor, we were finally single at the same time. I had gone through a series of short, frustrating relationships with guys who all seemed to have a lot of opinions on how I should live my life. As someone who had given my own future a great deal of thought, it was astounding to me how many dudes assumed I would leave my plans in the dust to follow them.

At this point, I had already been accepted to the Peace Corps upon graduation. I was just waiting to find out my country assignment, and I couldn't have been clearer about how excited I was for this next phase of my life. And yet, every guy I dated before Riley tried to talk me out of it. They couldn't imagine being in a relationship with someone who planned to live halfway around the world. I had known these guys for a matter of months, and they expected me to change my whole life plan for them? I couldn't show them the door fast enough.

So when I started dating Riley, I had convinced myself it would be a summer fling and nothing more. I'd accepted the fact that no guy was going to understand my ambition or respect that I had my own dreams to pursue. I can still remember the moment that I realized Riley was cut from different cloth. We were sitting on his hand-me-down couch, his black Lab sleeping under our feet. We'd had another marathon date on one of those perfect summer days that never seems to end. And then the topic turned to post-graduation plans. I felt a twinge in my chest because I didn't want to break up even a little bit, but I figured the next words out of my mouth would spell our demise as a couple.

I told him I'd been accepted to the Peace Corps, and after graduation I was going to teach English somewhere in the developing world, exact location unknown. His response caught me completely by surprise.

"Wow, that's great!" he said without a shred of resentment. "I'm really happy for you."

We were inseparable for the rest of the summer and as it turns out, made to stand the test of time and distance. Three months into my service in Ukraine, Riley flew halfway around the world with a ring in his pocket and proposed. Watching his plane take off and fly back to the US was agony. But I knew we'd have the rest of our lives to be together. And a year later, I joined him back in Texas, where we've happily made our home together ever since.

As time goes on, I realize even more how lucky I am to have Riley by my side. It's not as though we never disagree or have frustrations as a couple, but that underlying respect for each other's dreams and the willingness to sacrifice to make them happen is a rare quality that I hope I never take for granted. We're true partners, and our differences are complementary strengths.

Meeting new people is energizing to me, and I can easily get attached and begin to trust and build a relationship almost immediately. Riley, on the other hand, is much more discerning. His go-to mode is distrust. He really makes you earn his approval. It's why I love bringing him along to important meetings, even though he'd like nothing more than to stay far, far away. I use him sparingly, and I knew the Ryan Smith meeting was one of those rare opportunities to get Riley in the chair.

We chose Mi Cocina, our favorite Mexican restaurant in Dallas. I couldn't believe a producer from New York was flying across the country to buy me enchiladas. But just days after speaking for the first time, Ryan Smith was standing in front of me. At six feet, seven inches, he cuts an imposing figure. A corn-fed boy from Ohio with a degree from Columbia is a dangerous combination, and Ryan worked every bit of the small-town charm and big-city smooth talking.

He listened just as much as he talked, and when I expressed my concerns that I was handing over the keys for the national media to hijack my story, he said the words that changed the trajectory of my whole career.

"We don't want to do this story without you. We want to partner with you on it and give you a contract for the episode."

I was stunned. I hadn't even considered that such a level of equal footing was possible. Reading the temperature of the moment perfectly, Ryan excused himself to use the bathroom and left Riley and me to talk things over in private.

As soon as he disappeared around the corner, I turned to Riley and asked the million-dollar question. "Do you trust him?"

Riley didn't hesitate to give his approval, which has only happened a handful of times in the fifteen-plus years that we've been together. I took it as a very good sign, and when Ryan returned to the table, we all raised our margarita glasses to the promise of a new partnership.

The consultant contract took a few more weeks to iron out, and I was actually standing in the vacant house we had just made a lowball offer on when CBS business affairs called to confirm that the paperwork was awaiting my signature. At first, I wasn't sure which contract was going through, the house or my new gig with the national media.

It was a whirlwind of good fortune, and I couldn't believe the timing. One minute I'm working for a start-up that white knuckles it every payroll period and living in a split-level duplex. Next, I'm approved for a mortgage on a three-bedroom house and signing a contract with CBS News. I still had my job at CultureMap, and I was all too happy to have a backup source of income as a safety net for this next stage of life. It was the beginning of my new mode of operating, and for the next ten years, I'd always have at least two jobs to pay the bills. In the world of media, options and editorial variety are worth their weight in gold.

Now that I had the contract, the real work could begin. I had no idea how much time actually went into an hour of television, but I was about to learn. The first order of business was to get CBS up to speed with my reporting and read into the case. I compiled all my notes and gave them the full police file on Michele Williams, or at least I thought I did.

Turns out, because I wasn't working in television a few short months ago when I'd made the open records request, I had neglected to list the video files. As a print reporter, the written reports and audio interviews were totally sufficient to tell the story. But now the TV producers were asking for everything. It wasn't enough to have the still photos and 911 call.

I frowned at the idea of going back to the same public information officer at the Keller Police Department. She would surely remember me and not be thrilled at the firestorm of media coverage my story had set off. I shared my hesitation with Ryan, and he was happy to help. Since we already had the bulk of the evidence, all he needed to do was make a narrow request for the video files.

He jumped into action and onto the phone, quickly learning that the biggest obstacle in the request was the size of the video files. It would take forever to burn them all to discs, which is actually still the method of delivery at most police departments. Since money is no object for an outlet like CBS, Ryan simply whipped out his American Express business card and shipped the police department a $150 external hard drive, along with a written request as required by the Public Information Act. They'd have the video files ready in ten business days, perfect timing because there was a hearing scheduled in Michele's case for that same week.

Around this same time, I was introduced to the role of senior producer, which I learned was the TV version of a project manager. There are only a handful of them on staff at 48 Hours, and each one has a distinct personality and working style. The only consistency across the board is that they never leave New York. The highest-ranking senior producers were Judy Tygard, who had created her own 48 Hours miniseries called Live to Tell, and Anthony Batson, an Aussie turned New Yorker with a real affinity for Texas true crime. Batson was assigned as the senior producer for the Michele Williams episode, and while I didn't know it then, it was the first of many wild murder stories we'd work on together.

Ryan flew down from New York with a full team, including longtime producer Alec Sirken and his favorite correspondent, Peter Van Sant. They hit the ground running, setting up calls and meetings and dinner reservations from the moment they touched down in Texas. It was a whirlwind of activity, and I was right in the thick of it with them.

They asked for introductions to my sources, and I dialed them up. My main source had been Greg's first wife, Kathy Williams. She was the one who first told me about Michele's troubled background and the damage left in her wake from past relationships. Kathy agreed to meet with CBS, and she brought along her teenage daughter, Taylor, who was Greg's child.

Over a steak dinner, Kathy and Taylor agreed to do an on-camera interview later that week. They also opened the door to introduce us to Michele's side of the family, including her adult sons and her sister. It was all falling into place, and the team hadn't even been in town for twenty-four hours. But CBS had their sights on an even bigger "get" than those interviews. They wanted to interview Michele herself.

At least they knew where to find her. After my investigative series ran, Michele's bond had been revoked, and she was sitting in the Tarrant County jail. Authorities quickly realized she'd never been pregnant with twins. Ever the actress, Michele had actually tried to fake a miscarriage from behind bars, asking for maxi pads while screaming and crying from her cell. A jailer would later recall the whole scene in court, as the prosecution presented evidence that Michele's original pregnancy documentation had been forged. The exact sonogram image she provided was accessible under a basic Google search.

This was news to Michele's lover, who testified he'd framed the sonogram and kept it by his bedside for the past eight months. Michele was shameless, and she kept up the charade, insisting she'd been pregnant and miscarried despite zero evidence of either event. A pathological liar like this is TV gold, and CBS couldn't wait to put their request in to interview Michele from jail.

When you are awaiting a hearing to approve a plea deal for murder, I wouldn't recommend sitting down with the media. But Michele had no hesitation. I think the district attorney was just as interested to hear what Michele would say as we were, so the office didn't block the request.

"TV time," as it's called, runs about triple what you'd expect in real life. Need to interview someone for an hour? Plan for it to take the better part of the afternoon. And *48 Hours* correspondent Peter Van Sant was legendary for his lengthy interview style at CBS News. He'd chat easily with people for four or five hours, never wavering in his congeniality or interest. The crew, meanwhile, would be shifting on their feet, exhausted from holding camera positions and keeping focus the whole time.

Once, Peter was interviewing a detective and had instructed him to keep his posture steady so the framing wouldn't change. The poor detective didn't move a muscle the whole interview, and when Peter finally ended it, the detective shot up from his chair and screamed in agony. His leg had fallen asleep, and he'd been in pain for several hours. We never let Peter forget that one, and he wore it like a badge of honor.

Michele's interview was scheduled for the next available evening. Many jailhouse interviews are conducted at night, when everyone else is locked down in their cells. This allows more jailers to observe the interview and keep an eye on the inmate in question, since we usually request they are uncuffed and allowed to dress in civilian clothes. This creates a big security risk and so the police presence is heavy.

Michele's interview was no exception, even though they didn't allow her to change out of her yellow jumpsuit or remove her leg shackles. She was permitted to wear makeup, however, and she chose bright red lipstick for the occasion. (Fun fact: inmates don't usually have access to makeup, so they get creative with items from the commissary, such as using the red dye from Skittles as lipstick.) It was a bizarre scene, with Michele under camera lights inside an otherwise pitch-black conference room after hours at the jail. Peter Van Sant sat across from her, beaming. Jailers surrounded her on each side, watching and listening carefully to her every word.

It was quite a show, and Michele didn't fail to entertain. Although she had a plea deal alleging that she'd accidentally shot her husband and then cleaned up the scene in a moment of panic, now she shifted the storyline.

With cameras rolling, Michele told Peter she hadn't shot her husband at all. There had actually been a masked man in black who came in and shot her husband, and she was taking the fall for him out of fear. Fear also propelled her to clean up the scene to protect the real shooter's involvement, so he wouldn't come after her and her daughter. Peter pressed Michele on the mystery shooter's identity, and although she demurred at first, she eventually laid it out plainly. She believed the killer had been her own son.

It sounded sensational—a big reveal. But everyone in that room knew not to believe Michele's latest yarn; this was actually the third story Michele had spun about her husband's death. In another version, she'd told police that Greg shot himself, and she was covering up the suicide so she could claim his life insurance.

Her narrative was constantly changing, and each tale was equally problematic. There'd been no evidence of an outside intruder, despite canvassing the area with a canine unit and checking for signs of forced entry.

The shooter had come from inside the home; this much was clear. The suicide theory held water for a few weeks, until the autopsy report came back and showed the bullet was fired from at least twelve inches away from Greg's head. Hard to imagine anyone contorting their own arm into that position for a fatal shot. Left with no more options, Michele had then claimed it had all been a terrible accident and begged for mercy for the sake of her unborn children. It was a pretty impressive web of lies, and she nearly got away with a slap on the wrist. If only she could have stopped talking.

Despite Michele's bombshell jailhouse interview, the plea deal was technically still intact. No matter what you admit to a journalist or anyone else, the court has the final say. Since we weren't the local news, our interview with Michele hadn't aired yet. No one outside the jail and the DA's office knew that she'd changed her story and potentially jeopardized her plea deal.

Most importantly, the Keller Police Department had no idea about the development. They were still treating the case as though it was closed and had promised to have our hard drive full of video evidence ready the same morning as the hearing. An associate producer headed to the suburbs to pick up the loot, and Ryan and I headed to the Tarrant County district courthouse. From the outside, it still looked like a perfunctory plea deal hearing. But we knew better than to believe the listing on the docket.

The way courthouses are structured in Texas, the most serious cases are heard on the top floors. Word to the wise: If you get into a courthouse elevator and someone hits a double-digit number, they aren't there for a speeding ticket.

Michele's hearing was being conducted in the penthouse, and the courtroom was packed for the occasion. Judge Scott Wisch was presiding, and he was in no mood for games. He pounded his gavel, and the din of onlookers went silent.

The judge got down to business and spoke directly to Michele, telling her that it didn't matter what she'd said to the media. What mattered was the official court record, and as of now, there was still a plea deal in place. She meekly nodded her understanding before taking the stand for questioning by the prosecution.

In a normal plea deal hearing, the defendant doesn't even formally testify. She simply stands before the judge and raises her right hand to swear to the facts previously agreed upon. It's a brief, boring affair and ends with some signatures and a handshake. But this was not a normal day in court.

As the prosecutor began questioning Michele about what version of events she wanted the court to believe, she started to cry. Or at least she made the sounds and put her hands to her face. I couldn't help but notice her cheeks never got wet and her nose wasn't running. It seemed it was all part of the show, and our cameras were rolling. Although Judge Wisch gave her every opportunity to retreat to the safety of her plea deal, Michele was now adamant there had been an intruder in the house that night, and that mystery man was the real killer.

Flabbergasted, Judge Wisch delivered a searing assessment. "Lady Justice may very well be blind, but she is neither deaf nor dumb." Then he threw out the plea deal and set the case for trial. Instead of a maximum sentence of eighteen years, of which Michele would only be guaranteed to serve nine, she was now facing up to life in prison.

In disbelief, we gathered our belongings and headed out of the courtroom as Michele was led away in handcuffs. Downstairs in the lobby, we spotted our associate producer and asked the all-important question: Did you pick up the evidence? She said yes, and we shared a moment of relief.

But then she started patting herself down, and we noticed she was empty-handed. Where was the hard drive? Panic set in. We couldn't go back to the police department now that the plea deal had been vacated. We searched the lobby frantically and peppered her with questions.

Had she come into the courtroom? Could it still be inside? The hearing had already started when she arrived, and they wouldn't let her past the door. She'd sat on a bench right outside until it was all over.

We sprinted to an elevator and made our way back up to the courtroom. And there it was, all the video evidence in the case, sitting on a bench, hiding in plain sight. Ryan and I clutched the hard drive like a rescued child. The story was saved, but that associate producer was no longer trusted with anything besides lunch orders.

A lot had happened in the Michele Williams story since I'd first been con-
tracted by CBS, and there was still the matter of my own on-camera interview,
as the person who'd broken the story. As a journalist, one of the oddest experiences is being interviewed yourself. After spending countless hours on the
other end of the conversation, it's a trip to be the one answering questions,
not asking them. CBS wanted to do my interview at the CultureMap Dallas
offices, but there was just one problem: we didn't have any.

Once upon a time, when we were launching and flush with cash, we'd had
a whole floor in a historic building downtown. There was even a patio bar
that got internet reception. It was a plum situation, and it lasted about a year
before our investors realized we could just as easily work remotely and save
the exorbitant rent.

Now we had a handful of spaces at a coworking spot called Common
Desk in the Deep Ellum neighborhood of Dallas. A gritty area with lots of
brick buildings, street art, and public transportation, Deep Ellum was not at
all what you'd expect to find deep in the heart of Texas. CBS loved it immediately. We planned to film on Saturday evening, because as a coworking space
with twenty-four-hour access for members, this was our best bet for a quiet
set.

I was so anxious for my interview that I ran five miles that afternoon,
waiting for the sun to set and my opportunity to rise. If I'd only known how
long filming would run itself, I probably would have taken a nap instead.
Television types call the period of time right before the sun goes down "golden
hour" because everything outdoors is automatically bathed in the perfect
lighting. It's the most amazing film set you can imagine, but the clock is ticking. You have to hit it just right and move fast to capture the gold, or you'll be
on the hook for another day of filming.

My call time was golden hour, so they could grab some walking shots
of me coming into the office. It was supposed to look like I was arriving in
the morning, as one would do if they had a normal job. You can actually get
golden hour shots right after sunrise, but most creative types are night owls,
not early birds, so we fake it.

I walked up and down the street in front of my office and punched in the
access code to open the door about half a dozen times while camera men took
different positions to capture it from all angles. This was the "B-roll" portion

of my interview, where they grabbed shots of me in motion that they would later use to knit the story together and intercut with my sit-down interview, which is technically the "A-roll," although no one in TV actually calls it that. These ten-second clips took about thirty minutes to film. We were officially on TV time.

Once we knocked out the B-roll, we headed inside. Now the TV magic could begin. As the interview subject, I figured that would involve me. But instead, I was informed that the next order of business was "dressing the set," which would take a couple of hours. They told me to go to dinner and not to hurry back.

By the time I wandered back over to the set, formerly known as my office, it was looking very Hollywood. They'd strung up red yarn on a bulletin board and had a stack of glossy eight-by-ten photos from Michele's case, with a tin of clothespins at the ready. They'd moved most of the chairs out of view and had expertly lit a lone table in front of the bulletin board.

They asked me to pull out my laptop and open a blank Word document. Next, they shot close-ups of my blinking cursor and instructed me to start typing a few lines from one of my articles on Michele's case, as though I was writing it just then. After a couple takes of this, and a few nervous typos, they wanted me to dictate what I was typing and match my pace to the words on the screen. It's more challenging than it sounds, but it definitely looks cool.

Now it was time to create the investigative bulletin board prop, and I got out the red yarn and went to work, pinning up photos and stopping to ponder them as instructed. The number one rule of filming is never look directly into the camera unless instructed. So many otherwise perfect shots have been ruined by the interviewee turning to the camera and staring right at it, breaking what we call "the third wall" and totally messing up the TV magic.

It's ironic because we all know we are watching television, and it's not real life. But a great show will make you forget that fact, and you'll be lost in the storytelling, totally believing this is a bird's-eye view into the real world. And then a doofus locks eyes with you on camera and the illusion is shattered.

There is one exception to this rule: the Hero Shot. This is where you look down and then slowly bring your gaze up and into the camera lens and hold it there for a beat. This dramatic portrait is used to introduce a character over narration, and it works beautifully. It might sound funny coming from a journalist, but "character" is the term used for anyone who appears on camera and doesn't work for the network. Cops, attorneys, defendants, and victims' family members are all characters in TV land.

For anyone new to filming, the camera is a natural magnet. You can't help but stare into the blackness once or twice. I like to think I learned quickly. I was eager to shed the newbie label and appear like I knew what I was doing. *Fake it 'til you make it*, as they say.

We spent three hours in my new, perfectly lit office. I made phone calls, pinned up photos, typed and typed, and, finally, sat down for my actual interview with producer Alec Sirken. An East Coast native, Alec has the gift of gab, and an easy charm and quick wit that works so well on TV. Before joining *48 Hours*, he'd been an on-camera reporter for years at various NBC stations. The skill set still served him well, and he frequently stood in for the correspondent on interviews like this one, which were called "one-camera" shoots because you saw only the person answering the questions, not the person asking them. Alec and I went over the basics of the case, how I'd gotten involved and what I'd uncovered, and then we discussed the latest legal developments.

It was nearing midnight by the time the interview finished, and I was wiped out. But we weren't wrapped yet. They wanted to get even more B-roll shots, and they'd come up with the great idea to film me driving through the brooding streets of Dallas at night. "It'll be the perfect tone," one cameraman said. "We need more dark and mysterious shots of you."

Who was I to say no to that? They grabbed some GoPro cameras out of their gear bag and started rigging up a rental car, an SUV big enough for the crew to ride in back with their cameras and snag additional angles. It was quite the process, and there was no end in sight.

While this was going on in the parking lot, I was hanging out inside with the producers. And that's when things went sideways.

A burly man came out of the shadows, and I noticed he had "Security" stenciled on his shirt. This was news to me. Apparently in the production agreement that CBS had worked out with the building owners, the owners had agreed to provide security for our shoot—that is, until midnight. It was 11:55 PM, and keys in hand, he was kicking us out.

"Time to go," he said, clearly not in the mood for conversation. The New Yorkers tried to reason with him.

"Now wait a minute," producer Alec Sirken said. "We have a deal with you."

The security guard was unmoved. "Yeah, and that deal ends at midnight, so it's time to go."

Alec looked around and threw up his hands. "Do you see all this equipment? We couldn't get everything out of here in five minutes if our lives depended on it."

"Not my problem," the security guard said, crossing his arms.

We were at a standoff, and in Texas those don't typically end well. Time to bring in the big guns.

I stepped in between the warring parties—all five feet, two inches of me—and smiled.

"I'm so sorry we are running late," I told the security guard. "I'm exhausted too, and I really wish we could all get out of here right now."

He softened a bit but not much.

Now it was time to work on the New York side of the negotiation.

"Alec, how long would it take to clear everything out of here tonight?" I asked. He said it would be at least an hour, maybe two. The security guard was turning a new shade of red.

"Two hours," I repeated, and then gave him the closer. "What's your going rate for two hours of overtime?"

The security guard smirked and said, "One hundred dollars."

I looked at Alec for approval, and he was staring back at me with the utmost respect. We shook on the deal, hit up the ATM on the corner, and worked like crazy until 2 AM.

3

LIVING A DOUBLE LIFE

Six months later

I'm sitting on the tarmac in Abilene, Texas, trying desperately to get an internet signal on my laptop. Raindrops are smacking the windows, and the wind is blowing so hard that it's whistling against the plane.

I'm grateful that we're not up in the air right now, being thrown around in the storm. My stomach is doing cartwheels as it is.

I see a call coming through my phone from my boss at CultureMap, and I think I'm about to lose my lunch. She doesn't know I'm on a plane right now, stringing for the national media on a murder-for-hire case. She thinks I'm working from home, a few miles away from the office.

It's been six months since the Michele Williams episode of *48 Hours* aired. It was fittingly titled "Temptation in Texas," and Michele wasn't the only one being enticed by greener pastures.

After seeing my name on screen as a "CBS News consultant," I had officially caught the TV bug. Despite the glitz and glamour, I knew I didn't want to be on camera. I wanted to be a producer, the one making the stories happen. Finding the cases that everyone else had missed and putting them on prime-time television seemed like a dream job to me.

The first time Ryan Smith asked me to "field produce" a hearing for him because he couldn't make it down from New York in time, I actually Googled "what does a television producer do?" I learned the answer was basically everything I was already doing as an enterprising local journalist, except I'd get paid a lot more and didn't have to write daily stories.

Winning difficult people over, getting interviews and information from hostile sources, and problem-solving on your feet was all in a day's work for a TV producer. Correspondents and reporters, meanwhile, had to spend a lot of time in makeup chairs and wardrobe rooms, while producers read them into the story and fed them questions.

I prefer puppet mastering behind the scenes rather than sitting under the lights. Plus, who wants a record of everything they've said living in the archives of CBS News until the end of time? Definitely not me. My TV dreams were producer or bust, and I came up with a plan to make them a reality.

The week after the episode aired, I started pitching Texas murder stories directly to executive producer Susan Zirinsky and story editor Nancy Kramer. Susan Zirinsky often jokes that she might as well have been born at CBS, because they brought her right from the maternity ward to the broadcast center. In truth, she started as an intern in her twenties and rose through the ranks, producing stories for everyone from Walter Cronkite to Dan Rather. She was such a tour de force in political journalism that James L. Brooks shadowed her for his 1987 movie *Broadcast News*, where Holly Hunter played a character largely based on Zirinsky. Her nickname, "Z," is used industry-wide. You know you're a power player when your name graduates to a single letter.

Nancy Kramer, meanwhile, is an institution in herself. She's been at CBS nearly as long as Z, save for a brief stint at ABC News in the late nineties. Kramer, as she's known due to a multitude of Nancys in the building, also had a one-year run at *60 Minutes* before landing at *48 Hours* and never leaving. It's something of an open secret that Kramer would be happy to move on from the crime beat, but she never has managed to make the jump. She often pitches in as an executive on network specials, moonlights for *CBS Mornings*, and has flirted with positions on the West Coast. But at the end of the day, she always falls back into the comfortable arms of murder mysteries.

My late-night negotiation skills with the security guard had impressed longtime producer Alec Sirken, and he went to bat for me with the senior staff. I learned that years ago, *48 Hours* previously had a Texas-based field producer in Houston, but she left the company under suspicion of falsifying expenses. They didn't backfill the position, and it disappeared from the budget. But would they bring it back? I bought Texas stationery on Etsy and boldly threw out the idea of creating a position in Dallas for me as the new Texas-based field producer.

I had high hopes that they'd jump on the idea right away, but like most big decisions, it was a slow burn. Instead of giving me a real contract, they offered me a day rate and told me to keep my job at CultureMap. I could work for them on the side, when I had time, they reasoned. "Sure, sounds great," I said through gritted teeth. *I guess I can sleep when I'm dead*, I thought to myself as I hung up the phone.

The next few months were a blur. By day, I was the managing editor of a start-up digital media website. By night, I was stringing for the national media, developing true crime stories worthy of the CBS News name. How long could I keep up this balancing act?

Back on the plane, my phone is still ringing. I let it go to voicemail to buy time to plot my next move. If I can just get the internet to connect, I can maintain the charade. A few minutes later, the plane rumbles and we start taxiing to a new gate. Three bars appear on my phone, hallelujah. I quickly log into the CMS and pull up Google Chat.

"Hey, sorry I missed your call," I type in the chat box. "I'm in the CMS now editing the afternoon stories. Internet keeps going out on me."

It's not a lie, but it's definitely not the whole truth.

"Okay," my boss types back. "If the internet at your house is unreliable, you can always come into the office."

I grimace at the suggestion. I'm three hours west of Dallas as it is, and my final destination, weather permitting, is Lubbock, Texas. Over five hours and three hundred miles away from the CultureMap Dallas offices.

This is my first time traveling for *48 Hours*, and par for the course, I didn't ask CultureMap for permission to let me take the trip. I knew what the answer would be. Why would I volunteer for defeat? Instead, I'd hatched a plan to try to juggle all my responsibilities as the managing editor of CultureMap Dallas and still make my debut as a freelance field producer for *48 Hours* on CBS.

It was going about as well as you'd expect for one person trying to do two very demanding jobs. I feel my phone buzzing on my knee and see my new boss at *48 Hours* is calling. I hesitate a moment before remembering this is the call I can safely pick up, because this boss knows I'm on a plane.

"Greetings from Abilene," I say.

"Abilene, eh? Is that close to Lubbock?" Kramer asks.

New Yorkers are consistently clueless about Texas geography.

"Very close," I say, just to amuse myself. "It's a stopover for bad weather. We should be back up in the air as soon as the storm passes."

I'm trying to sound cool and calm about this development, as though it's a totally normal thing for me to be jetting off on planes in the middle of thunderstorms to cover murder trials—and not the first time I've done anything of the sort.

"Great," Kramer says, apparently fooled by my performance or otherwise unconcerned with my well-being. "When you get on the ground in Lubbock, go straight to the courthouse. The trial was scheduled to start this morning."

"Yes ma'am," I reply, and Kramer laughs as she hangs up. I guess they don't get much of that in NYC.

"Good morning, folks," the captain crackles over the intercom. "We should be cleared for takeoff in about fifteen minutes."

It's still storming outside, and I grip the armrests and steel my nerves. Fifteen minutes to edit three stories and get my first boss off my case. Here goes nothing.

I fire off some revisions, double-check the links to original sources, add captions to the photos, and hit publish on the first story. The next two stories require less TLC, and I polish them up quickly. Then I schedule them out to publish in two-hour increments across the afternoon. That'll buy me some time while we reroute to Lubbock.

I catch the flight attendant giving me side-eye and stow my laptop. I take a deep breath and close my eyes as we ascend back into the rain. Instinctively,

I start to say a little prayer to myself. But between the turbulent flight and the double work life I'm living, I'm not sure exactly what to prioritize. I feel the words "God help me" escape my lips as we climb into the clouds.

We touch down on solid ground, and I can finally exhale. Who knew I'd ever be this happy to be in Lubbock? The land of tumbleweeds, tortilla factories, and Texas Tech: a bitter rival of my alma mater Baylor University. You never really know what the future holds.

I hop in my rental car and punch in the address for the Lubbock County Courthouse on my GPS. Ironically the street is named Broadway. I follow the directions across a bleak landscape until I hear the magic words "You have arrived." I smile to myself and think it might actually be true.

Despite all the rush to get here, the trial hasn't even started yet. They are still picking the jury. I find a seat in the back and settle in. Hours go by and nothing of consequence happens. Finally, a bailiff announces that jury selection will continue into the next day. I guess I have time to go work on my other job now.

The rest of my evening in Lubbock is consumed with CultureMap Dallas duties, my actual job. I edit other people's stories, write a few of my own, and begin to plan out coverage for the following day. Somewhere in the middle, I fall asleep on my laptop and dream of getting fired.

It takes the better part of the morning before a jury is seated for Texas v. Thomas Michael Dixon. It's a capital murder case, and the details are coming out fast and furious in opening arguments. I'm taking the best notes I can, trying to keep up with the bizarre storyline.

"This is a case about love, jealousy, arrogance, wealth, and rage," the prosecutor says, before quoting the Bible. "Love is as strong as death. Jealousy is as cruel as the grave."

The way the state tells it, Dr. Mike Dixon was an accomplished plastic surgeon in Amarillo, Texas, who went down a dark path when his girlfriend broke up with him. She started dating another doctor, Lubbock pathologist Joseph Sonnier, and Dixon couldn't handle the competition. So he hired an unemployed pharmaceutical rep named David Shepard to break into Sonnier's home and kill him. A pawnshop receipt for three silver bars was found at Shepard's ramshackle apartment, and authorities traced them back to Dixon. They believed the precious metal was payment for murder, making it a capital offense and eligible for the death penalty.

Fearing the needle, Shepard pleaded guilty in exchange for a life sentence and was now going to testify against Dixon. To shore up his claims, Shepard had even led authorities to the lake where a dive team recovered an antique gun consistent with the murder weapon. The gun was originally registered to Dixon's brother. It all seemed pretty open and shut, albeit sensational.

But now it's the defense's turn to argue their case, and I get the sense the story is about to get a lot more complicated. Yes, they conceded that Dixon was friends with Shepard and had asked for his help in winning his girlfriend back. But all Shepard was supposed to do was take damaging photographs of Sonnier with other women. The defense is even willing to admit to trespassing and invasion of privacy, but not murder.

The silver bars had been a way to help Shepard out, as he was tight on cash and going through a messy divorce that put his bank accounts on blast. Frustrated and with a short fuse, Shepard had gone rogue and killed Sonnier all on his own, with a gun he swiped from his friend. Dixon had been as surprised as anyone when he found out.

"Mike Dixon did not pay, he did not plan, he did not participate in the killing of Joseph Sonnier," the defense attorney declares.

It's my first time covering a gavel-to-gavel murder trial, and I'm transfixed by the opposing storylines and alternate realities. Only one story could be true, but what will the jury believe?

After opening arguments, the state starts calling witnesses straight away. Cases typically go chronologically and begin with first responders taking the stand. Through the testimony, a pretty good ticktock of the murder develops.

Outdoor security cameras captured Shepard's arrival at Dr. Sonnier's home and subsequent backyard stakeout. He actually sat out there so long he fell asleep. Based on smudges on the inside of the window, it appeared Sonnier arrived home, spotted a disheveled man sleeping in his lawn chair, and rapped on the glass with his knuckles to wake him. Little did the good doctor know that he was rousing his own killer.

Sonnier's half-drunk cocktail was found nearby, surrounded by broken glass after Shepard had charged through the window. The murder had been a fight to the death, with Shepard shooting Sonnier multiple times with a .25-caliber pistol that the defense referred to as a "mouse gun."

The relatively small bullets hadn't done enough damage to kill Sonnier on their own, so Shepard pulled out a knife to finish him off. The final struggle had occurred in the garage, presumably as Sonnier tried to flee. He was left to die on the concrete floor. His body wasn't discovered until after he missed work the next morning and concerned colleagues reported his absence to police.

It was a lot of information to take in, and as court adjourned for the day, I called Kramer to get her up to speed. Needless to say, she was intrigued by this batshit-crazy murder case in the middle of nowhere, Texas. And best of all, it didn't appear that any other national media was in attendance yet. I told her about the local newspaper and television reporters I'd seen working in the courtroom, but everyone else looked like they were family members of one side or the other.

Small-town murders are big business, and *48 Hours* was hoping to keep a close eye on this case for the foreseeable future. That meant I wasn't going anywhere. Forget the fact that I did have this whole other job in another city, where my husband lives and where I thought I was returning the next day. I hadn't even packed two pairs of underwear.

Perplexed, I ask if CBS could send someone else from New York now that they knew the trial had started and it was the right brand of made-for-TV murder. Yes, and no, I'm told.

Yes, they could eventually send someone all the way to Lubbock, Texas, but it wasn't a direct flight from New York, and it would take some finagling. Plus, I was already there, and now I "knew the players and was invested in the story."

It was more cost-effective and logistically streamlined to just move me to the Marriott Courtyard in Lubbock for the duration of the trial. I cover the phone while guffawing at the characterization. The trial had been estimated to last two weeks. That was an eternity to spend on a business trip for a second job. *How am I going to explain this one?*

My husband was understanding of the situation and excited for my growing contract at CBS. But I knew breaking the news of my impending absence to my boss at CultureMap was going to take a more nuanced approach. The complicated thing was I really did love working at CultureMap. I had editorial freedom and friends on staff with a similar penchant for troublemaking reporting. But we didn't always make payroll, and even when we did, it wasn't like I was raking in the cash. It was fine for a few years, but now we were getting into that phase of life with mortgages, and student loan payments were increasing. And once you've seen the size of a national media paycheck, it's hard to go back to local budgets.

I pulled out my laptop and searched for the employee handbook. As a start-up, we had limited benefits and spartan vacation policies, but maybe there was something I could work with. It was November, and I calculated that I had three days of vacation left. I had earmarked it for Christmas, but my holiday was going to be a working one this year. I kept reading and discovered a section on "mental health days." Apparently, we had a week of time allotted for self-care. I was definitely going to need that to survive Lubbock.

I was somewhat conflicted about concealing the truth from CultureMap, but in the end I knew it was an opportunity I couldn't pass up. Plus, if I did eventually get caught, who better to understand my position than the leaders of a rebel-spirited, industry-disrupting website?

And at the same time I was bending the rules at CultureMap, I was getting a crash course in field producing for CBS News. As quickly as I learned their cardinal rules, I realized that I'd broken just about every one of them. My first mistakes had been booking a round-trip ticket and getting a rental car with the same end date. One-way tickets and two-week-long rentals were the norm. This way, you didn't have to deal with changing flights and extending rental agreements, both of which were time-consuming and expensive.

Another mistake with more personal consequences was packing lightly. What can I say—my Peace Corps training defaulted to just bringing the basics.

But I was in the TV world now, and I really needed some clean clothes for court.

I didn't have a CBS credit card yet, so everything I was doing was going on my account for reimbursement later. I was already out over a thousand dollars between the plane tickets, rental car, and hotel room. Kramer told me I could buy new clothes and that they'd reimburse me since I was staying longer than originally planned. But without the money to cover it up front, I was nearing the limit on my credit card. I needed to be thrifty, and in Texas there's no cheaper place to grab all the essentials than Walmart.

For less than fifty dollars, I got a week's worth of underwear, socks, and even a few tops to mix in under my standard courtroom blazer. I was rocking discount threads, but I still felt like a million bucks. I was working for the national media and watching a great story unfold before my eyes. How did I get this lucky?

Although I'd packed only a few professional outfits, there's one ensemble I never leave out of any suitcase: workout clothes and running shoes. Maintaining my sleep quality and overall spiritual Zen requires at least twenty miles a week of pounding pavement. It's cheaper than therapy. I'm usually a morning runner, but with court starting at 8 AM sharp and the West Texas heat making a post-run shower an absolute necessity, I opted for evening workouts.

I told my boss at CultureMap that I was "going through something" and needed to cash in on my vacation and mental health days right away. I felt a little guilty for using everything all at once, but I wasn't technically lying. Sure, there was a lot I was leaving out, but I was most certainly in a tight spot and needed room to work it all out. Good thing I no longer had to rush back to my hotel room and fire up my laptop all night to keep my day job.

When court adjourned at 5 PM, I couldn't wait to get off those wooden benches and into a good stride. By the time I hopped in my car and changed, I had about an hour until sunset to run my heart out. I'm not a pessimist, but I am a realist. And I know as a female runner, my greatest vulnerability is being out alone after dark. So no matter how great my run is going, when I see the sun dip below the horizon, I hightail it home.

Lubbock is a barren landscape, almost the desert but without the beauty of rock formations or open land. The one bright spot is the campus of Texas Tech, and so that's where I ran every evening, sporting a Baylor T-shirt, of course. I got some jeers, but it just made me run faster. I'm no stranger to pushing boundaries.

I had been stationed in Lubbock for two weeks with no end in sight. I'd burned through the rest of my CultureMap vacation days and was now using "mental health days." Only instead of feeling refreshed, I was nearing the end of my rope. Turns out that claiming a mental health day and spending it listening to murder trial testimony is not a recipe for relaxation. This was my first taste of the toll of working in true crime—and the unseen burden of absorbing graphic details of murder after murder.

Instead of taking it easy, I'd been taking it all in. And the case was growing more complicated and engrossing by the day. When triggerman David Shepard had testified for the state, he was expected to admit his guilt and implicate Dr. Dixon as the mastermind. But Shepard only kept up half of the bargain. He still admitted his role as the gunman, but now he said that he'd acted alone. Dixon hadn't hired him as a hit man at all.

The prosecutor couldn't accept the changing narrative and kept hammering on how Shepard had previously agreed to Dixon's involvement when he signed his plea deal removing the death penalty. But it was no use; Shepard had a new story to tell, and he was unwavering. Meanwhile, Dixon sat back in his defendant's chair and smirked. Was there another, secret deal in place between friends? All of us in the courtroom gallery discussed the possibility, especially considering what Shepard testified to was strikingly similar to the defense's theory in opening arguments.

One of the more interesting points in Shepard's testimony was his insinuation that his roommate may have played a role in the murder plot. Paul Reynolds was a former Special Forces operative for the army, a Green Beret who had served four years before being honorably discharged. He was currently working as a nurse. The knife used to kill Shepard had a tactical look to it, and the defense referred to it as a military-grade weapon, though there was never any actual proof of the affiliation.

But the suggestion was enough to raise eyebrows: Could one of the murder weapons have belonged to someone other than Shepard? What would that mean? It muddied the waters of responsibility, though the state was quick to point out that Reynolds was not the one on trial, nor had he ever been a suspect. He was a cooperating witness who allowed police to search their apartment and aided in their investigation against his roommate.

Despite Shepard repeatedly bringing up Reynolds in his testimony, the state didn't call the mysterious roommate as a witness. That's probably because they didn't realize Shepard was going to change his story on the stand and dramatically deviate from the plea deal parameters. Either decision, to hear from Reynolds or to leave him out of it, was a gamble. Who knows what he might say? Even after the state didn't call him, the defense still could have. But at that point, why would they? He was the wild card, the silent suspect lurking in the shadows. The devil you can't see is always more menacing than someone right in front of you.

As much as I wanted to approach Shepard and other witnesses after they testified to introduce myself and make a pitch for an interview with CBS, the prosecution was making that task impossible. They had escorts for every witness, bringing them in and guiding them back out, all under constant supervision. I found Shepard's mailing address with the Texas Department of Criminal Justice. I do love a captive audience. Paul Reynolds, meanwhile, was a lot harder to track down, and I didn't yet have access to the CBS subscriptions to public databases with cell phone numbers and known addresses.

Searching for every Paul Reynolds in West Texas felt like a dead end, so I kept my eyes peeled for better options. I noticed there was one prosecution witness who wasn't being escorted, Lubbock police detective Zach Johnson. He'd actually questioned Dixon after they found Sonnier's body, and Johnson had been the one to put the cuffs on Dixon himself. That's a pretty good perspective for TV, and coupled with his approachability, it looked like a winning combination to me.

After Detective Johnson testified, I followed him out of the courtroom and introduced myself. He was happy to chat and said he'd be willing to do an interview after the trial, provided he got departmental approval. Then he handed over his business card and cell phone number. Winner, winner, chicken dinner. We now officially had a voice from the state's theory of the case, and with the defense attorneys seemingly on board as well, the cast of characters for our episode was fleshing out nicely, in theory anyway.

With such compelling testimony, the days in court were flying by. Before I knew it, another week had passed, and I still hadn't been home. My Walmart wardrobe was wearing thin, and I pleaded with Kramer to let me fly home for the weekend for reinforcements. She finally relented, and CBS gave me a ticket home for Friday afternoon, returning Sunday night. Turns out the only round-trip flights they book are the ones that send you right back to work.

The Lubbock airport has one terminal with about ten gates, so flying out of there is about as easy as it gets. As long as the weather cooperates. I was so eager to get home that I left for the airport right after lunch, giving myself plenty of time to catch my 4 PM flight. But then the storm rolled in.

A good old-fashioned West Texas thunderstorm lit up the sky, and flight cancellations and delays followed. Rain pounded the windows and thunderclaps shook the terminal, and I felt like I was about to break down right then and there. I retreated to a bathroom stall, sat on the floor, and let myself go. The stress of working two jobs and not being home for weeks finally caught up to me. What in the world had I gotten myself into?

Just as all hope seemed lost, a voice came over the PA and announced my flight was once again scheduled for takeoff, and boarding would begin soon. I wiped my eyes with toilet paper, straightened my ragged clothes in the mirror, and got the hell out of Lubbock.

The weekend at home was a true respite, and Riley and I soaked up every minute together. I filled him in on my new crazy job as a national news producer, and we laughed at the absurdity of it all. Just a few short months ago, I was barely contributing to the household finances with my start-up salary, and now I had CBS News's deep pockets in my corner. But what would the next week hold?

I was burning through all my time off, and the trial had no end in sight. CBS was paying me more in a week than I made in a month at CultureMap, so sticking with them was a no-brainer. Still, I didn't know how it was all going to shake out. What would happen after this trial finally ended? How long would it be before they sent me to another one? Did I want to live out of a suitcase for the foreseeable future? As I went back and forth on all my options, Riley disappeared into the kitchen. He came back with a bottle of champagne and proclaimed, "That sounds like a problem for Monday, and it's still Saturday night."

We put away the work talk for the rest of the weekend, and by the time I headed to the airport on Sunday evening, I was ready to conquer the true crime TV world again.

CBS had made good use of the weekend as well, sending in backup from New York in the form of producer Alec Sirken, who I'd worked with on the Michele Williams case. Thirty years my senior, Alec had worked for *48 Hours* almost as long as I'd been alive. He quickly sized up the courtroom and alerted me to the competition. Producers from both ABC's *20/20* and NBC's *Dateline* were trial watching with me, staying under the radar in dark suits while taking notes on all the testimony. I hadn't even considered that they were members of the media. They just looked like attorneys to me. Lesson learned. And Alec was my unlikely teacher.

A lifelong bachelor, Alec had a boyish quality that comes from never settling down. He cracked jokes in court and played YouTube videos through his earbuds when the testimony bored him. Alec was an entertaining colleague to have around, and I was glad for the company. Plus, he had a CBS credit card, so I no longer had to eat dinner at 7-Eleven.

We discovered Lubbock actually had a few fine dining establishments and became frequent customers, inviting the defense to join us one night and the prosecution the next. The defense was the only side who ever took us up on the offer, and we all became fast friends. Wining and dining high-powered attorneys was a far cry from my digital media and local newspaper days, when I barely had the budget to buy a source coffee.

Still, I couldn't believe that we could bankroll an entire month of travel and expenses without having to turn around a single story or interview for CBS. I'd never had such open-ended assignments before and felt a little nervous about it. "Shouldn't we have an interview with someone by now?" I asked Alec, who brushed me off.

"Do you know the secret to success?" he quizzed me. As I started to say no, he cut me off in comedic fashion: "Timing!"

Alec was in no rush, so I took a cue from him and stopped stressing about our lack of production. I had plenty of other things to worry over, like my day job at CultureMap. I was praying the trial would end before my PTO days did, and I could get back to my desk at Dallas while keeping my contract with CBS. But that dream was dying before my eyes. The trial just kept going, day after day, week after week, until I was totally out of time.

It wasn't as if I hadn't seen this coming and expressly warned my CBS boss, Nancy Kramer, about it. But when the day finally arrived, she still acted shocked. I called her as I was walking down the courthouse steps to tell her I was headed for the Lubbock airport.

"I can't stay any longer. I am completely out of vacation days," I told her. "I am going to lose my job if I'm not back in Dallas tomorrow."

Even though I had already told Kramer that my days in Lubbock were numbered, she hadn't taken me seriously. She didn't believe I'd actually leave before the trial was over. But she'd left me no choice. I'd pitched Kramer and Z on a real, ongoing contract, one that would pay me almost double what I was making at CultureMap. And while it was a lot of money to me, I knew it was a drop in the bucket for a major network, a rounding error when it came time to balance the books.

They had kicked the contract can down the road every time I brought it up, saying we could discuss it after the trial was over. Well, that wasn't going to cut it. Just like getting that key interview, timing was everything, and I was walking out the door right now.

"Wait, you're leaving? Like actually leaving Lubbock?" Kramer said incredulously.

"Yes," I replied as I turned on my rental car and entered the airport address into my GPS. The directions started piping through the audio.

"Wait, don't go," Kramer said. "We have a deal."

Gobsmacked, I pulled over to the side of the road.

"What do you mean we have a deal?" I asked. "A deal-deal? Like a contract?"

"Yes," Kramer said. "Welcome to CBS."

Now that I was officially working full-time for CBS, I needed to get up to speed on a few things. In a traditional office, I've heard this is called "onboarding" and takes place with an HR representative. I've never worked in a real office, so all of my employee training has taken place on the fly, with questionable results. Since Alec was with me in Lubbock, he took it upon himself to show me the ropes. First up, the bane of all business travelers: expense reports.

My previous media gigs were so low budget that all I ever did was enter my measly expenses into an Excel spreadsheet. But places like CBS have entire software systems dedicated to reimbursements. Alec thought the easiest way for me to learn about it was to watch him input his own. Sounded like a snooze fest to me, but I put on my best eager-beaver smile and went with it. He typed away, and just as my mind was starting to wander, I noticed him entering expletives into a comment field.

"Uh, Alec? Why did you write 'Fuck you' in your expense report?"

"They never even read these things," Alec said nonchalantly as he shut his laptop.

Alec may have been my teacher and guide, but I wasn't going to follow his example on my expense reports anytime soon. Southern manners die hard.

As unorthodox as he was, I knew I could learn a lot about TV production from Alec, and I listened eagerly as he explained the highs and lows of the true crime story arc to me. I was picking up on all sorts of lingo, including the fact that no one at *48 Hours* ever called the show anything but "*48.*"

The first step to getting a story into production at CBS is writing the "bluesheet." Once upon a time, the notes were actually printed on baby-blue paper. And while the color went by the wayside, the name stuck. The bluesheet is a one-page, sexy summary of the story, and it's also called "the blue," because there's nothing TV insiders love more than a nickname for a secret code.

The idea is to pack in as many tantalizing details as you can, while also leaving room for mystery and intrigue. You want to leave the readers, who at this stage are all senior producers, wanting more, and asking questions with delicious answers that will bring to light new and exciting elements of the story that you can then pretend the senior producers discovered. There's no faster way to get your story greenlit, to use the preferred TV lingo for "approved." In addition to the brief summary, the bluesheet also has a list of potential characters and their photographs, along with a short description of where you are in the booking process.

Once you get the green light and go into production, the scripts for each episode are split into six acts, with commercial breaks between each one. Every act fulfills a certain purpose, moving the story forward, while still teasing out information and leaving the viewer wondering what will happen next. Because the show originated in linear, broadcast television, it's not designed for the binge viewer, who is streaming episode after episode.

The goal is to keep you on the couch for exactly one hour, and to create enough mystery and intrigue to last through four commercial breaks. Here's the TV formula:

Act 1: A glorified trailer that kicks off the episode "in media res," that is, with the action already in motion. Ideally, there's a 911 call, a crime scene video, and a breathless eyewitness account.

Act 2: A retreat from the action to go back in time to before the murder. Someone describes the victim along the lines of "She lit up a room." (That phrase appeared in so many scripts that it was eventually blacklisted, along with a handful of other true crime clichés, like describing a crime as "shocking" or saying that the victim "never met a stranger.")

Act 3: The real meat and potatoes of the case is presented by walking the audience through the evidence and introducing the suspects. If possible, most of Act 3 will revolve around red herrings, so that the actual killer comes as a surprise later.

Act 4: Typically, this is where an arrest or an indictment happens, though ideally there is still some level of uncertainty here. Maybe the first person arrested doesn't end up being the one charged for the murder, for example. Another option would be that former suspects will get arrested on unrelated charges that investigators discovered along the way. Drugs and embezzlement are the most common and intriguing false trails.

Act 5: The trial usually takes center stage, and this is where cameras in the courtroom make life so much easier. Roll camera on opening or closing arguments, and the script practically writes itself. Sprinkle in a few sound bites from friends and family, and it's gold.

Act 6: It's time for resolution, and in a perfect world, that means a verdict. But leading up to that, build suspense by casting doubt on the strength of the case, and by going back and forth on theories presented by the prosecution and the defense. Bonus points if a member of the jury weighs in on the deliberations, but the attorneys themselves will do just fine. Always try to give the victim's family the last word, teeing them up with questions about justice, closure, and the legacy their loved one left behind.

This tried-and-true blueprint has been the cornerstone of true crime television for years, and it works. It's an emotional roller coaster, but once you've been on the ride long enough, you anticipate the twists and turns, and your stomach no longer drops with every one of them.

In addition to thirty-plus weekly episodes each season, *48 Hours* would occasionally produce network specials under the CBS News banner, in which case Nancy Kramer or senior producers Anthony Batson and Judy Tygard were often tapped for executive producer roles. Terrorist attacks, natural disasters, and noteworthy deaths were all strong contenders. Pretty early on, I started hearing about one particular project already in production: "The Queen's Special." That was just a placeholder name for this memoriam, of course, because Queen Elizabeth was still very much alive in 2014. But she was eighty-eight years old, and with such a storied life and career as a working member of the royal family, CBS wanted to get a jump on things.

This is common practice at media companies. Journalists call it "the morgue," and on any given day in newsrooms across the country, there are pre-written obituaries and news scripts for the deaths of many world leaders. It's a little morbid, but it falls under the banner of working smarter, not harder. Plus, it gives us all something to do when the news cycle is slow. "Update the morgue if you can't find a story," editors yell to loafing reporters.

Like me, Alec had started out in local media before landing a job at the network. And if I thought I had an interesting path to *48 Hours*, Alec's was even wilder. He was a reporter for a CBS affiliate in Philadelphia when he overheard a colleague working on a story about a roundup of suspected mobsters. It was a touchy subject for the police reporter, but not for Alec. A jokester with a penchant for impressions, Alec thought it would be hilarious to leave the reporter a voicemail impersonating a mobster. In what he affectionately called his "hokiest mob voice," Alec demanded the reporter issue a retraction, "or else we know where your lovely family lives, and it won't be pretty."

Hokey or not, Alec did such a convincing job that the reporter called the FBI and was preparing to evacuate his family before he realized he'd been bamboozled. It didn't take long for the news director to call Alec into his office, where he admitted to the whole thing. Alec wasn't charged with a crime, but he was suspended from his job at the station for a couple days. And during that suspension, I kid you not, Alec drove up to New York and applied for a position as a producer for NBC's *Dateline*. He didn't get it, but he did eventually find his way to true crime reporting at CBS.

Years later, it came as no surprise when I learned one of Alec's close friends at CBS was Joe Halderman. An Emmy award–winning producer, Joe was working for *48* in 2009 when he tried to extort two million dollars from David Letterman over an affair with a show staffer. In the end, Halderman threw away his entire career for a phony FBI check. Working in true crime for too long is crazy. It can really addle your brain. Or maybe it just attracts people who already have a few screws loose.

I was both amused and appalled at Alec's antics, but who was I to judge? This was a senior member of the staff, and I was a day-old producer. He took me around the courtroom and made small talk with potential interview subjects, passing out his business cards and asking for their contact information. "Claire, you should give them your card, too," he suggested.

I pretended to fish around in my bag before saying, "Ah, looks like I'm all out. I'll just jot down my number." The truth was I didn't have any business cards, at least not ones that had my current job title. Once we were out of the courthouse, I let Alec in on my predicament.

"We can fix this," he said as he called the unit manager for CBS and told her that I needed business cards overnighted to our hotel.

Unimpressed, she informed him that all business card requests had to go through the "chain of command" and would be processed in the order they were received. Alec shouted expletives and hung up on her. Then he told me to drive to the nearest Kinko's printshop.

There was no question that what we were doing was unauthorized. The previous conversation I'd witnessed had left little in the way of doubts. But Alec was right in front of me, and this unknown, disapproving manager was 1,200 miles away. Plus, I really did need business cards to book interviews.

Alec approached the Kinko's counter and smiled as he handed over his official CBS business card. "So what we need is something that looks exactly like this, but it has her name and phone number on it," he said. A few hours later, we picked up a box of cards, hot off the press.

The trial had gotten all the way through the state's case, and it was finally time for the defendant to decide whether or not to testify. Thanks to our near-nightly dinners with the defense team, we already knew they were advising against it. This is the standard practice of defense attorneys everywhere, and, as they are all quick to tell you, it has nothing to do with guilt or innocence. Talking gets you in trouble, full stop.

The most important words in the American lexicon are "You have the right to remain silent." Why give that up? The majority of defendants listen to their attorneys and decline to testify. But there are some who just can't resist the opportunity to tell their side of the story and speak directly to the jury, and Dr. Mike Dixon was one of them.

Clean cut with a smart pair of glasses and a dark-blue suit, Dixon looked the part of the good doctor. He was well spoken and answered his attorney's questions with a relaxed expression, as though he was relieved to finally participate in his own trial. The death penalty was off the table for Dixon, but he was nevertheless fighting for his life, as the punishment for solicitation of capital murder was a life sentence without parole.

The prosecution's case against Dixon had initially seemed open and shut. But Shepard's testimony recanting Dixon's involvement and the introduction of a mysterious, ex-military roommate were muddying the waters. Would it add up to reasonable doubt for a jury? As Dixon took the stand, he tried to present himself as a regular guy caught up in a whole mess of trouble. He said he was blindsided by his arrest.

"It was quite a shock," he told the jury, turning to make eye contact with them.

His posture was a clear coaching move from his attorneys, and I wondered if it would help or hurt him in the end. Would the jury see through it as a strategy? Or would they connect with him and believe him?

Dixon stayed on the stand for two days, first taking softball questions from his own attorneys before getting the fastballs thrown at him from the prosecution. Through it all, he held firm that he never meant for his romantic rival to be killed.

"I tried to set in motion to get some photographs but never with the intent to murder someone or to hurt someone," Dixon said, but this time he used a slow, methodical cadence that sounded to me like it had been rehearsed.

It was a fascinating study in human behavior. Who was the real Thomas Michael Dixon? The quiet, smart doctor who was having trouble moving on after a breakup, or this revengeful, obsessive man who believed that murder was the solution to his problems?

I watched his every move on the stand, pausing only to observe the jury's reaction to his testimony. The most damaging parts of the case against Dixon were the silver bars with serial numbers traced back to him—and the text messages. Oh, the text messages. Dixon and Shepard texted thousands of times, which for two men seemed suspicious enough already. But the content of those messages was even more eyebrow raising.

"I'm ready to go south tomorrow," Shepard wrote the night before the murder.

The next morning, Dixon sent the messages "Put it on him" and "whip and spur."

On the stand, Dixon tried to explain the expressions as cowboy talk that he learned growing up on the ranch. It was not a coded message to kill anyone, he claimed, but simply good ol' boy encouragement about getting a job done. And the job, he was quick to point out, was to take damaging photos of Sonnier with other women and break up his new relationship. Shepard was the one who decided to bring a gun—and a knife—to the photography session.

The nearly monthlong trial was finally winding down, and soon Dixon's fate would be in the hands of the jury. Once deliberations start, the energy in the courthouse completely changes. There's an air of anticipation that everyone picks up on, because at any moment the jury could signal that they've reached a verdict. Some attorneys refuse to leave the courthouse and will hole up somewhere secluded, while others immediately decamp for their offices and wait for the word to come down. It could be a matter of minutes, hours, days, or even weeks.

As a jury deliberates, they communicate through written letters to the judge or by signaling with a red light that they've reached a verdict. The light is usually visible only in the judge's chambers, though I have seen some courtrooms that display the jury signal. Because of the palpable tension, and the fact that most trial attendees don't want to stray too far from the courthouse, jury deliberations are my favorite time to snag interviews. Everyone is just standing around, wondering what's going to happen next. It's the perfect time to strike up a conversation, and once you get them talking, you're halfway to getting them in the chair for an interview.

With the possibility of a verdict at any time, CBS had arranged a camera crew to sit with us at the courthouse. I've never been good at just waiting around for things to happen. I like to tip the scales and make the action when I can. So I asked Alec what he thought about approaching Dixon's family for a quick interview. He was ambivalent at first, explaining that we wouldn't get much from them without a correspondent on camera to ask the questions. But wouldn't something be better than nothing? I put the rhetorical question out there and let it hang. Alec smiled at me, and I knew I'd sold him.

I started scanning the halls for the Dixons and found them hanging out by the vending machines. I made a little small talk and then went in with my pitch. "It would be so nice to hear your perspective. I know this can't be easy."

Dixon's mom agreed to talk, and so did her husband. Dixon's adult children declined to participate, and I didn't press it. Two interview subjects were a win in my book. Now I just needed to find a quiet place to talk.

Hallways are problematic because you can't control the flow of people or noise. I needed a space big enough for the Dixons, a camera crew, and two producers. Ideally, we could use an empty courtroom. It wouldn't be the same one where the actual trial was taking place, but that wouldn't really matter. Of course, courtrooms are typically locked when not in use. That didn't stop me from trying the handles, but all the doors stayed firmly in place.

Pro tip: If you walk around a courthouse long enough trying to get into locked doors, someone will start asking you questions. A young bailiff speed walked toward me. "Can I help you, ma'am?" he asked.

"I sure hope so," I replied. "I'm supposed to be doing an interview in one of these courtrooms, but I can't remember which one, and they're all locked."

It was a fib, albeit a harmless one. Alec's eyes lit up at my improvisation.

The bailiff scratched his head and gave me a sideways glance. "Well, it can't be the 140th because there's a trial in there." I bit my lip to keep from smiling.

"I know the judge is out in the 237th today. Why don't you use that one?"

"Sounds perfect. Can you unlock it for us?"

He pulled out the biggest set of keys I had ever seen and started moving rings around.

"You've really got the run of the place, don't you?" I complimented him.

"Yes, ma'am," he said, selecting the proper key.

It was almost too good to be true. But I wasn't finished pressing my luck.

"You know, if you're not too busy, could you stand outside the door while we're in here and make sure no one interrupts? I'd hate for someone who wasn't supposed to be here to come waltzing in the courtroom."

"Sure thing, ma'am."

When the door shut behind him, Alec winked at me, and we got down to business. The crew threw up a couple lights and fired up the camera. We knew the jig could be up any minute, and we wanted to make the most of our newly sanctioned interview space.

After weeks of sitting silently in the courtroom while their son was on trial for murder, Dixon's parents were primed to talk. His mother was the strongest speaker, and you could feel the emotion behind every word.

Her son, a fifty-year-old plastic surgeon who'd never been in trouble a day in his life, was accused of orchestrating a murder plot and facing life in prison.

"You worry about a lot of things when you have a child," she said. "But I never worried about this."

It was exactly the sound bite we never knew we needed, and I felt the TV magic happening right before my eyes. We talked to his mom and dad for a few more minutes, and then our phones all started buzzing. There was action in the jury room. We grabbed our gear and loaded out.

Judge Jim Bob Darnell pounded his gavel to bring the court into order. He had news from the jury, but it wasn't a verdict. After deliberating for four hours, they were asking to go home for the night and to resume their work in the morning. The judge approved their request and put the trial, once again, in recess.

Even when the death penalty is off the table, a capital murder trial is a nerve-wracking experience. There is so much at stake, and in cases like the trial of Dr. Thomas Michael Dixon, you can't help but imagine the two alternate realities: he's found not guilty and resumes a career as a plastic surgeon and father; he's found guilty and spends the rest of his life in prison, losing everything in the free world.

The jury clearly wasn't taking their responsibility lightly. They had deliberated for more than six hours, over two days, before sending up a new note to the judge: They were unable to reach a unanimous verdict. A collective groan spread through the courtroom gallery. Had it all been for naught? Dixon's defense attorney practically leaped from his seat and asked for a motion for a mistrial. But the judge wasn't ready to give up just yet.

After reading the note, he denied the motion for a mistrial and sent back an Allen charge to the jury. This is a legal mechanism that instructs jurors to continue deliberating even when they are seemingly at an impasse. It specifically addresses those in the minority opinion to reconsider their verdict.

"We have invested a great deal of time and effort in this matter to flush it down the toilet," Judge Darnell said.

But in the end, that's exactly what would happen. A few more hours passed before the jury sent back yet another note, this time with the magic words declaring they were "hopelessly deadlocked" and could not reach a verdict. Having satisfied both the Allen charge and a second deliberation session, Judge Darnell reluctantly declared a mistrial. There had been two holdouts on the jury who wanted to acquit Dr. Dixon, and ten jurors who believed he was guilty. But there would be no verdict this time around because Texas requires a unanimous decision.

This halftime of sorts would have been a perfectly good setup for an episode of *48*, except for what happened next. Judge Darnell issued a gag order, preventing any party to the case—including attorneys, witnesses, and the defendant—from speaking to the media.

Our impromptu courtroom interview with Dixon's mom would be the only piece of tape we could get until the gag order was lifted, which wasn't expected to happen until after the next trial. All those dinners with the defense team had resulted in zero on-camera conversations, and now we were left holding the bag. We'd never even been close to getting the prosecution to talk, and although Detective Johnson seemed keen on the idea, no one was going to break the gag order and risk getting thrown in jail themselves for contempt of court.

This was devastating news for our story, and I couldn't believe our hands were tied indefinitely. We'd sat through weeks of testimony and knew the case backward and forward, but cameras had only been allowed in the courtroom for closing arguments and the mistrial announcement. We couldn't build an hour of television around those few sound bites without getting additional interviews from attorneys or witnesses.

The last month had all been a dress rehearsal for the next trial, which the prosecution wanted to put on the calendar as quickly as possible. For court cases, that typically means nine months to a year. It takes as long to bring a baby into the world as it does to get a trial date on the books.

I didn't realize it at the time, but as it turned out, both monumental events were in the works for me.

4
AN INSIDE JOB

While my first assignment for CBS had sent me clear across Texas, the next one was right in my own backyard. I was still smarting from the sting of a hung jury and no story, so a new case was a welcomed distraction. As a rookie producer, I tried to clear all of the Dixon details from my brain so I could absorb an entirely different storyline. I felt like I'd spent the last month cramming for an exam that had been unceremoniously canceled. But there was no time to dwell on the past. The capital murder trial of Eric Williams started in December 2014, one week after I got back from Lubbock. I know what you're thinking, but there's no relation to the Michele Williams case. Eric Williams is a killer in his own right.

The Dallas-area case had made headlines the world over. Three innocent people had been murdered during a targeted and methodical shooting spree in early 2013. The first victim was the lead prosecutor for rural Kaufman County. Mark Hasse was gunned down just a few feet away from the court-house as he arrived for work in the morning of January 31, 2013.

A single man with no personal enemies, Hasse was an unusual target for a violent crime. But his work life left decades of leads for law enforcement to follow up on. Hasse had been a career prosecutor with a stint in Dallas County where he'd put a number of white supremacists in prison. Witnesses described a professional hit, with a getaway car driver and a shooter dressed in tactical gear. The entire operation was executed in a matter of minutes. The Aryan Brotherhood was at the top of the suspect list, and the FBI was called in and opened a command center in Kaufman. The elite unit of the Texas Department of Public Safety, the Texas Rangers, was also investigating.

It was all hands on deck, which made it even more surprising when the Kaufman County district attorney, Mike McLelland, and his wife, Cynthia, were the next victims. They were ambushed on March 30, 2013, Easter week-end, in their own home, and once again the getaway car was the only clue. Surveillance video from nearby businesses captured grainy images of the sus-pect's vehicle speeding past neighborhood intersections in the early-morning hours before it dropped out of sight, seemingly into thin air.

While the FBI and the Texas Rangers had been looking at potential sus-pects all over the map, the real killer had been right under their noses. Eric Williams, a former justice of the peace, lived across the street from the com-mand center. A justice of the peace (JP) is an elected position in Texas, and they preside over minor civil and criminal cases. As a JP, Williams had gotten a small taste of power, and he liked it. In a made-for-TV twist, he'd often ride his Segway around the block, keeping tabs on everyone. He even gave local media interviews while zipping to and fro for the cameras.

Turns out, Mark Hasse and Mike McLelland had prosecuted Williams for theft when he was a JP, alleging he'd stolen computer monitors from the office. Williams was found guilty in April 2012, but he wasn't put behind bars. He was given a probated sentence, ordered to pay a fine, and was stripped of his law license. Less than a year later, both Hasse and McClelland were dead.

To their credit, law enforcement had Williams on their radar early on. In fact, just hours after Hasse's murder, the Texas Rangers knocked on Wil-liams's door. He answered it with wet hair and his arm in a sling. He chatted breezily with the investigators and even consented to a gunshot residue test, which came back negative. His wet hair was from a shower, and he claimed he'd recently had shoulder surgery. It was all very slick, and he gave investi-gators just enough information to keep them interested but not nearly enough for a warrant.

They'd be back, though, and after the double murder of the McLellands, they finally had enough probable cause to search Williams's home. He might have still gotten away with it, if it wasn't for a handwritten note with a nine-digit code scrawled on it, sitting right on Williams's desk. That code was traced back to an anonymous Crime Stoppers tip about the murder weapon. And lo and behold, the information about the weapon was right on target.

From there, authorities tracked down a secret storage unit that Williams had rented under a friend's name. Inside, they found the mother lode. Rubber-maid containers of evidence, handwritten hit lists, and most importantly, an expertly parked white Crown Victoria sedan that matched the description of the getaway vehicle.

Texas Ranger Dewayne Dockery described the joyous feeling in that moment as "second only to the birth of his children." They had Eric Williams dead to rights, now they just needed to find his accomplice, the driver. It didn't take long to realize there was really only one person close to Eric anymore: his wife, Kim Williams. She crumbled under questioning and turned on her husband, laying out the whole sordid plot.

It was even more twisted than most had imagined. Eric had relished the murders and celebrated with a steak dinner after he'd pulled off his deadly caper. If authorities hadn't stopped him, he'd planned to kill two more Kaufman County officials: another prosecutor and the judge who'd overseen his theft trial.

Unlike the Dixon trial, there really was no alternate theory of events for the defense. No boogeyman roommate or an unemployed hit man with question-able allegiances. All signs pointed directly to Eric Williams and his wife, Kim.

While the Dixon capital murder trial had taken three weeks for testimony, the Williams trial took just three days. The treasure trove of evidence coupled with his wife's cooperation had left little doubt about Eric Williams's guilt, and the jury returned in less than an hour. But now there was the matter of his punishment. And considering the premeditated nature of the murders, Williams was eligible for the death penalty. The defense focused the bulk of their effort on this portion of the trial, fighting with everything they had to save their client's life.

It's a hell of a thing to watch someone clearly guilty of triple murder defend their own right to live. As you might expect from a returned Peace

Corps Volunteer, I'm generally on the side of pacifism and don't support the death penalty. But this case made me question that firmly held belief. Sitting in court, listening to witnesses lay out the clear and convincing evidence of Williams's coldhearted murder was hard enough.

But then CBS asked me to get to Williams himself.

He hadn't testified in his own defense, which made the possibility of hearing from him all the more intriguing to TV execs. Scarcity is the name of the TV game, and Williams's exclusive interview was at the top of my wish list. Or, I should say, it was on the top of my boss's wish list for me. After hearing what Williams had done to his victims, how callously he'd laid waste to their bodies and then celebrated their murders with a steak dinner, I was terrified at the idea of occupying the same space as him. There was no training for this in journalism school, and it's not like CBS had given me any guidance on talking to a serial killer. I was entering wholly uncharted territory.

I half hoped my interview request would be denied, but I'd be lying if there wasn't another part of me that was intrigued at the idea of speaking with him. Before this murder, he'd presumably been a normal person—or at least masqueraded as one. He'd been elected justice of the peace, for crying out loud, and he'd served in the Texas State Guard. How did this civil servant become a serial killer? And would I still be able to see the humanity underneath his heinous actions?

I'm sitting face-to-face with Eric Williams, convicted killer. It's not a normal visitors' day, so the area is exceptionally quiet. The thin plexiglass separating us does little to comfort me as he sizes me up behind wire-rimmed glasses. He's not outwardly imposing. Five feet, nine inches, with a slight frame, and short gray hair neatly combed to the side. He brings his focus to my pen and paper, which was all I was allowed to bring into my interview.

I had put in my request for a no-contact, no-camera, media visit with Eric Williams through the Rockwall County jail, where he was being held during his sentencing phase. In addition to getting approved by the authorities, I needed Williams himself to consent to an interview with me.

There aren't a lot of rights afforded to inmates, but the decision of whether or not to meet with visitors is still one of them. I've found that nearly all accused murderers will agree to meet if you don't bring a camera the first time. Having a visitor, any visitor, breaks up the monotony of incarceration. And most people, killers or not, are flattered at the idea of being interesting enough for an interview.

I introduce myself and instinctively say, "It's nice to meet you." He laughs a big, spontaneous laugh that surprises me. He seems genuinely amused at the whole situation. And I quickly realize he's not here to talk about his case; in fact, he's droning on about everything but his case.

I'm allotted one hour to talk to him, which already felt about fifty minutes too long. But he's in no hurry and makes casual conversation, as if we're old friends catching up. I feel sick to my stomach and like I want to bolt. I'm trying to appear calm, but I'm sure he can see right through me.

He carries himself with a lightness that I never would have expected from someone in his position. He smiles while talking about the weather, conditions in the jail, and his countdown to be transferred to prison. His words fall to the background momentarily as I'm drawn to his eyes. In stark contrast to his demeanor, his eyes, a deep black, like inkblots, are totally devoid of warmth. I'm reminded of the infamous close-up of Charles Manson—same eyes, same dark, formless gaze. It's strange and striking, and I can't look away. Throughout my career, I'll start to recognize that deep-black void in the eyes of other killers. But you never forget your first.

I need to shift the pleasantries to the actual purpose of my visit. I'd sat through enough testimony to know he hadn't been born evil. He'd been a regular kid, a good one even, but somehow, he'd gone off course. So how did it happen? When did he turn off the straight and narrow and become a cold-blooded killer?

I take a shot in the dark and ask him, point blank. "How'd you end up here?" But he just laughs me off. The Eric Williams before me now isn't about to lay his soul bare and reveal any semblance of truth. It seems to me he is living in some fantasyland, with his time behind bars as an amusing sideshow. Stripped of his weapons and tactical gear, Williams knows he's no longer a real threat to anyone. But now he is chained up everywhere he goes, as though his small, soft frame is a formidable force.

He'd done his worst and gotten away with it. And no prison sentence can ever take that away from him. With nothing else to do but think, he probably replays the perverse killings over and over in his mind. And they call this his punishment.

A deputy interrupts Williams midsentence and tells us our hour is over. Williams hasn't agreed to do an on-camera interview, but he tells me I can write him in prison after he's transferred. As if I'm a pen pal. He twists his hand up from the cuffs to wave goodbye. "See you around," he says with a smile as he shuffles out of the booth in leg shackles.

I never thought much about evil before I took this job, but now it seemed I couldn't escape it. In the days after our visit, Williams started making eye contact with me in the courtroom. As he was led in and out, he subtly smirked back at me, like we shared an inside joke. It gave me the chills, and I had to stop myself from physically recoiling. It was all so bizarre. How was this even my life?

When I'd started out in journalism, I didn't imagine I'd end up here, buddying up to murderers. But I must admit, it gave me a thrill to think I'd fooled a master manipulator into believing I actually liked him. Killers like Eric Williams didn't deserve my honesty, and the last thing I'd feel was any guilt for playing them. Years into my career at CBS, a veteran *48 Hours* producer would remark, "You have a real talent for making friends with murderers. It's a good thing you work here, because I'm not sure that skill would translate to many other jobs."

While I'd been oblivious to the network competition from ABC and NBC in Lubbock, this time around I was on the lookout for the East Coast types who had found their way to this rural Texas courtroom. I realized they stuck out in their own way, if you knew what to look for. The shoes were the first indicator. Worn leather soles, the kind you get from actually walking miles a day like any true NYC resident. Once I identified the shoes, I followed them to the courthouse parking lot to see which car they got into, which was my next-biggest clue.

Rental cars were a dead giveaway for out-of-towners, and I learned to spot the "No Smoking" sticker on the window and the barcode on the dash. I'd discovered a handful of unidentified trial watchers this way, and I had good reason to believe that at least some of them were with *Dateline* and *20/20*.

The first person I approached was an older man, sitting by himself, who fit my shoe and car criteria. He was even taking notes on a yellow legal pad, which I'd seen other network producers do in Lubbock. I waited until the morning recess to approach him and feigned a reason to strike up a conversation by asking him for the time.

"It's ten thirty," he told me with a friendly smile, so I kept talking.

"What brings you to the trial?"

A cryptic reply would keep him in my possible competition category, while a straight answer would eliminate him immediately. I didn't actually expect anyone from network television to identify themselves that easily.

"Personal interest. I know the defendant."

Naively, I believed him. But as we continued to talk, I ferreted out the whole truth. He merely knew *of* the defendant, he didn't actually *know him*, know him. They'd lived in the same neighborhood years ago and crossed paths a time or two at social events. Yawn. He had no actual connection to the case and was a retiree looking for a place to pass the time. I'd later learn to give these trial watchers a wide berth, but this was my first rodeo with a courtroom lookie-loo. I was friendly but didn't bother to exchange contact details. I was keeping my counterfeit CBS business cards for the real-deal characters, thank you very much.

The next person I approached was an older woman who was also taking copious notes. She didn't appear to be working with anyone else and was laser focused on the testimony. Could she be a producer in camouflage? Her floral clothes didn't say New York to me, but I've never been a great judge of fashion.

I decided to go on the hunt and circled back to intercept her on the way out of the courtroom. I pretended not to know the way to the ladies' restroom and asked her if she could help. Then I steered the conversation to the trial.

"Pretty interesting stuff, isn't it?" She readily agreed. We chatted a bit more before she revealed herself as the true crime author Kathryn Casey. A media giant in her own right, to be sure, but not the kind I was looking for.

So I'd struck out twice already using this logic, but I was undeterred. Surely the odds were in my favor. The faces weren't the same as Lubbock, except for mine of course. But I just knew all three networks had to be in town once again. The trial was too high profile and the judge had allowed cameras in the courtroom, which was like catnip for true crime television producers.

It took a few more days of trial and error before I identified the producers from NBC's *Dateline* and *20/20* on ABC. Wearing dark suits and sitting up front, they'd blended in with the attorneys. Once I spotted them, I realized they were chatting up attendees during all the breaks, and from the looks of it, they were making some good inroads. They were in town for the long haul, and like me, they were working every angle they could manage. Was this how it was going to be at every trial? A battle royale for the story and interviews?

While CBS had eventually sent in another producer to help me on the Lubbock case, I was back to flying solo on this one. The other networks were using the buddy system, and my mind went into competition mode. I knew I was outnumbered and underexperienced. How could I compete with the big boys?

I focused on my strengths. Namely, I was a local. A native Texan. By the looks of it, I was also about twenty years younger than the other producers on the story. I'd have to find a way to make my youth an asset, not a liability.

I'm mulling all this over during lunch when my phone rings. It's Alec Sirken, and he's got a question for me.

"So I just got called into Z's office. Can you guess why?"

It took me all of two seconds to answer. "Because you wrote F-you in an expense report?"

"Ha! I can't believe you remembered that," Alec replied.

How could I not? It wasn't every day I encountered f-bombs in the workplace, but for a New Yorker in the national media, apparently it was forgettable.

An exception to this rule is senior producer Judy Tygard, who employs choice stingers rather than profanity.

I get Alec up to speed on my new story and tell him I'm in a hurry to finish lunch before court starts back up again. He asks me if I've made inroads with anyone from the case yet, and I admit I'm still trying to land my first character. As I crunch through my salad, Alec helps me strategize.

"Look around the café. Do you recognize anyone from court?"

When I tell him no, he gives me just the nudge I needed. "Well, they have to eat somewhere."

I hung up the phone and got on Yelp. What restaurant would stalwart Texans choose for lunch?

My eyes stopped on Soulman's Bar-B-Que, a local joint less than a mile away that had Texas written all over it. For my money, it seemed the best bet. And the following day, I hightailed it to Soulman's for the lunch recess.

I didn't really care who I cornered from the trial. I had a whole slate of interviews to fill, and thus far the only contacts I had made were with the deranged killer and some lookie-loos in the courtroom. I needed to get a winning character on my team, fast.

As I got in line at the buffet, I spotted two men in suits. Bingo. I'd found the prosecutors. I shuffled through the line and headed straight for their table with my cafeteria tray. Fortune favors the bold. They rose from their seats like good Southern gentlemen and pulled out a chair for me. Eat your heart out, senior *Dateline* producers.

The special prosecutors assigned to the case were giants of the legal system in Dallas. Toby Shook, a veteran prosecutor turned star defense attorney who'd dominated the private practice scene for the last decade. And Bill Wirskye, a career prosecutor who'd teamed up with Shook before, when they took down the infamous Texas Seven, a group of prisoners who escaped in 2000 and were on the run for a month before being apprehended.

Neither man was a stranger to the cameras, and they'd both had their fair share of interviews over the years. I knew I couldn't get them to agree to be exclusive to CBS for this story, which is the gold standard in the interview world. But maybe I could get the next best thing: the first interview after the trial. As our lunch was wrapping up, I wiped the barbecue sauce off my fingers and got down to business.

"I recognize this case is too big of a story for just one network to cover, but there will still have to be a batting order for interviews. And, respectfully, I'd hope that you'd consider CBS for your first interview after the trial."

I'd laid it all out there, and now it was just crickets. I still needed a closer.

"I'm a native Texan. I live in Dallas. Who better to get the first national interview with y'all on this case than a hometown girl?"

They smiled back at me. I was getting to them.

"You wouldn't let those smooth-talking New Yorkers steal you away from me, would you?"

How could they resist?

"Of course not. Let's get through the trial first, but then we'll talk to you."

We shook on it and exchanged business cards. I'm guessing mine was the only one printed at the Lubbock Kinko's.

After two weeks of testimony in the punishment phase of the trial, the jury returned a unanimous decision in favor of the death penalty for capital murder.

Upholding the jury's verdict, Judge Mike Snipes sentenced Eric Williams to death and assured the citizens of Kaufman County that their long nightmare was finally over.

"I know you've been scared for the last couple of years," he said. "Nobody's gonna be scared anymore."

He also spoke directly to Williams. "You made yourself out to be some sort of 'Charles Bronson *Death Wish* vigilante' in this case. I never bought that."

Family members from all three victims addressed Williams in court. Cynthia McLelland's daughter had the strongest words for the killer. "Fuck you, Eric Williams," she said. Now that's a justified use of an expletive if I've ever heard one.

A representative read aloud a statement from Mark Hasse's mother. "You are going to die, and our family will be there to watch it happen. And long after your corpse has been disposed of, and your name forgotten, this county and state will remember the good people—Mark Hasse, Mike McLelland, Cynthia McLelland—who gave their lives putting scum like you in prison."

Williams didn't have a visible reaction to any of the proceedings. At times he stared straight ahead and even locked eyes with those speaking, but he never showed any emotion. He appeared altogether unmoved by the gravity of the situation.

As he was led away in handcuffs, the once pin-quiet courtroom came to life. The collective relief was palpable, and everyone in attendance took a deep breath for what felt like the first time during the trial. While I had made small talk with the victim's family, especially a son who seemed about my age, I had been hesitant to approach them for an interview before now. But if I didn't do it soon, I might not get another chance.

I worked my way through the crowd, bobbing and weaving in between groups of people until I reached the inner circle of the McLelland family. I hated intruding on their space, but I had a job to do. I know how it might sound coming from a journalist whose mission is to get people to talk, but I've always believed in the Golden Rule: treating other people the way I'd like to be treated.

As disturbing as it is to think about, I've imagined how I would want to be approached for an interview if, God forbid, someone I loved had been murdered. I felt like I had to put myself in that mournful frame of mind to understand why anyone might ever say yes to a reporter in the aftermath of a tragedy. The way I looked at it, if I wasn't approaching a victim's family, somebody else would do it, and likely with far less care and sensitivity.

I've found that apologizing all over yourself is as good an introduction as anything else, and I led with a bounty of sorrys. I was sorry for interrupting them, sorry for the whole reason we were in this courtroom, and most of all, sorry that I couldn't leave them in peace. They smiled sympathetically back at me.

A ball of nerves, I handed out my business cards and gave them the shortest pitch in the history of my producing career. "I can't imagine what you're going through, but if you can find it in your heart to share your story, I'll be here to listen." And then I walked away.

Downstairs, the prosecutors were setting up for a press conference, and a small crowd was already gathering. With the hardest pitch to the victim's family out of the way, I was ready to work the room. I made the rounds, shaking hands, exchanging contact information, and taking notes on who was who.

There were members of Eric Williams's family, someone who served with him in the Texas State Guard, and a slew of investigators from every agency that had worked the case, including the Texas Rangers, the FBI, and the Kaufman County Sheriff's Office. In less than fifteen minutes, I had more than made up for my lack of usable contacts during the trial. My reporter's notebook was now full of names and numbers I could call on for interviews. I had everyone you could dream of putting on television for the story.

Everyone, that is, except for the victim's family, which is actually all that matters in true crime reporting.

You can substitute investigators, hire special consultants to analyze the case, and even call up a law professor from a local university in a pinch. The only thing you can't do is go to air without anyone representing the victim's side of the story. The closer the relative, the better. Parents, children, and siblings of the slain are the top rung in the booking ladder. Aunts and uncles, cousins, even friends and coworkers will do, and as a last resort, you can book a neighbor or a childhood friend.

It all sounds so obvious now, but this was only my second official story for *48 Hours*, and I had no idea that I was missing this crucial element. I'd approached the McLelland family but had nothing to show for it, so as far as anyone in New York was concerned, it hadn't even happened. There's a saying in TV that nothing is real until it's on camera, and I wasn't even close to lights, camera, action. All my confidence about the list of contacts I had on the story came crashing down when I called my boss after the press conference.

"Where are we with the victim's family?" Kramer asked me.

"I gave them all my contact information," I said, foolishly thinking this was an accomplishment.

"And?" she replied.

"Now I'm just waiting to hear back," I said.

I got an earful on that line, and I held the phone away. Timidity was not the way of the television world, much less on a major story like this one where all three networks were vying for characters.

I knew I had screwed up, and I was in full damage-control mode. Kramer was ready to pull me from the story, but I proposed a salvage operation. I was one more mistake away from being banished to the morgue, and, storied though it was, I had no interest in covering the Queen's life and inevitable death.

"Let me work the characters I do have contact information for, and I'll try to find a way in with the victim's family," I offered.

She wasn't happy about it but agreed to a one-week extension on the story. If I hadn't gotten ahold of someone in the McLelland family by then, she was throwing me on another case. I wasn't about to let all those long days in court go to waste without a fight.

I sorted my list of contacts by the highest value interviews. At the top of my page was Lenda Bush, an attorney and key eyewitness.

One of the first witnesses for the state, Lenda had recounted a first-person narrative of Mark Hasse's murder in haunting detail. She'd arrived early to the courthouse that morning and was still in her car looking for a parking spot when she'd noticed a figure in black out of the corner of her eye. She'd watched in horror as the man in black approached Mark Hasse and fired three bullets at close range.

Then the shooter fled the scene and got into a vehicle, which Lenda followed for several blocks while she attempted to call 911. She was so nervous that she kept misdialing the digits. Realizing that she probably shouldn't be following the shooter's car by herself, Lenda turned around and went back to the scene, where she performed CPR on Mark until an ambulance arrived. While delivering chest compressions, Lenda had a stunning realization—she knew the victim. Even though he was unresponsive, she called out his name. "You're going to be okay, Mark," she told him. "Hang in there. Try to breathe for me."

Lenda came by her toughness naturally. Born and raised on ranchlands, Lenda worked as a police officer before becoming an attorney. In other words, she was an ideal witness for the state and the stuff of made-for-TV dreams. The unique spelling of her first name coupled with her attorney practice made it easy enough to track her down. Now I just had to get her to agree to do an on-camera interview.

In her captivating testimony, she'd revealed her connection to every player in the case. As an attorney, she'd worked with Mark Hasse and Mike McLelland, and she knew his wife, Cynthia, as well. Plus, she'd even had occasion to work with Eric Williams, back when he was a justice of the peace. She was so much more than just an eyewitness.

I shared all this with the *48 Hours* brain trust in New York as we mapped out a plan to approach her. Considering her personal and professional connections to the case, we decided on first putting our pitch down in writing. While we didn't want her to feel like we were putting her on the spot with a cold call, we were still hoping for a pretty quick turnaround. I sent the letter certified mail and heard back from her office the next day. In an email through her assistant, Lenda said she'd participate in our episode.

I was new to the TV world, but I'd seen enough producer activity to know that a green light through a third party wasn't a sure thing. When you're asking people to talk about matters of life and death, sources can get cold feet and back out of interviews, especially if they've never even met you face-to-face. It was much better to establish a relationship in person and look them in the eyes when they commit to going on television.

So I set up lunch plans with her and made the hour-long drive from Dallas to Lenda's office in Terrell, Texas. Through my work covering trials for *48 Hours*, I'd eventually spend so much time on quaint streets that the locations would all blend together. But back then I was still new to the small-town beat. Every detail seemed unique and memorable, and I stopped to admire the original brick and mortar.

Most small towns have the same layout: courthouse on a square block, with law offices, cafés, and a few local businesses surrounding it. There's usually a hardware shop, a clothing boutique, and a bar to take the edge off. Terrell checked the same boxes as Kaufman, and I imagined how peaceful the morning must have looked before Mark Hasse was killed. It's unsettling how much damage one person with a grudge and a gun can do.

I spotted a sign that said "Law Offices of Lenda Ray Bush" and hustled into the historic building. Lenda gave me a quick tour and we headed to lunch. We were already getting along great. I liked her confident and direct nature, and she had stories for days. Turns out the Mark Hasse murder wasn't the first courthouse shooting that she'd been involved in, and she kept me on the edge of my seat with accounts of her earlier career as one of the first female police officers in North Texas. I knew I'd found a great character, and she didn't seem the type who would scare easily under the lights.

There was really only one thing left that could thwart our interview . . . well, two things: NBC's *Dateline* and ABC's *20/20*. Exclusives are the name of the true crime TV game, and while police officers, prosecutors, and any elected officials rarely give one network an edge, private citizens are another story. Friends and family of the victims and eyewitnesses are the key exclusive interviews that separate one show from another.

The trial had ended just a few short days ago, and I had to find out if anyone else had gotten to her first. Lenda told me a couple of producers had introduced themselves to her after she testified, but no one had followed up. I tried not to grin too big and instead gave Lenda my earnest pitch for her exclusive participation with CBS. I couldn't offer her a financial benefit, so I went with an emotional one.

"You've already been through so much. I'm sure every true crime show in America will want to talk to you, but it's your choice who you work with. If I were you, I'd want to tell my story one time to the media and then be done with it."

She smiled and said that all made sense to her, and she had no interest in making the rounds and giving multiple interviews. Talk about great news. We shook on it, and I hit the road back to Dallas, calling Kramer in New York on the way.

With Lenda Bush officially and exclusively on board, I knew I was one step closer to getting our episode launched. I still didn't have the victim's family or any way to contact them, but I couldn't dwell on past mistakes. I had to keep my momentum going, and so I reached out to my BBQ lunch buddies, the prosecutors.

I had been flying high after meeting Lenda, but I was about to come crashing down back to earth. When I called Toby Shook, he informed me *Dateline* had already set up an interview for next week. So much for the hometown girl getting first dibs.

Getting beat to the first interview is not the kind of news you rush to share. I decided to look for another exclusive interview before I gave my boss an update. It's always easier to deliver bad news on the heels of something positive. And I had already gotten all the mileage out of Lenda Bush's exclusive yesterday. This is the danger of sharing good news too quickly. You never know what's around the corner.

I went back through my notebook and desperately scanned my list for potential exclusive interviews. I called a man who said he'd served in the Texas State Guard with Eric Williams. We'd met shortly after the death penalty was pronounced at the press conference in front of the courthouse. He seemed interested in talking to me back then, but today he couldn't get off the phone fast enough. Swing and a miss. I put a line through his name and number and kept going.

Next up was a woman who identified herself as Eric Williams's sister. She'd been shy and standoffish at first, but by the end of our conversation she'd given me her cell phone number, and that was all the encouragement I needed. I took a deep breath to cleanse the last rejection and punched in her number. After it seemed like it rang forever, a woman picked up the line. I asked if she was Eric's sister, and she simply replied "wrong number" and hung up on me. Strike two.

My list of contacts was rapidly dwindling, and I really needed a win. I put my notebook down and started thumbing through a pile of business cards that I'd gotten from trial attendees. It was one sterile card after another: the court coordinator, the defense attorney, and a slew of investigators with tiny badges engraved beside their names. The job title might sound sexy enough, but trust me when I say there's nothing more boring than a real-life FBI agent on camera.

At the bottom of the pile, I saw a blonde woman's face staring back at me. Jenny Parks, attorney at law. I remembered that she wasn't directly involved in the case, but she'd come to watch the trial one of the days and had been chatty with the press. Her card showed she practiced in Kaufman County, and I ventured a guess that she'd been friends with Mike McLelland and Mark Hasse.

One way to find out.

Jenny was happy to talk to me, and I was relieved not to have three people in a row hang up on me. The call got even better when Jenny revealed her unlikely connection to the case. She hadn't really been friends with Mike or Mark, but she had once been close with their killer, Eric Williams.

Now this was a relationship I could work with for television. It wasn't a romantic one, but Jenny and Eric had been real friends. The kind that had lunch together and swapped stories about workplace drama. Back when Eric was a justice of the peace, he had even talked to Jenny about the theft charges against him. And years later, when the men who'd prosecuted him started getting picked off, one by one, Jenny had run into Eric around Kaufman. They talked about the murders, and Eric acted as flabbergasted as anyone about the turn of events.

I made plans to meet Jenny for lunch the next day and thanked her for her willingness to talk. I left out the part about her saving me from getting thrown off the story and into whatever fresh hell had dominated the headlines in the past twenty-four hours. You can't share every secret with your sources.

A great conversationalist with a penchant for storytelling, Jenny Parks was undoubtedly an excellent attorney. And it was ideal for our episode that she'd been actual friends with the killer, back before anyone dreamed what he was capable of. Plus, Jenny had lived in the Kaufman area for decades and could "set the scene" for us, providing context for the kind of quiet community Kaufman had been and speaking with authority on the characteristics of the town and its residents.

The only box Jenny didn't check was having photographs of Eric from the period of time when they were friends. For TV, those snapshots are worth their weight in gold. Platinum if you have videos. And while CBS News standards dictate that we can't pay for an interview, we can license photos and cut you a check. Without the ability to offer Jenny any kind of compensation, I tried to think of a way to win her over for an exclusive. She was already willing to talk on camera, but she gave it up so quickly that I worried she'd also say yes to a producer from *Dateline* or *20/20*.

We kept chatting and I took note that Jenny was decked out for our meeting at a roadside diner. Gone was the blonde from her business card, Jenny's hair was now a delightful shade of auburn. I estimated her contoured makeup must have taken hours to apply, and her outfit was impeccably put together, complete with accessories and high heels.

I told Jenny her perspective was exactly what our story was missing, and that we wanted to put our time and resources into securing her exclusive interview. Her eyes lit up, and I hoped she wasn't seeing dollar signs. I explained that we couldn't pay her outright for an interview, but we could provide transportation and her own hair and makeup artist.

I didn't have approval for this offer yet, but a little thing like permission wasn't going to stop me. One look at the smile on Jenny's face and I knew she was sold. This episode was shaping up nicely, if—and it was still a big if—I could ever get the family to call me.

It's Friday morning, and my weeklong leash to secure the story is getting tighter. I have two exclusive bookings plus a smattering of rejections. And that is just not going to cut it. Kramer has made it perfectly clear that unless I have a McLelland or Hasse family member, there's no story.

A lifelong bachelor, Mark Hasse didn't have much in the way of traditional TV talking heads to represent his family. His grieving mother had stayed away from the press, and I wasn't about to darken her door. That left the McLelland family, and they were a fractured bunch. Multiple marriages, stepkids, and the like.

Complicated relationships usually work to your advantage in the booking process. Without a united family, odds are there won't be an exclusive family interview, so no matter how far behind I was from *Dateline* and *20/20*, I still had a fighting chance to save my story. I just needed to find a friendly branch of the McLelland family tree.

When I hit a wall at work, the best use of my time is to step away from all my screens and go for a run. After five miles of pounding pavement, whatever problems I have seem much more solvable. Somewhere around mile three or four, I usually figure out my next right move and sprint home as fast as my legs will carry me. I'll fly in the door and land at my desk chair, sweat dripping onto the keyboard as I punch in my new game plan.

I've come up with nearly all my greatest ideas on long runs, and I've heard from other creative types that the combination of physical activity, being outdoors, and getting away from the actual problem is the right recipe for a breakthrough. Other people pull weeds, wax their car, or hit tennis balls against the wall. But I believe running is superior to all these brainstorming methods. We were born to run, not born to weed.

I tie up my laces and swing the door open. It's a beautiful day and before I know it, I'm in my rhythm. And like clockwork, as I reach mile four, it hits me.

Racing into my home office, I pick up the phone and dial Toby Shook, the special prosecutor who shattered my delusion of Texas grandeur. Yes, he'd already given *Dateline* his first interview, and there was no unwinding the clock on that one. But I still have a play in mind.

I explain to Toby that I'd chatted with the victim's son, J. R. McLelland, during the trial, and he'd seemed open to doing an interview with me. But, rookie mistake, I didn't actually get his number. Instead, I'd simply given J. R. my card. Now here I am, a week later, still waiting for my phone to ring.

He laughs and asks how he can help.

"I know you can't hand over a family member's contact info, but could you do me a solid and vouch for me the next time you speak to J. R.?" I'm intentionally emphasizing the last part, hoping he'll catch my urgent drift.

"Sure thing, Claire," he says. And I think he actually means it this time.

I hang up and pray my last-ditch effort works. I begin my bluesheet, laying out all the characters I had booked, including the prosecutors and some investigators I've added to my arsenal from the Texas Rangers. It always helps to have a man in a cowboy hat.

Kramer had already emailed and asked for an update on the family, so I knew I only had about an hour before she'd call me if I didn't respond. It was such a nice-looking sheet, but without the victim's family, it was a lost cause. I stare at my computer screen, my eyes glazing over.

My legs are shot from the run, and I need to stretch them. I grab my dogs and a tennis ball and head out to the park behind our house. I spot my cell phone on the desk and hesitate a moment before tucking it into my pocket.

I'm chucking tennis ball after tennis ball and watching the dogs play while the sun dips on the horizon. *Life is actually so great*, I repeat in my head to crowd out the overwhelming thought of going 0-2 in my first run as a national television producer, my entire professional life hanging in the balance.

I throw the tennis ball a little harder, a little farther to release my frustration. And then, I feel my phone buzzing. I freeze up, knowing it's my boss with another earful. I can't even look at the number and blindly pick up the call, steeling myself for the inevitable onslaught.

I'm pinching my eyes shut as I answer, "Hello?"

A man's voice booms through the other end of the line. "This is J. R. McLelland; I'm calling for Claire St. Amant."

Once I have J. R., everything else falls into place. He'd heard other members of his family were talking to *Dateline*, and he is willing to do an exclusive interview with *48 Hours*, and to bring his sister, Krista, along as well. Kramer no longer has any doubts about the viability of the story, and they assign a full production team. The Queen's long-suffering special will have to manage without me.

And with that I was really in the fold, the comeback kid who got the job done. The story was so rock solid that they even invited me to New York for the *48 Hours* Christmas party, all expenses paid. I couldn't believe my turn of fortune, and I enthusiastically accepted. Riley and I had never been to New York, and we decided to make a trip of it. We bought Broadway tickets to *Les Misérables* and found a CBS-approved hotel overlooking Central Park, where I planned to do the big outer running loop. The first time I traveled for CBS, I'd been marooned in Lubbock, Texas. Now, just a month later, I was jet-setting to the Big Apple.

Riley and I looked the part of tourists as we walked, our necks tilted back, marveling at the skyscrapers. We laughed and held hands and felt like we were in a scene from a romantic comedy. You know, the one where the small-town girl comes to the big city and finds herself. A plotline as old as cinema itself.

So much was happening so quickly, and I had butterflies in my stomach to prove it.

I'm shuffling into a large meeting room at the CBS Broadcast Center with mostly strangers. It's the *48 Hours* Christmas party, and even though Riley had flown all the way to NYC with me, significant others weren't invited. He's more amused by this than offended, thankfully.

It's 2014: pre–Me Too, pre-pandemic, and totally out of control. There's an open bar and a DJ, and it looks like a few of the higher-ups had a head start; it's already gotten a bit sloppy.

I grab a seat on a couch with a handful of other women in their twenties. One of them gestures to the dance floor, where I spy a senior producer headed our way. He saunters over and plops down next to us, a little too closely. "Is this where all the cool kids are hanging out?" he says, the smell of Jack and Coke wafting over his words. We laugh nervously and shift away from him.

But he doesn't get the hint, and worse, he's awkwardly putting his arms around us and leaning in for more conversation. I'm definitely getting uncomfortable, and I can see the others are, too. I don't even know this guy—I've just met him. But what's a girl to do?

Working for small media companies in Dallas, I hadn't exactly been trained in the nuances of the corporate predator. So when my first two couch buddies smile and excuse themselves, I know it's okay to walk away, despite the obvious pecking order here. It's clearly not the first time this has happened, but I sense I'm supposed to keep my mouth shut about it. I smile politely as I stand up.

It's the kind of tightrope walk women have learned to master. We have to be friendly enough so as not to offend a senior staff member, but still quick with the slip to get out of tight situations, lest they escalate and get someone into real trouble.

Not knowing exactly how to exit the scene gracefully, I begin to tiptoe backward, right into a row of tables set up with appetizers. So much for subtlety. I regain my footing and smooth my dress. I glance back over at the couch to make sure this hasn't drawn the wrong kind of attention. I see everyone has cleared out, leaving the senior producer to wander back into the crowd, drink in hand.

Extrication complete, I look around for familiar faces and spot Ryan Smith huddled with a group of producers eating pizza. Executive producer Susan Zirinsky is holding court nearby, and pretty soon she's clearing out space on the dance floor. I push to the front and make it just in time to witness a CBS party hallmark: Z's signature splits. And it is impressive. Everyone's still cheering as she gamely pops back up, knee-high boots, miniskirt and all. Z is such a natural entertainer that most people don't even realize that she rarely, if ever, drinks alcohol.

Figuring nothing else at the party could top Z, I decide to call it a night. Back in my hotel room, I snuggle up next to Riley. We order room service and channel surf, settling on *Home Alone 2: Lost in New York* before drifting off to sleep. I never did make it to Central Park for my run.

When we got back to Texas, the story was in full production mode. While I'd been a CBS News consultant for the Michele Williams episode, I'd never seen inside the process like this. Creating an hour of television takes months of work and requires a small army to carry out all the orders coming in from New York.

The first producer assigned to the Kaufman story was Chuck Stevenson. A wiry guy with frenetic energy, Chuck was known for his high production values and bursting budgets. His nickname was "Hollywood," and he earned it. His shows were beautiful and always had those extra touches: an exploding car, a fog machine, a reconstructed crime scene with every detail matched to perfection. Most producers wouldn't dream of pulling the stunts that Chuck came up with on a regular basis.

Need to film a location and the owners won't let you inside? Chuck will rent a helicopter and get aerials. He once had a duffel bag filled with two million dollars just to show the audience what it looked like. Rumor had it the cash was counterfeit, but no one ever confirmed it.

His reputation for outlandish requests was legendary among associate producers, who bore the brunt of his ambitious visions. APs, as everyone calls them, would trade "Chuck stories" about ridiculous assignments and wild-goose chases he sent them on. My favorite was when Chuck decided he needed goat's blood for a blood-spatter demonstration with a crime scene expert. He sent a poor soul all over town, trying to procure the actual blood of a goat. She ended up talking to a petting zoo and a vet tech and was awfully close to renting a goat and drawing its blood before Chuck mercifully pulled the plug on the whole operation.

To be fair, Chuck wasn't the only one who picked on APs. Producer Alec Sirken also had his fair share of fun with them. Without kids of his own to impart wisdom to the next generation, Alec decided to write a book called *The Young People's Guide to Success*.[5] He needed an image for the cover, so he called a handful of APs into the conference room and had them pose in a pleasing fashion. Just another day in the life of a budding television producer.

---

5   Alec Sirken, *The Young People's Guide to Success* (CreateSpace Independent Publishing, 2018), https://a.co/d/dROU54H.

Since I was new to the whole TV world, the thought of working with Hollywood Chuck sounded like great fun to me. Even though I was low on the *48* totem pole, I wasn't at the very bottom. By virtue of bringing my own stories to the show, I got to skip the lowest staff positions, including production secretary, broadcast associate, and associate producer. I was a field producer, one step away from the capital-P Producer, and I'd never even worked in television before.

As this was not the traditional way to join CBS News, it rubbed a lot of people the wrong way. I was still a team player, so I'd make coffee runs or pick up lunch in a pinch, but I left the true-blue gophering to the APs, who were typically the lowest-ranking members out on shoots. They were given every unpleasant task you can imagine, and Chuck could imagine a lot.

I got Chuck up to speed on the story by sending him all my notes from the trial. He called me and excitedly ran through his ideas for the episode. He was intrigued by the fact that Lenda Bush had been hypnotized as part of her witness interview with the Texas Rangers when she couldn't recall details about the suspect's getaway car. Chuck saw an opportunity for high drama and stylized filming, and he was already throwing out requests for a fog machine and a drone operator.

He also wanted to film in the Kaufman County Courthouse, which presented a bit of a problem because all my contacts had been at the location of the actual trial in Collin County. Undeterred, Chuck simply told me to find someone in the courthouse who we could say we were putting on camera to get us in the door. "Who knows, maybe we'll even use them in the hour," he said casually.

I'd soon learn the term for these types of ploys: "vanity interviews." We used them to grease the wheels of bureaucracy in courthouses, police stations, and any other entity that caused us headaches. We'd find a strategic person to interview as a Trojan horse. It might be a figurehead like an elected district attorney or sheriff who didn't actually have a role in the investigation, or it could be a keeper of the keys like a court coordinator or office manager.

Their actual connection to the case was inconsequential. We were really using them to get in the door and making them feel important and special by throwing up a light and turning on the camera. About 25 percent of the time, the character would say something interesting or helpful for our story, and so their interview actually made air. But most of the time, it was just a means to an end. We'd chat with them for five or ten minutes in their office, and then say we needed to grab some B-roll inside. That's when the real filming would begin, and we'd spend an hour or more getting all the essential shots for our story.

I heard from camera crews that in the past, they wouldn't even press the record button for a vanity interview. But then one time a character actually revealed a key piece of information, and the crew had to scramble to get the recording going and capture it again. This bumbling mistake was enough to change the vanity interview policy. Now, the cameras were always rolling, just in case lightning struck twice.

I was tasked with finding a vanity interview to get us inside the Kaufman County Courthouse, and it wasn't long before I found our mark: a court coordinator who'd been working the morning of the shooting. She remembered hearing the gunfire and going into lockdown mode. I was pretty sure this would be a usable interview after all, and told Chuck as much.

While it was great to have additional characters for the story, our main focus was still on the McLelland family. We needed to schedule multiple days of filming with them, including sit-down interviews and B-roll. It was winter in Texas, and while that may not sound like much of an obstacle to anyone up north, we do have dips below freezing that make filming outdoors most unpleasant.

With the rural setting of the story, we wanted to do as much as we could in natural spaces. Chuck was big on "organic interview locations," meaning places the characters normally inhabit versus hotel suites and studio lots. I learned that J. R. owned a livestock feedstore in the small town of Wortham, Texas. It had a tin roof, dirt floors, and actual bales of hay outside. It was picture perfect, except for the fact that it didn't have a heater or a restroom. "Minor details," Chuck said. We'd make it work.

The logistics for my first field producer shoot were further complicated by the fact that I was secretly pregnant. After feeling nauseated the whole time I was in New York, I'd finally forced myself to go for a run around our neighborhood back in Texas. About a block away from our house, I threw up in a bush. I walked home, doing calendar math in my head, and took a pregnancy test.

I still remember calling Riley's name from the bottom of the stairs, plus-sign test in hand, and seeing the positively joyous reaction on his face.

Although we'd gotten married just a few years after college, we'd made a pact that we wouldn't have kids until thirty. In Texas, that's what's called starting a family late in life. A few months after my twenty-ninth birthday, we were expecting. It happened so fast that it took us by surprise, and I was nearly out of my first trimester before we'd even realized I was pregnant.

We weren't ready to share the news with CBS yet, mainly because they'd only given me a six-month contract. I was far from an expert on business negotiations, but even I knew that I better keep this little miracle under wraps until I had a new deal inked. With my winter wardrobe doubling as pregnancy camouflage, I operated under the radar for the whole shoot. It helped that I was meeting many of my New York colleagues for only the second time, the first being my whirlwind trip for the company Christmas party.

The main event for our shoot week was the interview with J. R. McLelland and his sister, Krista, at the family store. We had to do the interview in the evening, after hours.

Shortly before it was supposed to start, J. R. threw us all for a loop when he said his grandmother was coming as well and wanted to be interviewed. This was problematic for several reasons. We'd prepared questions for J. R. and Krista, but we didn't have any written for Mike McLelland's mother, and on top of that, we'd already set up a two-on-one interview shot. To add a third person was not only an editorial challenge but a physical one as well. The camera angles were all lined up for a two-person shot, with the reverse on the correspondent, Richard Schlesinger.

A native New Yorker, Richard spent the bulk of his illustrious television career with *48 Hours*. Known for his searing wit and outlandish facial expressions, Richard was a blast to have on set. His interviews were always entertaining, and he relished asking difficult questions and painting suspects into a corner.

While Peter Van Sant specialized in bringing out emotion and connecting with characters, Richard was more adversarial and treated each interview like a boxing match. A consummate professional, Richard could interview the wall and make it talk. But because his strengths lay more in confrontational interviews than emotive ones, the idea of adding another sympathetic character was not overly appealing. There's really no hard-hitting question you can ask a grandmother. But it's not like we could kick her out of the room either. We hemmed and hawed about how to best handle this twist.

TV time perpetually runs late, and we were already behind schedule. It was after 6 PM, the winter sun was long gone, and it was now in the thirties outside. The tin-roofed building wasn't doing us any favors temperature-wise. We'd eaten up precious hours already tracking down space heaters, extension cords, and generators to run them on. With all the extra effort, it was still hovering just over fifty degrees on set.

The clock was ticking, the room was an icebox, and we had interviewees showing up in less than an hour. We ultimately decided to pull out a third camera and establish a wide shot that would include all three McLellands. We'd keep the original setup as two on one, so the main cameras wouldn't include the grandmother. I wasn't exactly comfortable with turning the family matriarch into a glorified vanity interview, but it didn't feel like my place to speak up.

So I bit my tongue as they set up an extra monitor to display the three-person angle that we all knew would likely end up on the cutting room floor.

A feed store made an organic, if chilly, background for Richard Schlesinger's interview with the McLellands.

No matter what it takes to get there, the moment you first see television come to life is magical. Being behind the scenes, watching the lights turn on and the shot go into focus is something special. You can see the monitor feed, which shows the image in the right dimensions for television, but you're also in the actual room where the real-life drama is unfolding.

For an episode of *48 Hours*, the conversations are always intense and revealing. You're hearing people share intimate details from the worst moments of their lives, and in so many ways, you feel like you shouldn't even be in the room. It's a therapy session, a confessional, and a eulogy all at once.

J. R., Krista, and their grandmother were the first people to sit down with us for the show. Bundled up in multiple coats, with a horse blanket warming them between takes, they took us through decades of their lives, leading up to the murders. By the end of it, we were all numb, emotionally and physically. The B-roll would have to wait for another day, when we could feel our toes and the Texas sun was shining again.

While Hollywood Chuck had left us to fend for ourselves in the frozen feed-store, he flew down from NYC for Lenda Bush's interview. I'd scouted half a dozen locations for him until landing on the winner: a historic building with floor-to-ceiling windows, wood floors, and original brick walls.

Although Lenda's actual hypnosis session with the Texas Rangers had taken place in a windowless, gray conference room, the re-creation was going to be in high style. It was more of a mood shot than an accurate portrayal anyway, Chuck reasoned. We were going for the ethos of relaxation and deep concentration, and we needed the scenery to match.

After being interviewed with traditional techniques and coming up empty for a license plate or a definitive make and model of the getaway car, Lenda had agreed to a hypnosis session with the Texas Rangers. In a state of deep relaxation, she visualized every moment of the shooting and the aftermath. Lenda recalled what she was doing and seeing in vivid detail, including the fact that she misdialed 911 as 991. The details that surfaced about the car included it being a smaller, older model sedan, either tan or silver in color, with a distinctive pattern on the back windshield that she remembered repeating from the bottom to the top.

The Texas Rangers used hypnosis in criminal investigation interviews for over forty years before the practice was discontinued in 2021, less than a year after a local newspaper started reporting critically on it. In April 2020, the *Dallas Morning News* published a two-part series called "The Memory Room," which questioned the science behind hypnosis and its use in Texas criminal cases.

Even back in 2013, authorities weren't fully convinced hypnosis was producing reliable intelligence in the Mark Hasse murder. They'd tried unsuccessfully to locate the getaway vehicle using Lenda's description, and then after the McLelland murders, it appeared the suspect's vehicle was something else entirely.

Surveillance video captured a white Crown Victoria with tinted windows entering the McLellands' neighborhood just minutes before the shooting and leaving shortly afterward. Police wouldn't learn just how accurate Lenda's

Setting up the shot to re-create Lenda Bush's hypnosis session, "Hollywood Chuck" style.

description truly was until after Eric Williams's arrest, when his wife, Kim, tipped off authorities to a different vehicle, hidden away in a junkyard.

The original getaway vehicle was a silver Ford Taurus, which had to be abandoned because the transmission blew out after the Hasse murder. On the back windshield, a clear pattern of cat tracks was still visible in the dust, going all the way across the glass. Lenda's hypnosis-induced memory had been correct and had even produced details no one else knew about the original getaway vehicle.

Despite the controversy around specifically labeled "hypnosis" interview methods, inducing deep relaxation has been proven effective in producing repressed memories. Victims of trauma are routinely led through breathing and visualization activities before being asked to describe their attackers for a sketch artist. In this relaxed state, witnesses will often recall details they couldn't otherwise remember and provide information that can be corroborated by physical evidence.

As I watched Lenda's interview and the reimagined hypnosis session, I could see her physically relaxing and appear to enter another plane of consciousness. I had no idea at the time, but I'd one day find my own way into trauma therapy, where I'd experience the revealing power of hypnotic interview techniques firsthand.

After Lenda's interview wrapped, we still had a few hours left on our rental of the historic building and the fog machine. Chuck tapped his fingers together and appraised the situation before deciding we'd use the extra time to shoot "stand-ups" with correspondent Richard Schlesinger in the expansive entryway.

Stand-ups have mostly gone by the wayside in true crime television, but back in 2015 they were still all the rage. It's a narration method where the correspondent speaks directly to the camera while standing up and looking "godlike" and all knowing. We actually referred to them that way to express the grandness of the shot and the camera angle we were going for. To make the correspondent appear larger than life, we'd shoot from down low, with the cameraman kneeling or even lying down.

Chuck fired up the fog machine and a soft layer of billowing clouds began to fill the room. It was spooky . . . too spooky. We weren't shooting a Halloween movie. We just needed a touch of ominous atmosphere to add depth to the space. But now we were swimming in a sea of clouds. Chuck looked around and summoned me and the associate producer on the story to go find something to waft the fog. "A large piece of cardboard would work well," he suggested.

We wandered the streets of Kaufman in search of discarded boxes and eventually came upon a dumpster outside a restaurant. We gave each other a look that recognized dumpster diving might be in our future, but thankfully we spotted empty cardboard liquor boxes nearby. We disassembled them and carried the flattened pieces triumphantly back to the crew. We'd successfully completed a Chuck mission in under thirty minutes. That had to be a record.

We took our positions off camera and began wafting the fog with sheets of cardboard to achieve the perfect godlike shot composition. The ten-second stand-up probably comprised more manpower than any other shot in the show. But it did look really cool.

An hour of television equates to forty-two minutes of content and eighteen minutes of advertising. And that means distilling down hundreds, if not thousands, of hours of footage to make our show. The decisions about which clips to feature and which ones to cut were an endless source of discussion between producers. We all had our favorite sound bites, "our darlings," that we'd go to war over, but not every battle could be won.

In the Kaufman story, there were so many interesting angles to choose from. The investigation had spanned months and included federal, state, and local agencies. Along the way, there were multiple tipsters and eyewitnesses who helped point the finger at Eric Williams. In the end, I think the main reason our episode focused on Lenda Bush's hypnotism had more to do with Hollywood Chuck's artistic vision than anything else. And I'm okay with that. They were some of the most beautiful shots in the whole show, and the cat tracks were the tiny, golden nugget of intel mined at the end.

The rest of the shoot was a blur of interviews with investigators and attorneys. We hit up the Texas Rangers, the Kaufman County Sheriff's Office, and the special prosecutors. There were lots of cowboy hats, glistening gun belts, and boots shined to perfection. The most vivid memory I have from that portion of filming was feeling my son kick for the first time, during our interview with the lead detective on the case. If he pursues a career in law enforcement, that'll be one heck of an origin story.

5

THE STAKEOUT

It's almost 9 PM, and freezing rain is pelting my windshield as I try to follow my GPS to Stephenville, Texas. This morning an ice storm had cut our shoot week short in Kaufman and sent all my New York colleagues home early. The Eric Williams story was officially in a holding pattern, but I wasn't going to stay still for long. The same storm that paused one shoot launched me onto a new one, my first assignment for *CBS This Morning*.

That afternoon, Kramer had called to inform me that I was being loaned out to the head of booking for the morning show's coverage of the capital murder trial of Eddie Ray Routh, a name that instantly made my blood run cold.

"They need more boots on the ground for the verdict, which is expected to come down today."

I barely had time to pack an overnight bag before hitting the road again. It was a two-hour drive on a normal day, but double that for navigating the roads in ice and sleet. As treacherous as that sounded to me, it was the best solution CBS had to their North Texas producer problem, since flights into the frozen tundra of Dallas were hard to come by, and the story was red hot.

Legendary Navy SEAL sniper Chris Kyle was murdered in February 2013, right in the middle of the mysterious Kaufman killings. While prosecutor Mark Hasse's murder had been front page news, the shooting of Chris Kyle by a fellow military man had blown that story out of the water.

Evidence showed that Eddie Ray Routh, a twenty-five-year-old former marine, had killed Chris and his friend, Chad Littlefield, at a gun range. Eddie fled the scene in Chris's truck, crashing the Ford F-350 into a police cruiser after a brief car chase. I'd actually attended Chris Kyle's funeral at Cowboys Stadium, where thousands of people had come to pay their respects to the deadliest marksman in US history. The movie *American Sniper* came out a year later, starring Bradley Cooper, and was nominated for half a dozen Oscars. The term "high-profile trial" was an understatement.

I spend most of the drive white knuckling the steering wheel as I navigate the country highways in slippery conditions. Texans driving in the ice and snow are a recipe for disaster, and I'm determined to make it to my destination in one piece. When I finally reach the parking lot outside the Erath County Courthouse, I breathe a momentary sigh of relief. But I know my real work is just beginning.

The area is crawling with media as the February rain comes down. There are satellite trucks, news vans, and about a dozen camera crews and lights set up for live shots. Every local station from Dallas and Fort Worth is here, along with crews from CNN, Fox, and all three national networks. It's alphabet soup, and everyone is jockeying for position in front of the rural courthouse.

I zip through the rainy media parking lot, trying to find an open parking space amid all the news crews. I squeeze in next to a van and grab my umbrella as I make my way toward the front of the courthouse.

The jury has been deliberating for hours, and there's a buzz in the air that the verdict could come down at any minute. There'd never been much doubt about Eddie's guilt, and the only possible mitigating factor was his mental state at the time of the murders. Eddie had been diagnosed with post-traumatic stress disorder and schizophrenia after his discharge from the marines in 2011. He'd been under the care of the VA hospital but had stopped taking his medications.

I spot the CBS News eyeball on an antenna and follow it all the way down to a satellite truck. I don't know anyone who works for *CBS This Morning*, but the freezing rain is soaking through my clothes, and I need refuge. Besides, I'm part of the family now. No need to knock. I pull the handle on the door and climb inside as if I'm returning home.

The surroundings are anything but familiar. Switches, lights, toggles, and monitors are everywhere. Two middle-aged men swivel around in their chairs and look at me quizzically. "I'm a producer with *48 Hours*," I say, and I almost believe it myself. "I'm here to help cover the verdict for the morning show."

They grunt in approval and pass me a slice of cold pizza. "You should probably get in there," one guy tells me as I'm midchew. "The verdict light came on already."

Don't touch anything: a view inside a CBS News satellite truck.

It's standing room only inside the courtroom as the verdict is read. Eddie Ray Routh is guilty of the murders of Chris Kyle and Chad Littlefield. The state had previously taken the death penalty off the table, and Routh is automatically sentenced to life in prison without the possibility of parole. The Kyle family declines to give a victim impact statement, but several members of the Littlefield family step up to the mic. They describe the men who were lost as heroes and call Eddie Ray Routh an American disgrace.

"The state of Texas has decided to spare your life, which is more than you were willing to do," Littlefield's father says.

My phone is buzzing in my pocket, and I see an unknown New York number coming through. I step out of the courtroom and take the call. A producer for the morning show tells me my assignment is to book a member of the jury. I wait, but there's no further instructions given. Perplexed, I try to ferret out some tips on how exactly I'm supposed to get an interview with the nameless jurors, who are all seated behind several layers of courthouse security.

"Approach them when they come outside the courthouse," an exasperated producer tells me before hanging up.

The courtroom doors fling open, and throngs of people start flooding out into the hallway. I push my way back in against the traffic to try to catch a glimpse of the jury. They are being led out in the opposite direction, past the judge's bench and into a hallway I can't access.

I've barely had enough time to register what they look like, and I wonder if I'd even recognize one of them if we were face-to-face. But the pressure to book someone propels me forward, and I take the stairs down to the lobby in hopes of intercepting the jury. Normally, I'd have no issue bounding down a few flights of stairs to beat the elevator crowd. But I'm three months pregnant and there's a questionable slice of pizza in my stomach. I make it down just in time to see a bailiff clear a path in the lobby and escort the jury members outside into a waiting van.

I dart back through the parking lot and jump into my car. Scanning the lot, I see the large van exiting and turning down a side street. I follow it, staying a few car lengths back. It turns into another parking lot, and all twelve members of the jury file out and go to their respective vehicles under the watchful eye of the bailiff.

What am I supposed to do now?

The cars are pulling out of the parking lot and taking off in every direction. I'm panicked. My assignment was the jury, and they are all disappearing. A truck turns down the street I'm idling on, and I start to follow it.

I'm not really sure what I was planning to do. It's a pretty impossible scenario to imagine booking someone after tailing their car out of a secure parking lot. But I had an assignment.

I follow the car for miles until it ends up in a residential neighborhood. I feel certain they must realize that I've been following them, and I make a last-ditch effort to memorize the license plate before turning off on a random street and berating myself. I probably gave that juror a heart attack, and for what? I wasn't any closer to booking them, and now I was miles away from the courthouse with no leads to follow. Talk about trial and error.

It's after midnight and I'm sitting cross-legged on top of a dipping mattress in a seedy motel room. It was the only lodging I could find in all of Stephenville, and I was too exhausted to go anywhere else. I fire up my laptop and see a chain of twenty unread emails. I've officially been looped into the *CBS This Morning* email thread. And it's buzzing with activity.

I sift through the missives, trying to decipher the TV shorthand. I've had all of three months on the job at CBS News, with no official training unless you count Alec's profanity-laced tour of Lubbock. I barely had a handle on the *48* lingo, and now I was being thrust into the morning show world: live daily television. The most intense variety of media, with the highest stakes and the lowest level of sanity.

I scan the emails looking for any assignments with my name but thankfully come up empty. I've been awake since 6 AM, which at this point feels like a lifetime ago. My eyes are glazing over, and I know I won't be good for anything if I don't get some sleep soon. I set my alarm for 5 AM and pass out on top of the covers.

The nightmare always starts the same way. There's a knock at my door, late at night. It's dark and I stumble down the stairs in my pajamas. There's a police officer at my door, dressed in full SWAT gear. He tells me he needs to come inside immediately, and I open the door for him.

That's when he pulls out his gun and starts hunting me down. I usually wake up right as the bullet fires. Heart racing, tears streaming down my face. I sit up in bed, frozen in fear. I look around the room and point out everything that contradicts my dream. I'm not under attack. It was all in my head. And the reason it's there is because it's exactly what happened to Cynthia and Mike McLelland at the hands of Eric Williams.

Back then, it was early enough in my true crime career that I was still poring over all the crime scene photos. I'd watch the body cam videos over and over, looking for clues and connections we could make in the scripts. But all that studying came at a price, and now the images were burned into my memory in ways I never imagined.

When I wake up again a few hours later in a strange hotel room, it takes me a minute to get my bearings. Then I grab my phone and see it's gone nuclear. Voicemails, texts, and oh so many emails. Apparently, there was a miscommunication. No one told me that I was expected to be on overnight duty. The morning show team had been trying to reach me all night and held actual meetings at 2 and 4 AM. What world is this?

Everyone is asking for an update on my assignment: the jury. I have nothing to show for my ten-plus hours in the field. I certainly wasn't going to tell them the truth: that I spent most of my time covertly following a probable juror's car home before chickening out and falling asleep at my motel.

My phone starts buzzing again, and I silence it while I brew some shitty in-room coffee and pace the shag carpet. I need a lead. A source. A juror. And fast. Because there's no way I am answering that phone until I have something to bring to the table.

I flip open my laptop as I sip my scalding-hot instant coffee. What has been my saving grace in every story I've ever covered? Connections to sources. I'm always leveraging my contacts to make a story happen, and while that's a whole lot easier when you live in the same city you cover, I wasn't about to let a little thing like geography stop me now. I may not have been from Stephenville, but I was from Texas.

I navigate to Facebook and do a contact search of all 1,200 of my "friends" to see if I have any connections to Stephenville. Three names that I vaguely recognize pop up. I quickly message them, giving a whitewashed version of my predicament and asking for any contacts they might have with a member of the Chris Kyle jury.

To my delight, one person replies right away and says she knows a juror. Even better, she gives me her full name. I still don't have access to the CBS News research database subscriptions, which let you run names for public records with alarming accuracy, but I do know how to use the White Pages, and I plug the woman's name into a targeted Google search. One of the many addresses it spits out is in Stephenville.

I call back the latest unknown New York number that's lit up my phone. It's a producer named Kaci Sokoloff, and she sounds pissed.

"Why weren't you at the live shot this morning? The correspondent had to produce his own segment and call traffic."

Considering I understood about 25 percent of that, I knew I'd have been very little help at the live shot, but there was no use trying to communicate that now.

I apologized all over myself and then threw in the magic words. "I've been working a source on the jury. I'm headed to her house right now."

Silence on the other end of the line. If you leave a New Yorker speechless, you're doing something right.

"But I can turn around and hook up with the crew if you need me on-site," I say, already knowing she'll never take me up on it.

"You have a juror?" she says, skeptical of my claim.

"I have a lead on a juror," I say, hedging my bets. "A source tipped me off to her."

Soon after, I carefully tiptoe up the icy steps to a nondescript one-story house in a quiet Stephenville neighborhood. It's 7:30 AM, and I'm hoping I'll catch the juror before she leaves for work. I can't tell if it's morning sickness or I'm-knocking-on-a-stranger's-door butterflies in my stomach, but I don't feel great.

At least it's not a murder victim's family member this time.

I take a deep breath and do the deed. A man comes to the front door in a bathrobe. So they haven't left for work yet. I introduce myself, name-drop my friend, and explain that I was told someone who lived at this house had been on the Chris Kyle jury.

As I'm giving my spiel, a woman walks up, hair in a towel. She's the alleged juror, but my intel was faulty. She had been summoned, but she wasn't selected. Dejected, I thank them for their time and am about to turn to leave when I notice the woman looking at my midsection. In my rush this morning, I hadn't thought to camouflage my baby bump. It's on full display and has caught everyone's attention.

Her gaze softens as she asks, "Do you want to come in? You must be freezing."

I consider myself a people person. I've always enjoyed making friends and meeting new people. In college, I remember having a light bulb moment when I took a survey called "Strengths Finder" and my top skill came back as "woo," winning others over. Because the truth is I get a kick out of making difficult people like me and actually turning them into allies.

The biggest lessons I remember from high school are finding a way to make the toughest teachers laugh and starting prank wars with coaches others feared. I just knew there had to be some common ground somewhere, and I wanted to see if I could find it. There are plenty of people in the world that I haven't been able to win over, but the thrill is in the challenge.

This delightful couple in Stephenville, who warmed to me nearly instantly, needed no special tricks. We chatted easily and discussed the case, which they had followed closely in the press. Although I'd only known them for five minutes, I felt like I could trust them with the truth. I told them I was a brand-new television producer, and I was trying to book my first interview for *CBS This Morning*. I'd been assigned to find a juror to go on camera, and I had no clue what to do next.

They seemed like they genuinely wanted to help me, this little pregnant lady who'd landed on their doorstep in the middle of an ice storm. And as it turned out, they were going to do just that.

They couldn't go on camera themselves, and they didn't know anyone who'd actually been on the jury. But they did have a valuable piece of information that would lead to the biggest interview in the story. They knew where Chris Kyle's brother, Jeff, lived. Not his exact address, mind you, but the name of the small town. This was way better intel than I could have imagined from a door knock born of a Facebook message.

I couldn't wait to relay this information to Kaci. She immediately saw the value and patched me through to a production secretary, who ran the name Jeff Kyle through their database and scanned the list for the right town. In a matter of seconds, I was punching the full address into my GPS and setting my course.

The biggest interview in the Chris Kyle story was undoubtedly his wife, Taya. But she was already fully locked on ABC and *Good Morning America*. She had a book deal and an agent, and there was just no room for CBS at the table. At the time of the trial, Chris's brother, Jeff, was more of a mystery. Four years younger than Chris, Jeff had also served in the military, as a marine.

I'd never even seen a picture of Jeff or his wife, and I had no idea if the address I was barreling toward was accurate. But I did have a secret weapon on board, my baby bump. I was still afraid to show it to CBS, but after what happened that morning, I was no longer hiding it from sources.

My GPS was leading me away from freeways and stoplights and into increasingly rural farm-to-market roads. I saw a tumbleweed blow by and figured I must be headed in the right direction. I'd seen the movie *American Sniper*, and this just looked like the kind of place the Kyle family would live. I spotted the street name and slowed down to a crawl as I tried to locate a house number. I saw only wooden fences, barbed-wire enclosures, and lots of livestock.

Up to that point, Google Maps had never failed me, but I'd never been this far out in the country. I was a native Texan, but a suburban one, and these dirt roads and farm plots were not my home turf. Completely directionless, I stopped at the first house that didn't have a privacy fence blocking access to the front door and steeled my nerves.

I knocked on the door and a man in denim overalls answered it. "Can I help you, ma'am?" he asked politely.

"I sure hope so," I said sweetly, hand on my belly. "I'm looking for Jeff Kyle, but I can't seem to find his house number."

It wasn't a lie, but it left out some key details, like the fact that I didn't actually know Jeff Kyle or have an invitation to come over.

The overall-clad man pointed to a plot of land in the distance. "You're on the right road. He's just a ways down there."

I thanked him for his help and headed back to my car, still having no idea what I was going to do if I actually found the correct address. It was one thing to door knock a potential juror or ask a neighbor for directions, but it was an entirely different proposition to show up on the front steps of a grieving family the day after a guilty verdict. And yet, this was my job now.

Before I started working at CBS, I never thought about how specific stories ended up on TV, and I certainly didn't realize that behind every tearful victim's interview there was a producer who'd convinced them to go on camera. Victims' families show the impact of crime in a way that no one else can. And if they are interviewed sensitively, as part of nuanced reporting that is trying to make a difference, then that's a job I want to do. But what if it's just sensationalized coverage of a horrific murder for the sake of big ratings? At this stage in the process, I never knew which side of the coin the story would land.

These thoughts are swirling in my head as I pull up to the property. I'm stopped in my tracks by a large, locked gate. Well, that answers the door-knock question. It wasn't like I was going to climb the fence. I didn't want to add trespassing to my list of accomplishments as a producer. And pregnant or not, going through a locked entrance to someone's house in Texas is a great way to get shot. They wouldn't even arrest the shooter for it.

I put my car in park and called Kaci back. She was thrilled that I'd actually found the house, and wholly undeterred by the locked gate. "Stay on the house," she instructed me. "They've got to come out—or come home—sometime."

Since I'd been unceremoniously launched into the story, I hadn't had a chance to read up on the trial yet. No time like the present. I recline my seat and search for daily articles on the trial of Eddie Ray Routh. There was no shortage of material to go through, and before I knew it, several hours had passed.

It was so cold outside that I had to periodically turn on my car and get the heat going again. My cell phone battery was also getting dangerously low. Is there anything that causes faster distress than a single-digit power percentage? My phone wasn't the only thing failing me. There was a tiny human playing bongos on my bladder. But I wasn't supposed to leave the house until I made contact.

I needed to cover all my bases. I didn't have another producer to hand off the baton to, so I'd have to improvise. I dug around in my bag for a piece of blank paper and scrawled a handwritten note, introducing myself, apologizing for the intrusion at their home, and asking for an interview. I wedged it in between the bars on the gate and hoped it wouldn't start raining anytime soon. Then I hightailed it to the nearest convenience store.

Bathroom break and power adapter secured; I was back in less than thirty minutes. And my note was still secured on the gate. I was tempted to keep driving, maybe get a real lunch and wait it out in a restaurant instead of my car. But I figured I was pressing my luck enough already by leaving my stakeout post once, so I stayed put. Just then, Kaci called from New York. "Are you still on the house?" she asked.

"Yes ma'am," I replied. I had made it back in the nick of time for that to be a truthful statement. I told her I hadn't seen any movement and was still waiting to make contact.

"New York is really excited about this booking," she said. "They want Gayle King to interview him in the studio."

This is escalating fast, and I don't even know if I'm sitting on the right house.

"I'll let him know," I said, trying to sound confident. Then I hung up the phone and rewrote my note to include Gayle King's name.

I half-jokingly considered including that Gayle was also working on a special about the Queen of England, but thought better of it.

I sat in the car for another hour with the note tucked into my pocket, just waiting for someone to come home or come outside. I was starting to think it was a lost cause, and I desperately needed to stretch my legs. I decided a little walk down the country road would do me good, and I set out on the gravel path.

When cars came by, they caused enough commotion that I knew I wouldn't miss anything as long as I kept the house in my sights. I must have been quite the image, a pregnant out-of-towner, pacing the street after sitting in her car all day. But what else could I do?

As I walked farther down the street, I noticed a bank of metal mailboxes. This was helpful information because they actually had address numbers on them.

I located the number for Jeff Kyle and felt like maybe I really was in the right place after all. I turned back up the road toward my car and saw the gate that I'd been bird-dogging was now open. My heart sank. Had I missed my opportunity to intercept Jeff?

Before I could beat myself up too much, I saw a woman walking down the driveway, headed straight for me.

"Can I help you with something?" I recognized her tone as Texan for *What the hell are you doing on my property?*

To an outsider, it would have sounded nearly identical to the sincere question from the overall-clad man who actually wanted to help me, but I knew better.

Southern women have their own way of communicating displeasure and still sounding polite to the rest of the world. I knew I was in deep shit, but I wondered if I could somehow dig my way out.

Shamelessly, I put my hand on my baby bump.

"I'm so sorry for doing this. My boss told me I couldn't leave your house until I at least made contact with someone."

She stared back at me.

"I work for CBS News. I wrote you this letter, and I was going to leave it in your mailbox. I can't even imagine what you're going through, or what this trial has been like for your family. But if you are interested in sharing your thoughts, Gayle King wants to interview you and Jeff on CBS *This Morning*. We can fly you to New York tonight."

The response I got was completely unexpected. She told me she wasn't interested in being interviewed, but that wasn't the end of the conversation.

"Jeff's already packing for New York. He's going on CNN and Fox tomorrow. The car should be here any minute."

I was floored. Here I thought I had a reluctant character, a camera-shy, private citizen who wasn't talking to anyone, but apparently Jeff Kyle had already been booked twice over. Even though I was new to the world of network television, I'd learned enough in the past few months to realize that the cable channels were not considered true competitors to the "big three" —ABC, NBC, and CBS. If I could get Jeff Kyle on CBS first, it would still be considered a huge coup.

Thinking on my swollen feet, I pivoted my pitch.

"That's great he's already going to be in New York. We could do our interview on the same trip," I offered.

As we were talking, I saw a black limousine approaching on the gravel road. Jeff Kyle walked down the driveway, suitcase in tow. I knew I had less than a minute to make my appeal in person. I kept the letter in one hand and extended the other to introduce myself.

"CBS News would really love the chance to have you on our morning show with Gayle King tomorrow. We can make whatever arrangements you need to work around your schedule and not interfere with the other interviews you have set up."

I handed him the letter, and he stepped into the limo and drove away in a cloud of dust. I stood there with his wife and watched the car disappear. I thanked her for being so kind to me and giving me the opportunity to make our case for an interview.

"I'll tell Jeff I think he should do it," she said. "Might as well make the most of his trip to New York."

Jeff Kyle appeared on *CBS This Morning* with Gayle King on February 26, 2015, about twelve hours after I made contact with him. To get in ahead of his schedule for CNN and Fox, CBS had to tape their interview with him at 5 AM, a full two hours earlier than they actually go on the air.

Back home in Dallas, I poured a cup of coffee and waited for the show to start. There were so many points when this could have fallen apart, including the 4:30 AM pickup from Jeff's hotel, circumventing the cable news channels. Producer Kaci Sokoloff was as giddy as I was, and she texted me behind-the-scenes photos of Jeff getting camera ready and doing sound checks on set.

I watched the show go live from my living room and couldn't believe my eyes. We'd actually pulled it off. I'd been the last producer to show up to the *American Sniper* trial and the first one to land an interview with the Kyle family after the verdict. I do love a good underdog story—especially after it's all worked out in the end.

The success of my Stephenville stakeout put me on the radar of every booking department at CBS News. If you needed someone to sweet-talk a character in Texas, I was the woman to call. No one knew my secret weapon was an adorable baby bump.

It's not like I'd planned to use my unborn child as a stepping stone in my burgeoning career as a television producer. It just happened organically, and who was I to turn away from a winning strategy? Plus, using it was easier than hiding it. When you're five feet tall, there's not much room for mystery in your torso.

Because the Chris Kyle story was of interest only to the morning show and not *48 Hours*, my involvement ended as quickly as it began. And I learned a number of valuable lessons from the whirlwind experience, not in the least of which was it's dangerous to be good at a job you don't want to do.

In addition to being on the call list for the morning show, I was getting thrown into all sorts of booking situations for other teams at *48*. You wouldn't believe how many roads led to Texas. The story might not start here but look long enough, and you'll find a character's sister or mother or uncle who lives in the Lone Star State. And that would be enough to send me to their doorstep, hand on my hip, asking for an interview.

My only reprieve was when I had assignments for my actual job.

As much as I wanted a 100 percent success rate, there were always stories that I couldn't land for one reason or another. One of the stories that got away remains an unsolved murder to this day.

6

PLAYING WITH FIRE

I'm sitting in a café in Highland Park. A wealthy enclave near Dallas, Highland Park has one of the richest zip codes in the country. Doctors, lawyers, and other professionals know they've made it when they get an address here. My lunch date chose the location and is a doctor himself, a specialist in fact, and he won't let you forget it. What is it with doctors and murdered spouses? The oath to do no harm seems to be having the opposite effect.

In addition to being a recent widower, Dr. Alan Wolter is also a former lead suspect in his wife's unsolved murder. Officially, police have stated that they've ruled out Dr. Wolter, but my sources tell me that it's more complicated than meets the eye.

Yes, it could be true that they no longer suspect him in the case, but authorities can also go public with misleading information as an investigative tool to get people to let their guard down. With the murder of Jena Wolter still open and active, it's anyone's guess. For now, I'll have to toe the line between sympathy and suspicion.

I reached out to Dr. Wolter after seeing a local news story on his wife's death, which was initially reported as an accidental drowning. He'd responded almost immediately and said he was willing to meet with me. His only question had been about how I'd gotten his contact information. A prominent doctor, he hadn't been hard to track down. And he'd given local interviews on the case already, which was nearing its one-year anniversary.

The tragedy had played out in their own backyard, and, the story goes, the good doctor was one of the first people on scene. Jena's adult daughter had discovered her mother, a fifty-five-year-old dentist, floating unconscious in the pool after coming home from work. Jena was still in her scrubs and tennis shoes.

Her daughter called 911 first, followed by her stepfather, Dr. Wolter, who rushed over from his nearby office. According to reports, Dr. Wolter informed authorities about his wife's family history of heart trouble, including two sisters who died of coronary complications before they turned fifty. He also mentioned that Jena was a heavy drinker and hypothesized that she'd had too much to drink and fallen into the pool.

With no sign of forced entry on the home, and several plausible theories for an accidental death, police called off the homicide detectives en route to the house. It was a Friday night in Dallas County, and there were more pressing matters needing their attention. Dr. Wolter said he asked police if he could have a moment alone with his wife before they took her body away. He lay down on the pavement beside her and wept.

Five days later, Jena was cremated, and hundreds of mourners packed her memorial service. In a touching eulogy, Dr. Wolter said he had chosen "not to ask why" Jena had died, but instead to remember how wonderful their life was together.

After meeting online, Jena and Alan were a couple for ten years. It was Jena's third marriage and Alan's second, and each brought a gaggle of older children into the mix: Jena had four kids, and Alan had three. The blended family had bonded together all the more through the tragedy, so when Highland Park police called them all up some five months after Jena's death, they were at a loss as to why. When someone dies outside of a medical setting, autopsies are routine before a cremation. But without foul play suspected, the results aren't given priority and can take months to come in.

The family gathered at Alan and Jena's home, just feet away from where her body had been found, and police delivered the shocking news. According to the autopsy and toxicology report, Jena had died with a perfectly healthy heart. She also had no trace of alcohol or drugs in her system. Her death was no accident. In fact, injuries indicated she had been brutally murdered. Her body showed evidence of a struggle, specifically of being held underwater while she fought for her life.

Turns out there were five million reasons to kill Jena, and her will was in limbo while the authorities worked to solve her case. With an insurance policy payable to five different people, everyone in the family was a suspect.

At the time of her death, Jena's dental business was running a $750,000 deficit. Alan was immediately caught in the police's crosshairs. So, too, were more family members, including Jena's son and her nephew. Both men had worked for Jena, and she'd recently learned they were stealing from the business. Jena had given her son and nephew a thirty-day notice that they were being fired. May 1 was to be their last day as employees. Jena was killed on April 25.

These disturbing details are fresh on my mind as I wait for Dr. Wolter to arrive for our lunch. He walks through the door in blue scrubs, white lab coat blowing in the wind. He'd suggested the time and place, telling me that he was off work that day, which makes his choice of attire all the more surprising.

I note that he'd worn the same uniform during a recent press conference, when police had announced that Jena had been murdered and there was a fifty-thousand-dollar reward for information on her case. Back in the café, Dr. Wolter talks gushingly about his late wife, telling me they had a fairy-tale romance and the kind of love that Shakespeare wrote about. I smile like I believe him, but I've seen this phenomenon before.

A tragic death often causes loved ones to remember a rose-colored-glasses version of history. It's understandable, admirable even, to remember the best of a person after they've passed and to dispose of the negative memories. But when there's a murder, you can't do that. You have to dig into all the dirty laundry and strained relationships to get to the truth of what happened.

With a little probing, Dr. Wolter tells me he passed a polygraph test in the months after the murder but claims Jena's son did not. As our food arrives, Dr. Wolter's eyes migrate to my midsection, and he asks when I'm due. It's always a bit of a gamble to assume a pregnancy when you've only just met, but the doctor was right, and we chat easily about my son's impending birth. I still have so many questions about his wife's death and their relationship, so I shift the conversation back to their life together.

He tells me they loved dancing and photography, and he would often set up a tripod on their dates. It sounds a little staged to me, but as a TV producer, who am I to turn my nose up at the promise of high-quality images?

I can see the shutter clicks playing out in our episode, and I keep him talking. I'm as surprised as anyone when he brings up their sex life, unprompted. I'm a gutsy interviewer, but even I wouldn't try to get these kinds of details in a first meeting, much less off camera. If I'm asking the tough questions, you'd better believe I'm getting it on tape, one way or another.

But Dr. Wolter is in the zone now, and I'm not about to cut him off. He tells me they had incredible sexual chemistry and would experiment with toys, role-play, and rough sex. Is he trying to shock me? See how I'll react? I can't make sense of it, and I try not to show how uncomfortable he's making me feel.

The waiter brings the check, which I scoop up with my CBS corporate card. I think our meeting is coming to a close, but Dr. Wolter has other ideas. He's picked up on the fact that I'm interested in photos of him and Jena, and he dangles the bait.

"I've got them all at the house. It's just right around the corner," he says.

In my gut, I know this is a bad idea. But there's also something in me that doesn't want to admit that I'm afraid.

"Okay," I say against my better judgment. "Lead the way."

In the parking lot, Dr. Wolter points out a red Porsche and tells me it belonged to his late wife. "I'll drive," he offers.

This guy just keeps upping the ante. It feels like he wants to see how far he can take it.

"No, thanks. I'll take my own car," I tell him.

He pushes it for a moment, trying in vain to convince me to get in his dead wife's sports car with him at the wheel.

I get out my own keys and say I'll follow him. He doesn't hide his disappointment but relents.

As I pull into traffic behind him, I can't shake an uneasy feeling about this whole field trip. It was one thing when we were in a public place and he was creeping me out, but now we were going to a second location. His private home, and no one else knows it.

Before I can even text my boss to tell her what's happening, we're pulling up to the house, and Dr. Wolter is standing at my driver's-side door. He was telling the truth about one thing. He did live just around the corner. I put my phone in my pocket and step out of the car.

As we walk up the steps, I realize that I've seen this house before, in local media coverage of the drowning. It's the same house where his wife was murdered, and more than a year later, he's still living there.

He unlocks the front door and I follow him inside the entryway. He doesn't stop there and keeps walking deeper into the house. He calls out to me and motions with his arm, but I'm frozen in place.

My body wouldn't let me take another step.

I reach for the phone in my pocket and improvise an exit strategy.

"I'm so sorry," I say to him, "I completely forgot that I had another meeting set up, and now I'm late. They're calling me. I really need to get this."

My legs come back to life, and I eye the front door handle. I press my thumb down on the lever and pray it's not locked.

Mercifully, it opens, and I hustle down the steps and back to my car without even waiting for a response.

I see the images so clearly in my mind. The brick walkway, the wrought-iron front door. I had gotten all the way to my car before it dawned on me that I didn't have my keys. I realized I must have left them inside, so I turned back the way I came.

Dr. Wolter opens the door for me. He was waiting. "I saw your keys over here."

I step back into the house, and everything immediately feels wrong. My heart is racing. My palms are sweaty.

I see Dr. Wolter in his scrubs coming toward me. What's that in his hand? A napkin?

He's closing the distance between us with big strides, and I'm frozen in place. He hooks me around the shoulder and presses a white cloth to my face. The whole room goes dark.

I wake with a jump. Safe and sound in my own bed. It takes me a minute to realize that I didn't really go back to the house a second time. It was a terrible dream. The emotional toll of working in true crime television was adding up, and it was seeping into my subconscious with alarming regularity.

In a lot of ways, I'm grateful that this experience happened, because it gave me a glimpse into a world I never wanted to reenter. Even though I loved my job, and the pursuit of a good story thrilled me, I had to draw the line somewhere. I realized there was no story that was worth putting myself in a vulnerable position with a suspected killer again.

In the years after this hair-raising experience, I would knock on countless doors, stake out dozens of homes, interview alleged hit men, serial killers, and cold-blooded murderers. But I'd never again do it without telling someone else where I was, and I tried my best not to be alone with a suspected killer.

While I was thoroughly creeped out by Dr. Wolter, I still had a job to do. And *48*'s interest in the story had not waned one bit. In fact, it was taken into overdrive a few days later once Dr. Wolter's stepdaughter Victoria told me she was planning to appear on *Nancy Grace* to talk about her mother's unsolved murder.

I'd gotten Victoria's number from Dr. Wolter, who still hadn't sent me those photos he'd promised he had at the ready in the murder house, if only I'd follow him down a dark hallway. I was starting to think they might not exist at all. But photos aside, the story was compelling. And I was a lot more comfortable talking to the victim's daughter than I'd ever been with the husband. My boss didn't want the daughter to go on any other show, much less *Nancy Grace*, a true crime free-for-all that often serves as a catalyst for coverage on network television.

In situations like this, when I'm asking a character to do something for me, I fall back on my Southern manners. I don't try to strong-arm them or threaten to abandon the story. I just lay it all out there and ask for their help as politely as I can manage. I needed to go for a run to put my own anxiety at bay, but I was six months pregnant and officially waddling. I power walked for two miles before I reached out to Victoria on the phone. My pitch was this:

"First of all, I totally understand that solving your mother's murder is your priority, not an allegiance to any one media outlet. If you think talking to Nancy Grace will help solve your mother's case, I fully support you doing that.

Personally, I've never heard of Nancy Grace solving a murder. But she is likely to bring a higher profile to the case and attract larger media attention from all three networks, where there's a better chance of getting results. For example, *48 Hours* has actually helped solve cold cases, gotten wrongful convictions overturned, and helped families find justice.

The best news, in my opinion, is that we are already interested and invested in your mother's murder. We'd like to continue working with you, but I know you have lots of options, and I'll respect whatever decision you make."

She thanked me for the call and said she was going to think it over and get back to me. A few hours later, she texted to tell me that she'd declined Nancy Grace's invitation to come on the show.

I was so relieved, and I couldn't wait to tell my boss the good news. For the moment at least, we still had the story to ourselves.

With Nancy Grace on the sidelines, I got to work writing the bluesheet. Thanks to my lengthy lunch with Dr. Wolter, I had plenty of material. I usually carry a digital recorder with me, and I'd wanted to use it with Dr. Wolter, but I was worried taking out the device would have interrupted his train of thought, which was flying down the tracks. I'd stopped short of recording our conversation at the restaurant, but I had taken notes. I went back over the snippets I'd jotted down.

"Fears for his safety. Got security cameras & CHL (concealed handgun license)."

"Says son is prime suspect. Failed polygraph test."

"Doc had wife cremated. Says she always wanted it that way."

Did this guy take a page out of the Michele Williams handbook or what?

The Wolter case had an added level of intrigue thanks to the five-million-dollar life insurance policy. An ideal episode would have interviews with all five beneficiaries, but that was a tall order. At the very least, we'd need to get in touch with the victim's son, the one who Dr. Wolter was accusing of the murder, to give him a chance to refute the claim. I tried every trick in the book to get reliable contact information but came up empty. Phone numbers were disconnected. Emails bounced back.

I put everything in the bluesheet and continued to work back channels in an attempt to reach the son. The open-ended, unsolved nature of the crime was what intrigued me most. We had a chance to really help the investigation, or at least that's how I saw it. But all the corporate execs saw was a legal nightmare with no end in sight. I pitched my bluesheet on the Wolter case to the senior producers at *48 Hours* and was told that without an arrest and conviction, the story was dead in the water. It was frustrating, but I held on to hope that one day, something might break in the case and allow us to tell the story.

For the next year, I kept tabs on the case. In fact, I was so close to it that I even learned through a source in the police department that ABC's *20/20* was in town filming interviews with the family a few months after my lunch. I held my breath, thinking that ABC would find a way to air the story in the new season. But it never came to pass. Instead, the family fought it out in civil court. Best I can tell, the insurance company paid out the five-million-dollar policy in equal measure to all beneficiaries, including Dr. Wolter and the victim's "prime suspect" son. Dr. Wolter later sued him for wrongful death. They reached a confidential settlement and have not spoken publicly about the case since the summer of 2015.

Unlike all the other stories in this book, I've changed the names and a few identifying details of this case. To this day, it remains an unsolved murder with no named suspects or arrests, nor an episode of *48 Hours* or any other crime show.

7

SAFETY IN NUMBERS

It's 2015, and I've covered so many murder cases in the past year that I'm having a hard time holding them all in my head. Just when I get comfortable with the facts of one story, I'm thrust into a new one. So when my boss tells me that the retrial of Dr. Thomas Michael Dixon is on the calendar, I have to jog my memory of the case. I'll do us both the favor of a quick recap:

A murder-for-hire case out in Lubbock where a plastic surgeon/jilted lover is accused of hiring a down-and-out friend to off his ex-girlfriend's new boyfriend.

The victim, Dr. Joseph Sonnier, had been stabbed and shot to death in his own home, and the shooter had confessed to the whole thing. An out-of-work, onetime pharmaceutical sales rep, David Shepard was not a typical assassin. And it showed. The crime scene was sloppy and haphazard, and the weapons used were far from professional grade. The knife was serrated, the kind used for wilderness expeditions. And the gun was an antique .25-caliber six-shooter. It belonged in a museum, not a crime lab.

I reported on Dr. Dixon's original trial back in 2014, when I was still working for CultureMap while moonlighting with a day rate for CBS. Never in my wildest dreams could I have imagined that my return to Lubbock would look so different.

Not only am I now a fully fledged TV producer, I'm also a new mom.

Riley and I couldn't have been more surprised and delighted to become parents as a result of my weekend leave from Lubbock the first time around. In the summer of 2015, I gave birth to a healthy baby boy. He was then, and remains to this day, my greatest production.

As a first-generation working mom, I had no road map to follow. Riley also comes from a stay-at-home-mom household, but we never considered that option for our family. The idea that I would retire at thirty, or take an extended absence from my career while I was still building it, seemed counterproductive for our family's future.

Now the end of my maternity leave coincides with the start of Dr. Dixon's second trial. And I have an unconventional idea how to handle it all.

What if I bring my baby along?

I have a childhood friend who lives in Lubbock and is a stay-at-home mom. She has two kids in elementary school, and I wonder if she'd take on a third, a newborn. I laughed at the boldness of my request, but you never know unless you ask. And besides, the worst that could happen was she'd say no, and I'd be right where I was already. I had met up with Susie and her husband a few times during the trial last year, and they were following the case and knew all about the looming retrial.

Because CBS had already covered the first trial "gavel to gavel," they didn't expect me to be at every single day of testimony this time around. But they did want me there for the end of the trial, when a verdict, God willing, would come out. That's when the great post-gag-order interview scramble would begin. So I was looking at a weeklong favor, not a monthlong one. Maybe it was doable. After all, what are friends for?

I call my friend Susie and make the pitch. She's surprised by the idea, and I tell her I wouldn't blame her one bit if she declined. More than anything, I think Susie said yes out of solidarity for a young mom trying to figure out how to nurture a baby and a new career. Susie had taken a few years off from the workforce, but she never intended to stay out forever, and helping me find my own way back seemed to resonate with her.

Grateful for her help, I can't wait to hit the road with my newborn. While packing, I start a photo essay called "Baby's First Business Trip," and add extra pages to the back of my son's baby book.

I'm parked at a rest stop outside Sweetwater, Texas, about two hundred miles away from Lubbock. My son is on my hip, and I'm looking at a sagging tire on our SUV. I'm not really sure what to do next.

I call Riley to share the dilemma. This wasn't quite how I pictured this business trip starting out, and I'm trying not to lose my cool.

It's November, but the West Texas sun has no off season. I find a shady bench and wipe the sweat from my brow as I appraise the situation. I have the back of the car packed full of baby accoutrements, and the idea of unloading it all to get to the spare seems unnecessarily onerous, especially because I can only go fifty-five miles per hour on it, and I still have hundreds of miles to cover.

While I'm on the phone explaining my predicament, an older couple in an RV pulls up next to me. They get out to stretch their legs and can't help but overhear the pickle I'm in, baby and all.

As soon as I get off the phone, they offer to help, air compressor in hand. I'm extremely grateful for their aid, and before I know it, I'm back on the road, cruising to a local mechanic.

Here I had thought my pregnancy was my strongest secret weapon, but it turns out an actual infant is even more irresistible.

I didn't expect my first big assignment post-baby to be five hours from home, but I'm making the best of this new adventure. And figuring out a way to bring my son along for the ride is an added bonus. No one really knows what to think of a baby on a business trip, and even checking into the hotel is comical.

"What brings you to town, business or pleasure?" the front desk clerk asks quizzically as she eyed my luggage, dry cleaning bags slung over a baby bouncer.

"A little bit of both," I reply.

Although I hadn't been present in the courtroom for opening arguments or the witness testimony, I stayed up to speed on the action thanks to my partner in crime, producer Alec Sirken. He was attending the trial daily and giving me recaps, plus I was following the case in the local Lubbock media.

At first it appeared that this trial was shaking out exactly the same as before, but a key difference soon emerged: David Shepard's roommate, Paul Reynolds, would take the stand this time around. And he wouldn't be alone. Because Shepard had implied that his roommate was involved in planning the murder, Reynolds had his own criminal defense attorney by his side as he testified.

Considering Reynolds was the one who called Lubbock police and said his roommate had confessed to the murder of Dr. Joseph Sonnier, I found it hard to believe that he wasn't a prosecution witness in the first trial. But it's always easy to play Monday-morning quarterback, and with the hung jury at the top of everyone's mind, the state was trying a new game plan.

Reynolds testified that yes, he'd waited two days before calling police to turn in Shepard, but he did the right thing in the end. "I'm a Boy Scout. I'm a Christian," Reynolds said.

No longer the faceless boogeyman, Reynolds was unmasked before the new jury. Yes, he'd served as a special forces Green Beret in the army, but he didn't present like a GI Joe gone rogue. As hard as the defense tried to paint Reynolds into a sinister corner, the fact remained that he was now a civilian, working as a nurse, of all things. Plus, he had been the one to sound the alarm on the whole murder plot. If he really was the mastermind, as Shepard claimed, what did he gain by calling the police? All the evidence pointed to Shepard pulling the trigger and getting paid in silver bars from Dixon. Any theory involving Reynolds required both a serious stretch of the imagination and putting your faith in the post-plea-deal testimony of David Shepard.

But the state wasn't going to open the door to that theory this time around, choosing not to call triggerman Shepard as a witness at the retrial. Instead, prosecutors relied on his plea deal as his only statement in the case. I couldn't blame the prosecution for wanting to keep Shepard out of the courtroom. His testimony had been such a wild ride last time.

With these key changes afoot, I wondered if Dr. Dixon would take the stand in his own defense a second time. Perhaps reasoning that his testimony contributed to the hung jury, Dixon again elected to testify.

I arrived just in time to see Dixon's encore performance on the stand. He had clearly aged in the past year—hard time in prison will do that to a person. He'd made it out on bond for one month of freedom before the second trial began, but that's not much of a reprieve when you're facing the possibility of life in prison without parole.

He stayed consistent with his statement, repeatedly insisting that he'd never intended for anyone to be physically hurt, and that Shepard had gone rogue when he murdered Dr. Sonnier.

"I never in my wildest dreams thought anything could happen to Joseph Sonnier," Dixon said.

But with Paul Reynolds no longer in the shadows, the details of the state's case against Dixon came into clearer focus. Despite Dixon's testimony that he didn't plan or pay for the murder, the silver bars and the murder weapon that Shepard used were both tied to Dixon.

The case that had once appeared gray and murky was turning black and white before my eyes. I wondered if the jury would see it the same way this time around.

As unusual as it was at first, I quickly found my rhythm as a working mom out in West Texas. Each morning, I'd drop my son off at my friend's house and drive to the Lubbock County Courthouse, laptop and breast pump in tow. I had to pump twice a day, which sounds about as inconvenient as it was, but Mother Nature always wins, doesn't she?

On my first day at the courthouse, I scoped out the building for a suitable room to do the deed. I had three basic requirements: a door that locked, a power outlet, and no windows. In a courthouse, this is actually not that difficult of a request. The hardest part of the equation was finding an unoccupied space and ensuring that it would be available daily. I enlisted a bailiff to help me location scout and pretty soon we'd identified a suitable room. It checked all my boxes, plus it was on the same floor as the trial court, and no one had reserved it for that week. He pulled up the online system and blocked out the room for me, and just because I like to be thorough, I also asked him for a piece of paper that I could tape to the outside of the door that said "Occupied."

Between my friend providing childcare and my makeshift breastfeeding room, I had gotten into the groove as a newly minted working mom. When I first started out in journalism, I couldn't have predicted that I'd one day be juggling a capital murder trial with infant care, but such is the juxtaposition of life. And I was up to the challenge. I had gotten so comfortable with my routine of ducking out of court around 11 AM and 3 PM to pump that I didn't even think twice about it. I'd just give Alec a nod and head to my secure room. Usually, I could time it so that I'd sneak out between witnesses or during an attorney sidebar conference with the judge.

But now it's time for closing arguments, and the schedule is no longer so laid back. Each side will get about an hour and a half to present their arguments. Since I usually went four hours before taking a break, I figure I can power through the whole of closing arguments without needing to pump.

I settle in next to Alec and get ready for the show.

Because the state has the burden of proof in US courts, the prosecution always goes first—and last—during closing arguments. They are able to divide their time so that they present their case for guilt first, the defense gets a turn in the middle, and then the prosecution returns to finish and rebut any arguments from the other side. As Lubbock County prosecutors took the jurors through the bizarre details of the violent murder of Dr. Joseph Sonnier, Dixon remained emotionless and listened intently.

"It is a completely senseless murder," the prosecutor declares before asking the jury to return a guilty verdict.

The defense takes its turn and uses the lion's share of their allotted time to point to the physical evidence of triggerman David Shepard committing murder. Dixon's attorneys claim their client is guilty only of criminal trespassing for hiring Shepard to surveil Dr. Sonnier. It was a case of greed and jealousy, but there was no murder plot.

I'm transfixed by the bombastic statements of both sides, and I'm craning my neck to catch glimpses of Dixon as the arguments bounce back and forth. His life hangs in the balance. The prosecutors are up front again, bringing home their case when I feel a pang in my chest. I'm instantly aware of one thing: a need to leave the courtroom so I can pump, right now.

It's not an ideal time to stand up and exit, and with so many onlookers joining the gallery for closing arguments, I've somehow ended up in the middle of the row. But I have an emergency situation brewing. I grab my bags and make my way down the crowded aisle, stepping over angled knees on wooden pews like I'm ducking out early at church.

I bust out of the double doors and make a beeline for my secure room, locking the door and getting down to business immediately. I'm so relieved that I actually made it that I don't even mind missing the end of closing arguments. I'm just glad I won't need a wardrobe change.

Twenty minutes go by, maybe thirty, and I hear a knock at the door. But who would be knocking on a reserved room that's locked and has an "Occupied" sign taped to the outside? Except, did I remember to tape up the sign this time? I call out "Occupied!" as I hear the distinct sound of a key jangle. I turn my head to see the locked handle moving counterclockwise. My back is to the door, and I keep it that way as I call out louder, "This room's occupied!"

A stunned jailer and an inmate in an orange jumpsuit make it through the threshold of the door before realizing they are truly not welcomed in this space. "I'm so sorry, ma'am," the jailer says as he backtracks out of the room.

Hazards of the job.

While the first jury agonized over their decision for two days before coming back deadlocked, the second jury had no such crisis of conscience. It took only four hours to reach a unanimous verdict: Dr. Thomas Michael Dixon was found guilty of capital murder on November 18, 2015. Because the state had already agreed to waive the death penalty, Dixon was automatically sentenced to life in prison. As the news came down, the courtroom came alive, and the judge had to admonish the gallery back into order. But the fireworks were just beginning.

Dr. Joseph Sonnier's family had waited four long years to speak to the man at the heart of the murder plot, and they didn't mince words. His sister called Dixon "trash" and a "lowlife" before labeling him exactly as the state of Texas did: a convicted murderer. Sonnier's son opted for the nickname "Mike Guilty," and another relative called Dixon a "douchebag." It was surreal to watch, and I wondered how much of this we could actually put on network television. But that was a problem for another day.

Our CBS camera crew was back in action, and we grabbed hallway reaction interviews with both the prosecutors and the defense. We spent the next hour running and gunning all over the courthouse, getting as many shots as we could to capture the chaos of the moment. The Sonnier family felt vindicated, and that justice had been served. But for the Dixon family, the nightmare was simply entering a new chapter.

In their eyes, their son, brother, and father had just been wrongfully convicted of murder and was facing a life sentence. We tried to do justice to these dueling viewpoints, while acknowledging that this time, the jury had spoken with a clear voice. We stayed in Lubbock one more day, picking up odds and ends and making plans to come back and interview Detective Zach Johnson and other Lubbock Police investigators. But there was one person my boss in New York really wanted to interview, and he wasn't anywhere near Lubbock. "How fast can you get to David Shepard?" Kramer asked me.

In the fall of 2015, triggerman David Shepard was serving a life sentence at the John B. Connally Unit in a place called Kenedy, Texas. Prisons in Texas are strategically placed in the middle of nowhere, and the Lone Star State has a lot of real estate to choose from. There are plenty of wide-open spaces with clear sight lines for guard towers to see for miles, all surrounded by twelve-foot razor-wire fences. And while most places in Texas are easy to navigate by car, Shepard's prison wasn't one of them.

It was a seven-hour drive from Lubbock, and I didn't even have approval from the prison to interview Shepard yet. Plus, I wasn't crazy about the idea of diverting Baby's First Business Trip to a maximum-security prison. With Thanksgiving on the horizon, we decided I'd return home to Dallas and make the request to visit Shepard in December.

A few weeks later, I'm pulling up Google Maps to chart the path of least resistance. It was a five-hour drive from Dallas, which meant I'd have to stay overnight in Kenedy. The hotel options were about as appealing as a night in prison, but I could suck it up if I had to. The question was: Did I really have to?

The nearest airport was in San Antonio, so if I caught the first flight out of Dallas, rented a car, and drove the hour and a half to the prison, I could conceivably interview Shepard for two hours and still make it back to San Antonio to catch the last flight back home. And worst-case scenario, I'm spending the night at the Westin in San Antonio, not the Budget Suites in Kenedy. Game on.

My alarm goes off at 5 AM and I tiptoe into my son's room to kiss his head and get a whiff of that newborn scent. What is it about infants' newly formed skulls that smell so amazing? I wish I could bottle it. Speaking of bottles, I'll be taking along a couple of empty ones in my carry-on luggage. No, I don't plan to actually pump at the prison, but considering how long I'll be away from home, I will need to find a private, secure location of my own. Those nursing pods in major airports were still a few years away from popping up and making the lives of working moms slightly less complicated, so I was left to scavenge for places to pump in the wild. I like to think all my crazy pumping stories somehow contributed to the availability of public nursing spaces, mostly by making men uncomfortable, which is how so many societal changes eventually turn the tide. Never underestimate the power of making dudes squirm to change the world.

I'm sitting on a metal chair bolted to the floor in the Connally Unit of the Texas Department of Criminal Justice. I've been granted an interview with David Shepard, the admitted triggerman in the murder-for-hire conspiracy of Dr. Joseph Sonnier. There's nothing that prepares you for sitting face-to-face with someone who took an innocent life, and unlike the other murderers who I'd interview in my career, Shepard wasn't denying it.

As the prison guard opens the steel door, a hulking man bends through the door frame. David Neal Shepard is six feet, five inches and over three hundred pounds. I try to put on my best poker face, but he definitely looks the part of a hit man, and even through plexiglass, I'm scared shitless.

While I'd been to a handful of jails already, this is my first time in a prison. In jails, where there is still the presumption of innocence, the mood is a bit lighter. Hope springs eternal in a county jail visiting room. But in prisons, everyone has already been judged as guilty. I've heard I'm lucky to be visiting in the winter, because Texas prisons aren't air-conditioned. It regularly tops out at over one hundred degrees inside. After I get through security, the public information officer gives me a casual tour of the prison on our way to the visiting room. He cheerily points out plaques and law enforcement memorabilia encased behind glass.

I'm struck by how incredibly clean everything appears to be. The floors are gleaming, and there's not a smudge in sight. Just then, I see an inmate in a white pressed jumpsuit pushing a broom down a spotless hallway. He's alone, and I look around, unnerved. Sensing my concern, the officer laughs and tells me that the inmate is a "trustee" and has special privileges to work in the prison, unmonitored. Of course, that's a loose term, and he points up at the dome cameras every fifteen feet, capturing a 360-degree image of all the common areas.

Back in front of Shepard, he's eyeing me up and down with a crazy look on his face. "Thanks for coming to see me," he says, grinning. I'm feeling anything but thankful to be there, and I try not to wriggle in my seat. I'm wearing a blazer, long pants, and a high-neck blouse, so why do I feel so exposed? There's something unnerving about Shepard leering at me, and even though I know he can't physically touch me, I fight the impulse to back farther away from the visiting booth.

I'm still trying to book Shepard for an on-camera interview, and as much as I hate it, he's the only one with the power to make it happen. I have to play nice. I take a deep breath and put on my best bullshit smile. "Glad to be here," I tell him, lying through my teeth. We talk about the first two trials and how his plea deal entered the picture. "I was scared they were going to kill me," he says. "I would have signed anything."

While Shepard admits he killed Sonnier, his latest version of events is that it was all an accident. There's no leap of logic that allows for six gunshots and eleven stab wounds to be "by accident," but I'm not here to confront the killer. I'm here to win him over. I nod along and search for words that I can say and not hate myself for later. "That sounds awful," I tell him truthfully. "I can understand why you were scared."

As our allotted visiting time ticks down, I go in for the kill. "Everything you've said to me is what's missing from our story, and we can't tell this part of it without you. Will you grant us an on-camera interview?"

"I'd like to do that," Shepard tells me. And for a moment, I actually am grateful that I made the trip. But then he keeps talking.

"I'm meeting with *20/20* next week, so it'll have to be after that," he says matter-of-factly.

I leave the prison with a pit in my stomach, and I call my boss, Nancy Kramer, on the long drive to the San Antonio airport. "We're screwed," she says. "If *20/20* is already bringing cameras into the prison, we can't move fast enough to beat them."

I clench the cheap steering wheel on my rental car and navigate the rainy highway back to civilization. I dial up Lubbock police detective Zach Johnson and learn that he too is already filming interviews with the other networks. His interview with NBC took place the day after the verdict. It's an exercise in futility, but I dial up the defense attorneys as well. Our standing dinner dates did nothing to curry any favor. They've filmed with both NBC and ABC already. I've spent two years of my life covering this insane case, only to have it booked out underneath me post-verdict.

In the end, CBS would be the only major network not to get any mileage out of the trials of Dr. Thomas Michael Dixon. NBC's *Dateline* was the first out of the gate, playing spoiler and running their episode "Obsession in the Lone Star State" on December 4, 2015. ABC's *20/20* followed suit, touting their "exclusive interview" with triggerman David Shepard.

We could have still batted cleanup and been the third to air our story on the case, but the powers that be decided it would be a bad look to finish last. So we didn't even play.

Back on that lonely stretch of highway outside the prison, I'm still clamoring for an angle to salvage the story. I try to think of any remaining avenue I hadn't explored yet, but I come up empty.

At that time in my career, the only definition of owning a story that I knew was getting it on the air first. It would take me years to understand another level of control was possible, and that the real power in the media isn't just who gets there first, it's who stays the longest.

After spinning my wheels on the Dixon story, I desperately needed a win. I couldn't rewrite the past, but I was going to do everything in my power not to repeat my mistakes. I turned my full attention to the Kaufman story and the completed trial of Eric Williams, the former justice of the peace turned serial killer.

The ice storm had thrown a frozen wrench in our shoot week, and we still had a lot of work to do to get the story ready for air. But when the senior producers looked at the budget from our first shoot with Hollywood Chuck, they didn't see much money left to pull it off. They promptly pulled Chuck from the story and assigned a pair of no-frills producers to finish out the show on the cheap.

Instead of another high-end, stylized week of shooting in Texas, they wanted to fly the McLelland family up to New York and film in a studio. The interview with J. R. McLelland and his sister, Krista, at the family feed-store had been the first domino to fall on the story, but the freezing-cold temperatures resulted in stiff answers delivered underneath a distracting volume of winter clothing. Plus, the buzz from the generators created a background noise that our post-production team couldn't eliminate. The interview was barely usable for television.

Thankfully, the McLellands were enthused at the idea of an all-expenses-paid trip to NYC, courtesy of CBS News. It helped that we let them bring along significant others and extended the dates to cover a weekend. Amazingly, this was all cheaper than shooting in Texas because we didn't have to transport in the crew or correspondent. We still needed to do a week of pickup shots in Texas, but we'd work the schedule so we could piggyback on another CBS assignment and split crew costs. I was learning a lot about the business of making television.

One of the more interesting lessons took place at the location of the double homicide, the former residence of Mike and Cynthia McLelland. Unless you work in real estate or true crime television, you've probably never thought about the rules that govern what happens after someone has been murdered in a residential location.

In Texas, real estate agents have to disclose if a murder has taken place on the property or face a potential lawsuit under the Deceptive Trade Practices Act. This means that whoever buys the house generally falls under one of two categories: they are looking for a good deal on a house and don't care how they get it, or they are actually interested in owning a macabre property.

As strange as it may sound, the latter has proven more common in my experience. In the McLelland case, the new owners took their interest in the murders to a whole new level. While I'd been nervous to call on them, my hesitation was completely unfounded.

The new owners invited me over and gave me a tour of the house, which they'd purchased the year after the massacre. Much to my surprise, they'd opted to keep several of the bullet holes and simply cover them up with curtains and picture frames, which they gamely pushed aside for me. They even said they hosted a Halloween party and allowed their guests to view the damage. It was a bizarre stance to discover, but welcome, since they practically rolled out the red carpet for us to film inside.

Everything was shaping up nicely for the story, and we had all the components we could have dreamed of for our episode. Well, except for our own interview with the killer, Eric Williams. After he'd been shipped off to death row, I'd written him a letter as instructed, requesting an on-camera interview. I was so creeped out at the idea of corresponding with Eric through my home address that I got a PO box for the occasion. I'd end up keeping the account for the entire time I was at CBS and using it to communicate with dozens of accused murderers.

When I wrote Eric, I had no idea if he'd actually respond. But a few weeks after I sent him a letter, he replied. "If/when the circumstances change/improve in my legal case, that may be the appropriate time for me to have an interview. Until then, I'll continue concentrating on my post-trial issues."

He signed the letter and included a reference to a Bible verse, Numbers 35:30. "Anyone who kills a person is to be put to death as a murderer only on the testimony of witnesses. But no one is to be put to death on the testimony of only one witness."

It struck me that he wasn't claiming to be innocent. Pointing out this technicality from ancient times seemed more like an admission of guilt than anything else. And if he wanted to go the biblical route for justice, I could think of a couple of verses off the top of my head that were more relevant, such as "Thou shall not kill" and "an eye for an eye." But it wasn't like we would put any of that on television. And as it turned out, we already had a pretty good interview with Eric Williams on camera.

The Dallas CBS affiliate KTVT had interviewed Eric before he was arrested, back when he was still free to zip around Kaufman on his Segway. Although only about thirty seconds of it had aired, we were able to get the raw footage from the interview and had plenty to work with for our episode. Plus, their veteran investigative reporter would go on camera with us and provide commentary on the whole thing.

By the time the episode "Target Justice" was slated for February 13, 2016, I thought nothing could stop it. But there's a rule in television that says anything that can go wrong will go wrong when you're on the air.

Our episode was in full swing, with all the anticipation building for the big reveal that former justice of the peace Eric Williams was the masked murderer, when the screen went black. All over the country, regularly scheduled programming was interrupted for a news bulletin from President Barack Obama. Supreme Court Justice Antonin Scalia had died suddenly while at his ranch in West Texas. He was seventy-nine years old and appeared to suffer a cardiac event, with his death ruled the result of natural causes.

It was a stunning piece of news, delivered nearly in real time to the American people. By the time President Obama ended his address, our episode's time slot had also expired. *48 Hours'* social media erupted with viewer outrage, demanding to know the outcome of the story. Normally an episode is available online the next day, but our digital team went into overtime to create a link for the "Target Justice" episode and had it up and running before midnight.

It was a chaotic end to an unbelievable story, but I didn't have much time to dwell on it. There was already another Dallas-area case on New York's radar: the disappearance of Christina Morris.

8

EVERY WOMAN'S WORST NIGHTMARE

It's hard to believe there was once a time when I didn't know about every murder in a hundred-mile radius. But those days are long gone. Now I'm intimately familiar with violent details on dozens of cases, and the numbers are always growing. But even in the dark world that I currently inhabit, Christina's case is especially disturbing.

The surveillance camera image is grainy, but you can still make out the basics. A woman, maybe early twenties, is walking down a sidewalk at 3:57 AM on Labor Day weekend in suburban Dallas. There's a young man next to her, and they turn together into a parking garage. It could have been a perfectly innocent scene, two people who just happened to cross paths on their way home, except for what happened next.

The man drives out of the parking garage, and the woman disappears into thin air.

When twenty-three-year-old Christina Morris doesn't come home that night, her boyfriend isn't immediately concerned. They'd had a fight, and he knew she was hanging out with friends for the holiday weekend. He ends up waiting three days before calling the Plano police, who spring into action on the missing person investigation. The couple's recent argument doesn't look good for Christina's boyfriend, who quickly becomes the first suspect in her disappearance.

Police begin retracing Christina's steps and find her silver Toyota Celica parked in the garage. There's no sign of a struggle inside, and her purse and keys are still missing. They discover the parking garage was equipped with two security cameras, one on the entrance and one on the exit. The latter caught a black Camaro leaving the garage shortly after the pair entered it. The camera angle captured the license plate, leading to the identity of the male driver as Enrique Arochi. Police interview Enrique and learn he'd been visiting friends at a nearby apartment complex on the night in question. He said he knew Christina from high school, and they'd been hanging out with a group of friends, barhopping and partying together.

Enrique admits he left the party around the same time as Christina, but he claims they parted ways *outside* the parking garage, and he didn't see her again. Police know that's not true, and they take a closer look at the surveillance video to see if there's anyone else riding in Enrique's car when it exits the garage. But the windows are darkly tinted, and all detectives can make out is a shiny reflection. Even without proof of Christina in his vehicle, the investigators gather enough circumstantial evidence to get a search warrant for the Camaro.

Authorities comb the car for any sign of Christina. The vehicle appears to have been recently cleaned and vacuumed, and there's a toll tag inside, which documents a portion of Enrique's route that night. Retracing his use of paid roads, investigators find more surveillance video, this time at a gas station, where Enrique not only fills up his car but gives it a thorough scrubbing with paper towels and a squeegee. He seems to be paying extra attention to the trunk area, so crime scene technicians go there as well, dusting for fingerprints, DNA samples, and any other evidence. When the lab report comes back, there's only one hit, but it's a big one: a single drop of blood belonging to Christina Morris.

Police now believe they're working a murder case. The body, however, is still nowhere to be found. Enrique is charged with aggravated kidnapping, and police ramp up their search efforts, fanning out teams across an increasingly wider swath of the Dallas area.

The disappearance of Christina Morris was one of the last stories I covered for CultureMap Dallas before becoming a producer at *48 Hours*, and it was also one of the first I pitched to CBS. It seemed like a natural fit for true crime television: a beautiful young woman vanishes, her boyfriend falls under suspicion but is ultimately cleared, and the bad guy gets busted CSI-style.

Although the crime took place in 2014, the trial wouldn't come up on the docket for years. Despite regular searches dating back to the initial missing person's report, there was still no sign of Christina. As the years dragged on, authorities decided they would go to trial with what they had rather than wait for a day that may never come. Enrique was put on trial for kidnapping in the fall of 2016 in Collin County, Texas.

A few weeks before the trial began, there was a hearing to make sure both sides were ready to proceed. I had my own reasons for attending, namely the fact that Judge Mark Rusch hadn't approved my request for cameras in the courtroom.

Before I started working in television, I thought it was a given that every courtroom would allow the media to record the proceedings. After all, this is America. Our courts are open to the public, and the freedom of the press is guaranteed right there in the First Amendment to the US Constitution. But it's not that clear-cut.

While I've never encountered a judge who didn't allow a journalist to take notes with a pen and paper, there have been plenty of them who wouldn't allow any electronic recording devices, including cell phones, computers, and cameras, to be used. If you're a print reporter, it's no big deal. But for TV people like me, that's practically a death sentence for the story.

With so much at stake, asking a judge for permission to have a camera in the courtroom is among the first conversations any good TV producer has on a story. And I had my pitch to judges down to an art form. I'd start by stroking their ego, and I'd always do my homework before I got an audience in front of them.

If they'd covered any high-profile trials before, I'd compliment them on how well the case had gone and their command of the courtroom. If they'd never allowed cameras before, I'd talk about how it was an opportunity for people to see justice at work, and an example of a courtroom run to perfection.

If they had allowed cameras before, I'd commend the judge for their wisdom in allowing the court to be truly open for all to see. And I'd still make a point of asking for permission for this trial in particular. I couldn't always win the judge over, and if I lost the camera battle, I still had a way to win the story war. Because after several of my stories were killed when cameras were kicked out of the courtroom, I came up with a new strategy.

I'd spin the lack of cameras in the courtroom as a positive development to my bosses in New York. "No one will have anything on tape from the trial, so we don't have to worry about *Dateline* or *20/20* going to air right after the verdict. They will be starting from scratch and have to build their episode out without any trial filler."

But as Nancy Kramer famously says, "No is just the beginning of a conversation." And I wasn't going to surrender our cameras without trying everything else first.

I approached the bailiff and asked if I could meet with the judge during a break in the proceedings.

By this point, I'd already attended a handful of trials for *48*, and I was beginning to recognize the competition. The *Dateline* producer at this trial was the same one who'd attended the Kaufman trial, and we exchanged pleasantries. I could tell we were scoping each other out, seeing which sources each of us seemed closest to and where there might be an opportunity to poach someone.

Because I'd first reported on the Christina Morris case for CultureMap, I had to reintroduce myself to the characters as a *48 Hours* producer. I remembered Christina's mom, Jonni, from those early searches on the outskirts of Plano. I had already interviewed her multiple times and even had her cell phone number. Plus, she was now in the CBS ecosystem, having gone on *Dr. Phil* to talk about Christina's case and the heartbreaking reality that they may never find out what truly happened to her.

Although the trial hadn't even started, I was feeling particularly poised for success considering the other events that had taken place. The bailiff motioned to me and said I could talk to the judge during the next recess. I thanked him and waited patiently for my window of opportunity.

Nothing could have prepared me for what happened next.

I approach the bench and introduce myself to the Honorable Judge Mark Rusch. I tell him that I am a member of the media. Seemingly confused by my last name, St. Amant, Judge Rusch repeats what he thinks I've said: "Claire Sandoval?"

I smile and correct him, giving the Texas pronunciation of my name first, before going into a rudimentary French lesson. "My name is Claire Saint Amant. It's French, pronounced Sa-na-ma, rhymes with Panama."

I'd had this portion of the conversation so many times in my life that I don't even bat an eye. Outside of Louisiana, I've listened to every possible mispronunciation of my name, including people who think "St." is an abbreviation for street and not saint. In college, the campus satirical newspaper coined the nickname Claire Statement. I'm generally good humored about all the varieties, though the one where everything runs together ("Stamant," rhymes with dammit) is my least favorite.

But Judge Rusch can't get past his mischaracterization and fixates on the mistaken belief that I am Hispanic.

"Do you know what they do to journalists in Mexico?" he asks me expectantly.

I am thrown off by his question, but I know I need to respond.

"No, Judge. I'm not very familiar with Mexico," I tell him.

"Oh, they do not treat journalists so well there," he says, looking me up and down and putting his hand on his chin.

"You would not fare well in Mexico," he continues. "They do all kinds of awful things to journalists like you. Kidnap, rape, and torture. It happens all the time."

I'm speechless for a moment, and the judge seems to enjoy my obvious discomfort at his wildly inappropriate comments.

"I guess it's a good thing this isn't Mexico then," I say, before trying to steer the conversation back to my request for a camera in the courtroom. But Judge Rusch cuts me off.

"I've never allowed cameras before and I'm not going to start now, for you," he says. "There's no recording of any kind allowed in my courtroom, audio or video. Is that understood?"

"Yes, Judge," I say, gritting my teeth.

I look around to see if anyone else is listening to this bizarre conversation in which a sitting judge had insulted an entire country and effectively told me I was a good candidate for kidnapping and rape. But since the court is in recess, the attorneys and other members of the gallery have already left, as has the court reporter. The bailiff is the only other witness, and he won't even make eye contact with me anymore.

I gather my belongings and go into the hallway. I see benches where the rest of the media is hanging out, but I don't stop there. I walk all the way down the hall, take the stairs to the first floor, and exit the building. There is no way I am going back to that courtroom today. The rest of the pre-trial hearing remains a mystery to me, but I don't have any regrets about leaving. My sanity is more valuable.

I would later recount this story to another *48 Hours* producer, an older woman who'd worked at CBS for decades. She took the opportunity to inform me how lucky I was that this was "all I had to deal with," before launching into a story of her own about a legendary *60 Minutes* correspondent who used to slap associate producers on the ass around the office, in full view of everyone. "Can you imagine what he did in private?" she asked me rhetorically. "Things are a lot better now."

Although no one knew it yet, the 2017 revelations about film producer Harvey Weinstein that would ultimately usher in the Me Too movement were just around the corner. In the years ahead, all the major news networks would face repercussions from the wide-ranging scandal, including bombshells from female producers about CBS's Charlie Rose, NBC's Matt Lauer, and Fox News's Bill O'Reilly that led to the powerhouse anchors being fired.

Along the way, *60 Minutes* executive producer Jeff Fager would also get the axe, leading to a shake-up at the most venerable news program in broadcast television. I had no idea then that my path at CBS would eventually lead to *60 Minutes*, and that I'd get to peek behind the curtain of the infamously secretive show. Because of a belief that true crime is beneath the *60* pedigree, there are very few criminal justice stories that make it onto the coveted Sunday evening schedule. But I'd find one that would break the mold and send me across the street to *60*, where I'd first hear the disturbing refrain: "You're working at *60 Minutes*? They eat their young over there."

Opening arguments in the Enrique Arochi trial kicked off in September 2016. There were no cameras to capture the action, but the media was still there in force. With so many of Christina's supporters attending the trial, every seat in the courtroom was taken. Despite the heavy attendance, you could hear a pin drop. No one was going to risk the wrath of the judge, least of all me, Claire Sandoval.

"Where is Christina Morris?" the prosecutor asked the silent room. "The truth is, I don't know, and at the end of this case, you won't either."

It's a bold move to tell that to a jury, but Texas courtrooms are known for tough tactics. Enrique probably thought he'd never go to trial if they couldn't find the body, but he wasn't counting on a kidnapping charge stemming from a single drop of blood inside his otherwise squeaky-clean car.

The defense still had a job to do, and they tried their best to muddy the waters that clearly spelled Enrique's guilt. Their strategy focused on Christina's boyfriend, Hunter Foster, who was the first suspect in her disappearance. And at the time of the trial, he was already behind bars himself, facing federal drug charges.

"There's a lot more to this case than out of nowhere he decides to be an abductor," the defense said, pointing to Enrique. Pivoting to Hunter's history of drug use, the defense proceeded to discuss a number of hypothetical reasons for Christina's disappearance, including drug cartels, human trafficking, and the Aryan Brotherhood.

But the prosecution wouldn't be drawn off course, telling the jury: "Each piece of evidence points to one person, and that's the defendant, Enrique Arochi."

Sitting ramrod straight in a black suit, twenty-three-year-old Enrique showed no emotion as the two sides drew their battle lines for the trial. If found guilty of aggravated kidnapping, Enrique faced a punishment ranging from probation to life in prison. Before the DNA tests came back and Enrique was arrested, he gave multiple interviews in the local media, including one with the CBS affiliate where he proclaimed his innocence.

"I had nothing to do with her disappearance," Enrique told CBS at the time.

Desperate for answers, Christina's friends and family had begun to protest outside Enrique's house in Plano. Calling themselves "Team Christina," they'd hold up signs and march up and down the public street, asking Enrique what happened that night and where he'd taken Christina.

Enrique told CBS that the group was asking for him to give them answers he didn't have.

"Everything I know, I've told police," he said.

In addition to speaking to the media, Enrique gave multiple interviews to Plano police, waiving his right to an attorney.

At the time, a police spokesperson told *48 Hours* that Enrique had cooperated with their investigation and was not believed to be involved in Christina's disappearance. Remember what I said about authorities giving out misleading information to the media? Enrique was arrested less than two months later, with a laundry list of circumstantial and forensic evidence backing up the case against him. Shortly after that, Judge Mark Rusch put a gag order in place, preventing any party to the case from speaking to the media until after the trial.

High-profile missing person cases are usually flush with media attention by design, because the more people who hear about the case, the better the chance of actually finding the person. But the state had accepted the fact that for the time being, they wouldn't be able to harness the public's help in locating Christina.

As the parade of prosecution witnesses took their turn on the stand, the state's case seemed to grow stronger with each one. Friends who'd been with Christina and Enrique on the night she disappeared remembered that Enrique was wearing a short-sleeve shirt, and that he didn't have any visible injuries to his hands or forearms. But in photos the police took of Enrique during his interview three days later, he had visible scratches on his hands and something that resembled a bite mark on his arm. There was also recent, unexplained damage to the front right fender of Enrique's Camaro. It painted a grim picture of a violent struggle on the night Christina vanished.

If the defense was hoping to score points by questioning Christina's boyfriend, Hunter Foster, they were in for a surprise. When Hunter took the stand, he pleaded the Fifth and refused to testify. His attorney told the judge that Hunter couldn't answer any questions about his activities the night

Christina disappeared without incriminating himself for dealing drugs. Later in the trial, prosecutors brokered a deal for Hunter on his drug case, offering him a reduced sentence in exchange for his cooperation. He testified that he was at a club in Dallas, selling cocaine. He was texting with Christina on and off throughout the night, until around 4 AM, when she stopped responding.

Christina's parents offered heartbreaking testimony about their daughter's fear of walking alone at night. She was also claustrophobic and afraid of the dark, her dad said. The fact that Christina most likely spent her last moments in the trunk of Enrique's car was not lost on anyone. Cell phone tower pings showed Christina's and Enrique's location as being together as they left the parking garage and headed north on the tollway. Shortly after that, Christina's phone was turned off and disappeared from the grid forever.

Disturbing details like these would stick with me long after our reporting ended. I'd try to wipe them from my memory when the next story came around, but I'd find them lingering in the recesses of my mind. They'd come to me in nightmares or show up when I'd find myself alone in dark parking garages. To this day, when I drive past the Plano shopping center where Christina disappeared, I say a little prayer for her family.

As the trial entered a second week of testimony, the media had all fallen into a familiar rhythm. We were there every day, often sitting side by side with our competition in the packed courtroom. We'd dutifully followed all of Judge Rusch's rules, silently taking notes and only approaching friends and family members outside the courtroom on breaks.

We still didn't have cameras inside, but we knew we had another window of opportunity coming up to ask for them: closing arguments. In a perfect world, you get cameras in for the whole trial, but in a pinch, even just having closing arguments and the verdict on camera is enough to carry the trial portion of an episode. In closing arguments, each side ties up the case in a nice little bow, summarizing their best points and putting forth a theory for the jury. There's passion and drama and sound bites for days. As a producer, it's painful to watch closing arguments without a camera to capture the action, because you know you'll have to try in vain to re-create it when you interview the attorneys afterward. And it's never as good as the live show.

While I'm normally happy to revisit the camera conversation when the trial is winding down, I had zero interest in going before Judge Rusch a second time. I didn't share the details of my first conversation with the producers from *Dateline* and *20/20*, but I did let them know I'd struck out on my initial request.

"I'm not going back up to that judge," I said in no uncertain terms. "It's somebody else's turn."

Meade Jorgensen, the salt-and-pepper-haired *Dateline* producer who I recognized from the Kaufman case, stepped up and volunteered to give it a shot. "Wish me luck," he called out as he headed into the courtroom during the afternoon recess.

A few minutes later, he popped back into the hallway with a big smile on his face.

"He's letting us have a pool cam!" he told us.

And for a moment we were all on the same team. A pool camera is when one network is allowed to film but they have to share the feed with every media outlet present at the trial. Because exclusives are the name of the TV game, it's not an ideal situation. But it is still far better than no cameras at all.

To get everything ready for closing arguments, the judge was adjourning court early. I was so tired of being imprisoned on those courtroom benches that I actually pumped my fist in celebration. Jorgensen couldn't help but rib me. "Now, Claire, don't get too excited. It's still a school night," he said with a twinkle in his eye.

The gag order was still in place, and so the camera in the courtroom for closing arguments was our only chance to get anything we could use in our episode until after the verdict. Christina's family had stayed friendly with me, and we'd exchange pleasantries during breaks and chitchat in the hallways. But I was always mindful not to break the judge's rules and try to go for an interview. The last thing I wanted to do was get crossways with the victim's family—or Judge Rusch.

I took my seat as closing arguments were set to begin. Enrique was led into the courtroom and sat down next to his defense attorney. Worn down by a two-week trial, he now appeared hunched over in his black suit, elbows on the table in front of him.

The prosecutor returned to his line from opening arguments, asking the jury rhetorically, "Where is Christina Morris?" before reminding them that he never promised an answer to that question. But he did have something else up his sleeve.

"Where *was* Christina Morris? In the defendant's trunk," the prosecutor said plainly. "We've answered that question, and the scientific DNA evidence has proven it."

Facing an uphill battle to counter forensic evidence, the defense tried to suggest that Christina's DNA could have been introduced to Enrique's car through an unintentional transfer by a crime scene technician, who also searched Hunter Foster's car earlier in the day.

It was a far-fetched theory, but I had to give the defense credit for concocting something that attempted to explain the otherwise damning evidence against their client. In the end, the jury deliberated for seven hours before returning with a unanimous guilty verdict. I had hoped that the verdict might signal the end of the gag order and finally allow the victim's family to give interviews again. But after pronouncing the verdict, Judge Rusch said the gag order would remain in place for the punishment phase of the trial.

In Texas, criminal trials are split into two phases: guilt-innocence and, if necessary, punishment. If a guilty verdict is returned and automatic sentencing guidelines do not apply, then there is a separate trial, complete with new opening arguments, witnesses, and closing arguments, to determine punishment. The defendant can choose to have the judge or the jury decide the sentence, and in Enrique's case, he chose the judge.

He was facing a wide range of punishment, anywhere from probation to life in prison, and both sides agreed to take a long weekend to prepare. It was only Wednesday, but the court would remain in recess until Monday. With the gag order renewed, I exchanged only sympathetic smiles with Christina's family as we shuffled out of the courthouse. Her mother, Jonni, silently raised her fist for the cameras gathered on the courthouse steps as she made her way to her car.

I'd spent the weekend blissfully unaware of the true crime world, choosing to take a much-needed break from anything resembling work. Because this trial was taking place in the Dallas area, I wasn't staying in a hotel or flying back and forth each week. But in some ways, that actually made the experience all the more jarring. It was one thing to be marooned in a random city and engrossed in a murder trial that felt so far away from your normal life. It was another to attend one in your own backyard and return home to your son and husband after spending eight hours listening to horrific testimony down the street.

I tried to put the trial out of my mind for a few days, and although it was a challenge not to check the headlines at first, by the end of the weekend I was totally in my domestic groove. I'll admit that I'm one of those people who actually looks forward to Monday mornings. As much as I enjoy the weekend, I like getting down to business, and I rarely dread the start of a new workweek. I see it as a chance to start new projects, finish old ones, and tackle my to-do list. This Monday was no exception, and I woke up before my alarm, ready to take on the world. But I was about to get a rude awakening in the ways of true crime television and learn firsthand what it takes to get a killer story.

As soon as I approached the hallway outside the courtroom, I could sense something was off with Christina's family. They were huddled together and talking in hushed tones with *Dateline* producer Meade Jorgensen. I didn't want to intrude, so I slowed down and took a seat on a bench a few rows away from them. It was early, and the courthouse hadn't fully come alive yet. I flipped through my phone and waited for Jorgensen to make his exit. When he finally broke off from the group, I went over to say hello. But before I could, Christina's stepmom cut me off.

"Don't even try to talk to me," she said.

Flustered, I didn't even get a word out. I was left with my mouth hanging open as she brushed past me into the courtroom.

Now I was really confused. Christina's family and I had always been on good terms, dating back to two years ago when I'd met them at one of the volunteer searches. Her parents were divorced, and I had gotten to know her mom, dad, and their new spouses. I'd interviewed them a handful of times on the record, and we'd spoken dozens more off the record. I had no clue what I could have done to offend Christina's stepmom considering I'd barely spoken to her since the trial began with a gag order. Was my lack of communication causing the offense?

At first, I gave her space, but as the day went on, I felt like I had to try to address the issue. The last thing I wanted to do was upset a grieving mother, but somehow, I'd done just that. After the lunch break, I waited outside the courtroom to speak to her. I started out by apologizing, even though I didn't know what I was apologizing for. She was still clearly upset, but she was finally ready to talk to me. And that's when she told me that I was completely out of line for calling her during the break, and that she didn't appreciate being pressured to give an interview while there was still a gag order in place.

I was blindsided by this information and earnestly explained that I never called her during the break. At that moment, I could see a light bulb go off in her head. Her anger faded away, and then *she* started apologizing. As she listened to the sound of my voice, it had dawned on her that it wasn't actually me on the phone.

"It was another Claire from *48 Hours*," she said to me. "I'm so sorry, I thought that it was you. She said her name was Claire and she worked for *48 Hours*."

My head was spinning because I'm the only Claire who works at *48 Hours* and was covering this trial. There's no one else from the show who would have called her, much less another person named Claire.

Even as she apologized to me, I could see the damage had been done. After believing that it really was me on the phone, she'd promised to give *Dateline* her first interview after the trial. That was the conversation I'd stumbled upon this morning in the hallway. I'd been totally schooled, on my home turf, right before my own eyes.

I tried to stay calm. It wasn't this poor woman's fault that someone from *Dateline* had called and impersonated me. How in the world could she be expected to see that coming? I certainly hadn't imagined this level of trickery, so why should she?

I assured her she'd done nothing wrong, and that it was all a big misunderstanding and that we'd sort it out together. Meanwhile, I went into overdrive trying to book other characters exclusively, but it was a fool's errand. I didn't realize then that my senior producers would be so incensed that they'd eventually kill the story. I'd covered the entire trial, we finally had cameras in the courtroom, and there was a guilty verdict. What could go wrong? Apparently, a lot.

And it wasn't just CBS who pulled the plug on production. Despite attending the entire trial, ABC's *20/20* also never aired an episode on the disappearance of Christina Morris. I might never know what shenanigans went on to kill the ABC story, but in the end, only *Dateline* would make it to the finish line. Enrique Arochi was sentenced to life in prison on September 30, 2016, and *Dateline*'s episode "Frantic" aired on NBC six months later.

As much as I hated getting beat, it hadn't been for nothing. I'd gained a valuable lesson in the war games that go on in the national media. And I'd adjust my strategy accordingly. From that point forward, I always explained to my contacts early on that my cell phone number was the only way that I'd ever communicate with them.

"This probably sounds kind of crazy, but just because I've been burned before," I'd tell them as I leaned in over the dinner table. "I want you to know that this is the only number that I'll ever call you on. If one day in the future, you get a call from another number, and that person says they are me, don't believe them."

9

WRONGFULLY ACCUSED

To me, getting a story killed was the worst insult. It meant I'd wasted my time, and worst of all, now I had to find a brand-new case and start developing it from the ground up. While I tried to avoid this at all costs, other producers seemed to enjoy getting their stories killed. They'd sharpen the axe themselves, arguing to can a story after spending a few days in the field working on it.

I started to realize that these producers were more into travel than TV production, and they looked at their assignment as a free trip with no strings attached. No one ever seemed to notice that all these people did was visit an exciting city and come back with reasons why the case wasn't good enough. And somehow, these fatal flaws had never occurred to them until they were on-site, despite all their years of research from their cushy home offices.

I always looked for ways to get the "yes" from New York, where saying "no" comes much more naturally. In the fall of 2018, I was covering a highly anticipated serial killer trial in Austin, one that I had fought to keep on our planning schedule for years. The crimes, a series of home invasions, had taken place in 2014, and they had rocked the community.

It was a baffling set of circumstances. Three seemingly unrelated victims all brutally murdered in their modest homes, their killers taking almost no loot. One of the more disturbing lessons from my time covering true crime is just how little some people will kill over. There is actually not a "normal" amount of motivation that's common to murderers. The stakes can be as little as ten dollars or as much as millions. Some people kill just for the thrill of it and take jewelry or cash as a trophy. Other people leave valuables in plain sight because the crime was never motivated by money anyway.

In this case, the crimes were not random at all, though they'd appeared to be on first blush. The first known victim was a middle-aged choir teacher who lived alone. Kathy Blair was an attractive single woman who liked to wear costume jewelry. She didn't have much, but she always looked her best, and she was careful with her money.

She'd hired a local landscaper to help fix a drainage problem in her back-yard, and she'd complained to the company that the worker took long lunches and left the job unfinished. This was months ago, and it was likely not even on her mind that December night when she was getting ready for bed early and left the back door unlocked for her son, who was on weekend leave from the navy.

He would be the one to discover her body in a pool of blood the next morning, setting off an investigation that would eventually lead to that dis-gruntled landscaper. Authorities would learn his name was Timothy Parlin, and he was an accomplished ex-con who specialized in jewelry theft. He'd recently started working with a young protégé named Shawn Gant-Benalcazar, a college dropout with no priors or history of violence. They were very much the odd couple, and two more people would die before police could connect the dots. As sensational as the cases had been, the five-year gap between the murders and the trial meant that the rest of the national media had completely forgotten about it.

It happens more than you'd think—when there's an arrest in a big mur-der case, and the headline runs in all the major papers, and New York–based producers from *Dateline* and *20/20* fly to Texas for the initial hearings. But when the trial gets delayed for years, it often falls off the radar for network coverage. Because there's always another murder fighting for attention. The crime beat never sleeps, as disturbing as that is to think about.

At this point in my career, I had developed so many Texas stories that CBS often had to fly in producers from New York to help me cover them all. In fact, when I came to Austin for the capital murder trial of Shawn Gant-Benalcazar, I was also in the process of booking interviews for a separate Travis County story about the 2015 attempted assassination of District Judge Julie Kocurek.

I was totally in the zone, taking calls and meetings on both stories and enjoying myself immensely. Austin is a great town, even when you're there for tragic reasons. I had made plans to meet up with friends while I was around for the week, and everything seemed to be going my way. Isn't life like that, though? When you least expect it, the universe comes in and kicks you in the teeth.

I arrived in Austin the day before the trial was scheduled to start. I had attended pre-trial hearings for years, and I'd already introduced myself to the judge, the prosecutors, and the defense team. More than once, I had broached the topic of allowing a camera at trial with Judge David Crain, and he'd been open to it but never fully committed.

I'd sold my bosses in New York on the idea that I could win him over, and now we were on the eve of the big show. I showed up with confidence and a stellar track record on my side. I'd patiently and politely attended every hearing, never asking for a camera in the courtroom for those occasions and reserving my request for the future trial.

I approached the bailiff during a break in the jury selection and reintro-duced myself, snazzy business card in hand. He told me that opening argu-ments would take place at 8 AM the next morning, and the judge was allowing us to set up our camera equipment the night before so everything would be ready to go when he struck his gavel. I smiled and said that sounded perfect. All my years of courteousness hadn't been for naught. I was getting the green light.

It probably seems like all we'd have to do is set up a tripod in the corner and press the red button to record. But for network TV, it's a lot more compli-cated than that. Because we want to be able to use the actual sound, we have to wire the front of the courtroom with our own mics and run cables back to the main camera. Plus, we usually try to have two camera angles, one pointed at the attorneys and one that covers the witness stand and the judge. We were aiming for the perfect vantage points that included the key players but excluded all the jurors. We needed at least two hours to set up if we wanted it done right. And what other way is there?

I waited in the hallway with my camera crew: director of photography Dave Roberson and sound engineer Steve Osmon. At this point, we'd already covered a handful of trials together and had a pretty good working relationship. These days, crews are independent and don't work exclusively for any one network. They are guns for hire, shooting for all three crime shows, plus sports and entertainment across the premium and cable channels. They might be at a murder trial one day, a championship game the next, and round out the weekend on the red carpet.

I liked working with Dave and Steve, and I was always happy to see them attached to one of my stories. Plus, they were from Austin, so it made logistics a lot easier, and we got the hometown discount because we didn't have to put them up in hotels or fly them and their gear across the country.

That day, we spent about four hours killing time in the hallway outside the courtroom, waiting to set up our equipment. The judge had told us we could come in "as soon as jury selection finished for the day." We had hoped things might wrap up soon after the lunch recess, and we'd arrived around 1 PM with all the optimism and energy you'd expect from three Texans. But by the time 5 PM rolled around and the jury had finally been empaneled and sent home, we were feeling a little deflated.

The work life of a crime producer is feast and famine. When I'm out in the field for a story, I can easily work fourteen hours straight. But when I'm back in the office, I might piddle around at my desk for four or five hours on a good day. I've learned it all evens out in the end and to take my breaks when I can get them.

Back in the Travis County courthouse, I was in the thick of it. With a little luck, we could be out of here by 7 PM and get a whole twelve hours off the clock before we had to come back to be in position for opening arguments. Courthouses close at 5 PM on the button. They run a tight ship, and unless a jury is deliberating, everyone typically heads out the door when it's quitting time.

But our day was far from over, and as all the attorneys, court clerks, and bailiffs were leaving, we were loading gear into the building. This raised more than a few eyebrows, and before we knew it, a Travis County sheriff's deputy was striding across the marble floor to question us.

He was all decked out, bulletproof vest, nightstick, Taser, and gun belt gleaming. He had so many pairs of handcuffs affixed to his body that it was comical. *Was this guy expecting a riot?*

"The building is closed," he told us with his hands on his hips. "You'll need to take all this equipment outside, right now."

I approached GI Joe with a big smile and extended my hand, as though I was thrilled to meet him.

"I'm so glad you're here. We are working with Judge David Crain's court, and he said we might need a police escort. You look like just the man for the job."

He visibly bristled at the comment, and I hoped I hadn't underestimated him.

"No one is allowed in the building after five PM," he told us without removing his hands from his hips. "You have to leave."

I told him Judge Crain gave us special permission to set up our camera equipment in his courtroom for a trial that was beginning tomorrow morning.

"If you come up to the courtroom with us, you can talk to the bailiff and confirm our story," I offered.

He begrudgingly agreed and motioned us down the hallway. As we grabbed our camera gear and hustled to the elevators, I tried to make small talk. I asked him how long he'd been with the sheriff's office and if he liked working in the courthouse. Then I told him I had a son who wanted to be a police officer when he grew up. He was a toddler in a cops-and-robbers phase, so it wasn't a total stretch.

But I was laying it on thick, and Dave and Steve were trying to keep a straight face. They knew me well enough to recognize my favorite tactics, and flattery is definitely one of them. Compliments can be so disarming. And this guy had a lot of weaponry to account for.

Once we got upstairs to the courtroom, the sheriff's deputy went right inside and found the bailiff sitting at his desk, feet up, playing on his phone. As you might imagine, this did not go over well with GI Joe. The bailiff slowly rose to his feet and the two lawmen appraised each other. I popped in between them, trying to defuse the situation that appeared to be escalating rapidly.

"Hi there, do you two officers know each other? We're so grateful for your help in allowing us to get the courtroom set up for tomorrow."

They looked at me like I had two heads. Dave and Steve were frozen behind me, not feeling comfortable enough to actually start setting anything up yet.

The sheriff's deputy and the bailiff were still sizing each other up, and the deputy spoke first.

"No one told me about anyone being in the building after hours today. That has to be cleared with me in advance."

The bailiff said that the judge himself had approved it and authorized the bailiff to stay with us to supervise the setup. It seemed like an open-and-shut case to me, given the latitude that judges are typically afforded. But GI Joe was unimpressed, and he told the bailiff that he needed to speak to the judge himself to confirm the permission.

At this point, the bailiff threw up his hands. "It's after five PM, I don't need this hassle. I'm outta here." And then he picked up his lunch box, and walked right out the courtroom doors, leaving us all slack-jawed.

Except GI Joe, who was grinning for the first time that evening. "Well, that decides it then. You no longer have anyone to supervise you, and you can't be in the courtroom alone, so you have to go too, right now."

My camera crew groaned and threw up their hands. We'd been in position for five hours, waiting to get inside the courtroom, and as soon as we entered, we were being kicked out.

But I wasn't through trying to win over GI Joe. What did I have to lose?

"Oh man, my boss is going to kill me. I really messed this up."

I paused to wallow in my feigned self-pity for a moment.

"I wish I hadn't put my faith in that bailiff. What was I thinking?"

GI Joe kept grinning. He was enjoying my misfortune. I took a deep breath and squared up to him like a basketball defender. Time to go for the win.

"You're probably the only person in the world who could fix this for me, if you wanted to."

He looked back at me quizzically.

"You're in charge of the whole building, and that includes this courtroom. I bet you could supervise us while we set up real quick."

GI Joe considered my offer and looked around the room as if to survey the audience. Dave and Steve smiled innocently back at him, gear still frozen in their hands.

"How long will it take?" he asked.

I lied my ass off and said, "Fifteen to twenty minutes."

"Okay. I'll give you twenty minutes."

I avoided eye contact with my camera crew as long as I could, because I knew the daggers that were awaiting me.

Twenty minutes was barely long enough to unload the gear, much less set up a two-camera courtroom and wire for sound. But the goal of the field producer is to get in the room, and I knew that if I didn't underplay the time commitment, we'd have been kicked out before we even started.

Now, all I had to do was keep our police escort happy long enough to let my crew work, and to somehow make two hours feel like twenty minutes.

I pulled up two comfy desk chairs from the attorney's table and motioned GI Joe over. I started asking him every question I could imagine about life as a sheriff's deputy, and before I knew it, he was telling stories of foot pursuits, car chases, and shoot-outs. But what I really didn't expect was where the conversation went next, when he asked me what my first job was after college.

"The Peace Corps."

He was stunned. He'd been in the Peace Corps, too.

For the first time all night, I was truly interested in GI Joe, and we spent the next two hours swapping stories of our Peace Corps adventures. It's a very small club, and when you meet another returned volunteer, there's an instant kinship. I had been faking something like friendship with GI Joe, and now we had a real-deal bond. My crew was happily working away, without a fear in the world of being booted from the courtroom, when GI Joe suddenly popped up from his chair.

"Holy cow, it's eight PM! I have to go do my rounds and check the perimeter real quick. Are y'all about done?"

The truth was, we could have been done about an hour ago, but since everything appeared to be going so well, my crew was giving the courtroom the deluxe treatment, and they were currently in the middle of wiring up addi-tional mics at the attorney tables.

He looked over at the crew, on their hands and knees in front of a mess of wires, and offered up a concession.

"Just keep working. I'll be back in about fifteen minutes."

As soon as he walked out the door, and we heard his heavy metal boots track down the hallway, we burst into laughter. What a coup this had been! Our biggest obstacle was now our new best friend, the gun-toting Peace Corps Volunteer.

We recalled the story with triumph, enjoying our victory and working quickly to finish wiring the sound. Producers don't usually handle the equip-ment. There are even union regulations about it. But in this time crunch, it was all hands on deck, and I pitched in with the gear.

By the time GI Joe returned from his rounds, we had all but finished in the courtroom. We shook hands and parted as friends, heading off into the night feeling like we had really pulled off something special. Little did we know, there was another version of events, hiding in plain sight, that would soon land us all in a world of trouble.

I don't remember much about opening arguments in the capital murder trial of Shawn Gant-Benalcazar. All I know for sure is that the cameras and mics worked great, and the courtroom was packed.

While most of the day was tedious and uneventful, I vividly remember what happened around 4 PM. I was stealing a glance out the window, day-dreaming of a run around Town Lake, when the judge pounded his gavel and brought me back to reality.

"There are some matters the court needs to attend to, so we are adjourn-ing early."

What luck. Early dismissal. On the very first day.

As I zip up my bag and start to make my way out of the courtroom, I notice two strange things. First, the judge has already left the bench. If there were mat-ters to attend to, where was he going? And second, the doors are being blocked by a handful of plainclothes investigators from the district attorney's office.

I recognize the type. Dark suits, guns harnessed in strategic locations. And no smiles on their faces. What in the world is going on?

My journalistic senses are heightened, but my evening run is calling my name, and after giving them a once-over, I head past them. Or so I think.

"Excuse me, we need to talk to you for a minute," a female investigator says.

"Me? Okay," I say, genuinely intrigued.

"Actually, all of you," she says, gesturing to Dave and Steve, who are still futzing with the equipment behind me.

"Oh boy," Dave says with a nervous laugh. "What's up?"

At this point, I'm not even worried. It is more amusing to me than anything else. I had been lectured by law enforcement when covering a high-profile trial before. I figure it's the typical finger-wagging "don't film the jury" and "no recording sound when the judge goes into sidebar with attorneys." Rookie mistakes that Dave, Steve, and I would never make.

But when the investigator asks us for identification, and then makes a show of taking pictures of all our driver's licenses, I start to get the feeling this is going to be a different conversation.

I glance back and realize the doors are being locked, and we aren't going anywhere. This is a first for me. They hand us back our IDs and then go straight for the jugular.

"This will go a lot easier if you just tell the truth," the woman says, pausing and looking us each in the eye.

We all turn to each other incredulously and shrug our shoulders. We have no idea what she is talking about.

"What's going on?" I ask her.

"You stole something from us, and now we need it back," she replies.

Now we are really confused. We hadn't stolen anything. How would we have even gone about that, in a courtroom with cameras everywhere?

"Hold on a minute," I say. "We didn't take anything from anybody."

"We have you on camera," she says. "You can't deny it."

At this line, Dave throws up his hands and Steve lets out a guffaw. I am too stunned to speak, and I stand there, frozen, while my mind runs in circles.

Another investigator makes a show of turning on a digital recorder and placing it on the wooden pew in front of us.

"What are we supposed to have stolen?" I finally say. "How can we help you find it if we don't even know what you are looking for?"

They consider my question for a full minute before answering. I can tell they are trying to read us, but we are genuinely in the dark on this one. We just stare back with blank expressions and wait for them to enlighten us.

"Last night when you were setting up your equipment, you took a flash drive with all the evidence on it. We saw you."

This is a surprising accusation for several reasons. One, we know we didn't take their flash drive, and two, we had a sheriff's deputy with us the whole time. Well, almost.

"We didn't take your flash drive," I say, even though I know denial is futile. They have already decided we are guilty.

The investigator confidently says that they have us on camera, in the courtroom, taking the flash drive in the period of time when the sheriff's deputy left to go do his rounds.

"I don't know what you think you saw, but we didn't take a flash drive. We wouldn't do that. We are filming the whole trial. We will get the evidence at the end, like we always do. There's no reason to steal it."

Unconvinced, she tells us, "If you let us look through your laptop and search your vehicles, then you can go."

Now I am the one guffawing. The idea that I will give up my laptop and vehicle to the state of Texas, without a warrant, is truly laughable.

While I'm reeling, another investigator pipes up.

"You might as well have a seat and get comfortable then. Because you aren't going anywhere until you let us search your stuff."

I survey the room. The crowd has grown to about a dozen law enforcement officials, and they have encircled us.

So much for my jog around the lake. I look up at Dave and Steve. They are both old enough to be my dad. And they are looking at me for a cue on what to do next.

"Have a seat, guys. I think I need to call New York."

I sit down and position my laptop bag in between my feet. It is coming up on 6 PM in New York, and I am thankful that the creative types on the East Coast typically work nights. The office doesn't even come alive until 11 AM, which means most people leave around 6 or 7 PM.

I punch in the number for senior producer Peter Schweitzer, an old-school New Yorker who knows a thing or two about a thing or two. Schweitzer has always been a great sounding board for story problems and anything else that comes up in my professional life. He's also a dad and a fellow long-distance runner; what's not to love? There were several senior producers who didn't care for my particular brand of Texas attitude, but Schweitzer wasn't one of them. He was in my corner, always. The line rings, and rings, and I am starting to worry I won't catch him before he heads home.

Mercifully, he picks up. I relay the situation to him, explaining we are essentially being detained and accused of stealing evidence in a capital murder trial. Oh, and the whole thing is being recorded, including my side of this phone call. It's a lot of information for the end of the day, but Schweitzer takes it all in stride.

"Sit tight. I'm going to patch in our attorneys."

I stay on the line and wait for the legal calvary to come. In a matter of seconds, Nicholas Poser, chief legal counsel for *48 Hours*, is ready to advise me.

I've never been so happy to hear an attorney's voice before. He tells me that I do not have to give the authorities my laptop under any circumstances without a subpoena. It is a work product and property of CBS News.

I tell him they also wanted to search our personal vehicles. He thinks for half a second and then weighs in. "Those are being used in the process of news gathering, so they are protected as well. You can consent to them searching your car, but I would advise against it."

Nick says he is going to make some calls to attorneys in Austin and see if he can find someone to come to the courthouse and sit with us. I thank him profusely and promise to keep him updated.

Then I take a deep breath and look around. Everyone is watching me, and several people are taking notes. I am not used to being on this side of the reporting process.

I notice Dave and Steve are getting up from their seats, and I intercept them as they are walking toward the doors. I am puzzled; where do they think they are going?

"New York said we don't have to let them search our cars because they were used in the process of news gathering," I say somewhat cheerily.

This is good news, right?

Dave laughs and rolls his eyes.

"I've been through this kind of thing before. We didn't steal anything. The best thing we can do is just let them search our van and see for themselves." Steve is already digging the keys out of his pocket.

I am incredulous. Why in the world would you consent to an unlawful vehicle search? Who knows what they might find or accuse you of? What if they seize our equipment? I tell them I see no upside to this decision.

"The upside is, we get to go home," Steve says as he turns to walk away.

"Not necessarily!" I shout out to him as he waves me off and heads out with a police escort.

Now *I'm* pissed. What the hell are they thinking? Haven't they seen our show before? When you are accused of a crime, you lawyer up and don't do anything stupid. Letting them search your van definitely classifies as stupid in my book.

On top of that, they have now left me alone with all the investigators. I am surrounded and totally vulnerable. It's the end of the day. I am hungry and I kinda need to pee. But the last thing I want to do is admit they have any power over me by asking to go to the restroom. Sit tight takes on a whole new meaning.

Suddenly, the doors swing open, and a petite blonde woman marches through them. It's Margaret Moore, the elected district attorney for Travis County. This night is just getting more and more troubling.

My phone rings; it's my attorney. I say a silent prayer for good news before I answer it.

Nick tells me he found a local media attorney who is going to come to the courthouse, but she needs someone to let her in the building since it's after hours. Nick tells me to put him on speakerphone and hold the phone out for whoever is in charge so he can explain the situation.

"This is very important. Do not hand your phone to them. That would constitute a consent to search."

I walk over to where District Attorney Moore is standing and announce, "Excuse me, my attorney would like to speak to you."

Still firmly grasping my phone, I punch the speakerphone button and hold it out.

Nick introduces himself and explains that I have legal representation trying to get into the building where I am being detained.

"What kind of law does she practice?" the DA asks.

Nick says she is a media attorney specializing in the First Amendment.

The DA laughs. "You need to send a criminal attorney, not a civil one. They are being investigated for felony evidence tampering."

I feel my stomach drop, and I put out a second hand to steady my phone.

Felony evidence tampering? Am I about to be arrested? Despite my penchant for troublemaking, I've never spent the night in jail. I've been detained before, but I've never been arrested. It's a distinction I want to keep intact.

Nick is apparently making the same connections I am, and he blurts out, "If you arrest members of the national media who are covering a trial, you are going to end up in court yourself!"

As much as I appreciate Nick standing up for us, it is getting pretty awkward holding that phone just inches away from the DA as the shouting match intensifies.

"Call us back when you find her a criminal attorney. She'll need a good one."

And with that, she walks away. I take the call off speaker and swallow the lump in my throat.

Nick tells me he will find a good criminal attorney and call me back.

"Don't worry. We will take care of this. And if they do arrest you, we'll spring you as fast as we can."

I hang up the phone and sit back down on the bench. I take some deep breaths and try to mentally prepare for the idea of being arrested in this courtroom and taken out through the back doors to the jail. I've seen countless defendants shackled and shuffled through those courtroom tunnels that connect to the county jail. I've even been in those tunnels a time or two with defense attorneys. But I never imagined being the one in custody.

As I am staring at the jail doors, wondering if I will see the inside of them that night, another set of doors swings open behind me. It's Dave and Steve, flanked by police, and looking incredibly forlorn. They are pale, and Steve is holding a clear plastic pencil case. I can see highlighters and pens and some sticky notes peeking through.

The investigator stands up eagerly. "That's the pencil case that the prosecutors are missing," she says.

My jaw hits the floor. I look up at Steve and his expression is tortured. "I must have grabbed it by accident when we were loading up our gear. I thought it was one of mine. I am so sorry."

If you don't know Steve, I can see how this story might sound. But the thing is, bless his heart, Steve is one of the least daring people I have ever met. I don't mean this as an insult, but there is very little I can imagine Steve risking for a story. He's just not that brand of journalist. He's kind and cautious and not at all a person who bends the rules to get ahead. Trust me; I know the type.

An old-school sound technician, Steve spent twenty years on staff with the CBS affiliate in Houston. Punching the clock and paying his union dues. He was good at his job, and maybe twenty years ago, he had something resembling mischief in his eyes and a fire in his belly, but certainly not today.

Steve is hapless but harmless. Except in the eyes of Travis County, where he is a criminal mastermind, stealing a flash drive full of evidence on the eve of a capital murder trial, under the full view of courtroom security cameras.

I feel so badly for Steve. He looks like he might pass out at any moment. The investigators take hold of the pencil case and begin picking through it, searching for the missing flash drive. It takes less than a minute for them to realize it isn't in there. But this only further excites them about getting their hands on my stuff.

"Of course it's not in the pencil case anymore," one investigator says. "They had to get the evidence off of it."

All eyes turn back to me, the producer.

"Now would be a great time to tell the truth and let us look at your laptop," the lone female investigator says to me. "We can get to the bottom of this right now."

It sounds good enough, but I know that it's a lie. Because they aren't going to find any evidence on my laptop, which is only going to convince them that they have to look elsewhere. There is no way they are suddenly going to believe me and stop searching.

"Look, we all have bosses," I say. "And mine told me not to let you search my laptop. So my hands are tied."

I immediately regret my word choice, and I hope it isn't a premonition of things to come.

Soon we've been detained for hours. It is pitch-black outside, and I look down at my phone to see several messages from a friend I'm supposed to be meeting up with for dinner. Oops.

We hadn't seen each other in about fifteen years. But back in the day, Catherine Campbell had been a close friend and high school basketball team-mate. Although she'd wisely stayed out of trouble herself, she was a witness to many of my youthful shenanigans. When I realized she was living in Austin, I had arranged to meet up.

Now, I fire off a blunt text. "Hey. Going to have to miss dinner. So sorry. Being detained, literally, in the courthouse. Will explain later tonight if I can."

Catherine doesn't miss a beat.

"Let me know if you need bail money!"

What does it say about me that someone I haven't seen in over a decade has no further questions upon learning I've been detained by authorities?

The next number that pops up on my screen is my attorney's. I answer before it even rings.

"Sorry it took so long. We are still trying to find a criminal attorney in Austin that has a working relationship with CBS."

Then Nick tells me to put him on speaker again so he can talk to the DA.

I groan, and the investigators turn in my direction. "My attorney wants to talk to you again." I stand up and bring my phone over.

"Look, we don't have criminal attorneys on retainer at CBS News," he says with a laugh. "I've called a bunch, but it's late and we're across the country. The best I can do is get a civil attorney there. I still have one on standby."

The DA has clearly been thinking about this and discussing it with her team because she has an offer ready.

"We have local criminal defense attorneys that we work with to make arrangements for high-profile cases."

The phrasing makes me grimace. *High profile? Criminal defense?* Kill me now.

"We can have a criminal attorney in this courthouse in a few minutes to represent your people. That's the only chance they have of leaving this building tonight."

Nick says he needs to talk to me privately, and I take the call off speaker and huddle in the farthest corner of the room.

"You don't have to do anything you don't want to do. And I normally wouldn't advise using a defense attorney that was handpicked by the prosecution, but in this case, I think it's your best bet."

"If I don't do it, do you think they are going to arrest me?" I ask him.

"Probably. And they still might. But at least you'll have an attorney with you if they do."

I hate all of these options, but I agree having an attorney present seems like the way to go. I walk back over to the DA and her cohorts and press the speakerphone button again.

"We'll agree to the counsel of your choosing for the purposes of tonight's negotiation only. Who is it?"

The DA says it is the firm of Minton, Bassett, and Flores. I chuckle. I actually know them. And they are high-profile attorneys. They are in the middle of representing a trust fund kid accused of hiring a hit man to kill his parents.[6] I'd chased them around this very courthouse trying to get interviews on that case recently. I'd welcome their undivided attention.

"Great. I already know them," I blurt out.

The DA shoots me a look. "Small world," I shoot back.

We get off the phone, and I go over to Dave and Steve to give them the update. Steve still looks like he is not long for this world, and I can tell Dave is trying to hold it together for his sake. When I tell them about the attorney, they seem suspicious.

"Is he *your* attorney or *our* attorney?"

I tell them that my understanding is that he is representing all of us. But Dave and Steve are unconvinced.

"New York only cares about producers. The crew always gets screwed in situations like this."

"Good thing I'm not from New York then. I won't let them split us up. If one of us gets arrested, we all get arrested."

---

6 Associated Press, "Texas teen, wife accused of hiring hitman to kill his jeweler father," CBS News, May 31, 2018, https://www.cbsnews.com/news/texas-teen-wife-accused-of-hiring-hitman-to-kill-his-jeweler-father/.

This doesn't have the comforting effect that I'm hoping it will, but at least they know I'm not going to leave them high and dry. I'd rather go to jail on bogus charges than desert a fellow Texan.

As I am still reassuring them, our attorney walks through the courtroom doors. I guess the wheels of justice spin faster when you're the DA.

I immediately recognize Samuel Bassett as a named partner in the firm. I'm glad they didn't send some first-year associate. He hustles over to us and suggests we talk in the far corner, which is as close as we can get to attorney-client privilege in a courtroom with a dozen government employees.

I get him up to speed, including the fact that Dave and Steve let them search the van and they found a pencil case belonging to the prosecution team.

"A pencil case? They detained y'all for office supply theft?"

I explain that they believe there was once a flash drive in that pencil case, and it contained all the evidence in the capital murder trial we were covering.

I tell Sam we did not take their flash drive, and that we have no idea where it is. We didn't remember seeing a flash drive when we were setting up the courtroom the night before, and Steve taking the pencil case was an honest mistake.

Sam listens sympathetically to our plight, and I immediately feel better just having him on our side of the courtroom. He tells us to follow him, and we all walk over to the DA, who is standing with her arms crossed, looking very law-and-order-y. Winning her over is not going to be easy.

"Here's the deal," she says. "We have reasonable cause to believe that they stole the flash drive of evidence, which is a felony. We can't let them leave tonight with that laptop, because they could destroy the evidence."

Sam thinks for a minute and then offers a solution.

"If she can't leave with the laptop, and her company says she can't give it to law enforcement, would you be willing to let her give it to me instead?"

The DA is listening. Sam explains that he'll keep the laptop secure in his office overnight, and in the morning, with me present, he will perform keyword searches with my consent for the evidence. If he finds anything, he will be legally obligated to tell the DA and the case can go from there. But if there is nothing on my laptop responsive to the search terms that the DA provides, then I get it back.

I don't love this idea, but it sure beats spending the night in jail.

The DA and her team confer for a minute before agreeing to the terms. And then I have to unzip my bag and hand over my laptop to my newly minted attorney. He hands me back a business card and instructs me to come to his office at 7 AM the next morning so we can search my laptop together.

And then come the magic words from the DA herself. "You are free to go," she says. "For now."

Finally outside the Travis County courthouse, Dave, Steve, and I breathed a huge sigh of relief. The whole thing was so absurd, but we were far from out of the woods yet. We said good night, and I made them promise they were coming back in the morning. We laughed in that exhausted, punch-drunk way that I've come to associate with long television shoots.

I got in my car and called my friend Catherine. "I'm free! Want to get a drink?"

I met Catherine at a burger joint with a wall of beer on tap. Freedom never tasted so good. Shortly after I popped up on a barstool and relayed the story to her, my phone started ringing.

It was a retired detective with the Austin Police Department. Derek Israel had worked the Kathy Blair murder case, and I'd interviewed him several times before for CBS. But I knew he wasn't calling me about that. I apologized to Catherine and said I probably needed to take this one. She waved me off with an understanding flick of her wrist.

"Are you calling me as a friend or a detective?" I asked Derek by way of greeting as I stepped outside.

A veteran homicide detective and skilled interrogator was on the other end of the line. Considering my predicament, I knew I was playing with fire by even talking to him. But I also couldn't resist hearing what Derek had to say. He was someone I considered a friend—and a smart investigator. Maybe he could actually help my case. Or maybe he was recording the call for the DA's office.

"I'm calling you as a friend, but you know that I am also a detective."

I told him I was glad he called. "Can you talk some sense into the DA and her gung ho investigators? They have lost their minds."

Derek tried to rein me in. "Look at it from their perspective. The flash drive just happens to go missing the one night that your crew is in the courtroom? It doesn't look good. You have to explain yourself."

It had been a long day, and I felt like I'd already explained myself until I was blue in the face. So I decided on a new tack, hoping it would get Derek thinking I might actually be innocent.

"I'm not a Girl Scout, okay. It's not that bending the rules would be so far afield for me. But think about this: I have no motivation to steal *this* particular flash drive. I gain nothing from it.

"We are already in the courtroom with a camera. We are rolling on every piece of evidence. Why in the world would I commit a felony for a story I already own? There is no upside."

Derek was silent. Then he clued me in. "They think you're going to put it on the internet. They are checking CBS News's website for it right now."

It was so ridiculous I had to laugh.

"What exactly would be the story there? 'Producer steals evidence and outs herself online.' Does that sound like a headline that would ever run? Do cops even watch the news?"

Derek told me he would try to talk some sense into them, but he ended the call the same ominous way he started it. "It doesn't look good, Claire. Trust me."

I got off the phone and wondered what evidence they had against me that could make someone as smart as Derek question my innocence.

I rejoined my friend Catherine inside the restaurant, and she tried to make me feel better about my plight.

"You have a way of getting into—and out of—trouble," she said. "Either way, it always makes for a good story."

At 6:55 AM I was parked outside the law offices of Minton, Bassett, and Flores in downtown Austin. I had barely slept the night before. I had tried to tell myself the hotel bed was a much better place to get some rest than a jail cell, but somehow that wasn't the comforting thought I needed to drift off to sleep.

I had been wide awake when my alarm went off at 6 AM, and since it was still dark outside, I went for a run on the treadmill, my least favorite way to work up a sweat.

I was in a horrible mood and drinking shitty instant coffee from the little machine at my hotel because I hadn't had time to go anywhere with a decent brew. My morning run and latte were two simple pleasures that I was already being robbed of. I wasn't cut out for a life of crime.

I walked into my attorney's office and was ushered into a conference room where he was waiting with my laptop.

"How was your night?" Sam asked with a bemused smile on his face.

And with that we were off to the races. The DA had given him a list of keywords to search for that they believed would reveal whether or not I had copied the evidence to my computer. Even though I knew I didn't have the evidence on my laptop, it was nerve-wracking to watch him perform these searches. First, he put in the defendant's name: Shawn Gant-Benalcazar. About a dozen files popped up. He raised his eyebrows at me.

"I'm covering the story. Of course I have files with his name in them."

He looked through the files, which were mostly Word documents and email messages. Then came the probable cause arrest warrant affidavit and the indictment. He turned to me for an explanation.

"Public records. I got them online through the court's website."

He raised his hands in mock protest. "I'm just the messenger. I wanted to make sure you had the right source."

He ticked through the rest of the search terms with similar results. There were no evidence-tagged files on my laptop, or at least none that he could find. Sam rang the DA's office and delivered the news. They were less than enthused, and Sam confirmed that he was returning my laptop back to me.

As I was going to leave, Sam gave me the best lawyerly advice I've ever gotten. "You aren't guilty, so don't act like it. And you should assume they are watching you."

With that foreboding instruction, I headed out the door and down the street to the courthouse, where I hoped I would be allowed to leave at a time of my choosing for a change.

I got through security and made it into the courtroom just as the jury was being seated. As I whipped out my laptop to start taking notes, I couldn't shake the feeling that someone was looking at me. I turned around and spotted the female investigator sitting in the row behind me. The same woman who had spent the better part of last night grilling me was now attending this trial. How about that? I guess my attorney knew that it was going to take more than a clean laptop to stop this investigation.

I don't blame them for taking an interest. It was almost too easy for them to tail me. They knew exactly where I would be from eight to five for the foreseeable future. I was probably the easiest mark the DA's office had in their sights that week. I use that criterion on my own work schedule all the time, first selecting the stories that are within closest reach from my front door, before venturing out farther. Low-hanging fruit gets picked first, no matter what your trade is.

Still, I didn't have to like it. And being tailed has a way of making you self-conscious of every choice you make. Was I going to the bathroom too much? Did it look suspicious? Maybe she was so good that she already knew I had a lot of hotel coffee in my system, and it was going to have to come out.

She followed me everywhere, from the stall to the street. I started referring to her as my shadow and introducing her to people I was meeting with. "Have you met my shadow from the Travis County DA's office? She's a peach," I'd tell my lunch companions, to their confusion.

If I had to be tailed by a surly investigator, I was going to at least try to have some fun with it. Because fun can be hard to come by in the courtroom.

A big part of my job as a field producer is to take meticulous notes during trial. Yes, there's a court reporter, but those transcripts take months to finalize and cost thousands of dollars. CBS has the money, but they'd rather not spend it on transcripts when they have perfectly capable producers who are getting paid to sit in the courtroom.

It's grunt work, but it does help pass the time, and I enjoyed finding sound bites that I could flag for scripts later. Plus, I saw it as an easy way to get in the good graces of other producers. Thorough court notes made everyone's job easier, from fact-checking associate producers to the script-writing capital-P Producers. Everyone loved the colleague who came home with perfect notes.

As one of the handful of CBS producers who lived and worked outside of the Tri-State area, I had to do whatever I could to claw my way into their little club. I realized I was never going to make it into the inner circle from my home turf in Texas, but I'd get as close as I could while still firmly planted in the Lone Star State.

Living in New York just wasn't in my blood. I like the sun too much, and I can't stand crowds, or relying exclusively on public transportation. I loved visiting New York, taking in a Broadway show, jogging in Central Park, and then flying home to my three-bedroom house with an attached garage.

The thought of actually living in New York with my family gave me hives. And that's the kind of statement I could never make inside the walls of CBS, where New York is considered the mother ship, the grand prize, the holy grail of broadcast television.

I had made the mistake of hinting that I didn't aspire to live in New York once, years ago in a contract negotiation with the legendary Susan Zirinsky. She'd asked where I saw myself in five years, standard boss-type temperature reading. I told her I wanted to write for the show more and to have a seat at the table picking the kinds of cases we would cover.

"A seat at the table means New York. Are you okay with that?"

"That would be a pretty big sacrifice," I said honestly.

As soon as the words left my mouth, and I heard silence on the other end of the line, I knew I had royally messed up. Z is rarely at a loss for words. I tried to cover my tracks by adding qualifiers.

"But for the right position, I'm sure it would be worth it," I blurted out.

For most people in this profession, getting a promotion to New York would be the highlight of their journalism career. But I didn't worship at the altar of NYC. And this was the equivalent of blasphemy in the media world.

From where I stood in Texas, though, this admission should actually be a good thing for my colleagues at CBS. If I wasn't willing to move to New York, I shouldn't be a threat to 90 percent of the producers at the show. And being perceived as a threat in the cutthroat world of national media is definitely a hazard of the job.

The politics of working at one of only three network true crime shows in the country is not for the faint of heart. It's a coveted job, and most people assume you'd do anything to keep it. This is the kind of workplace culture that can get people to fly to a trial on a one-way ticket with instructions to stay until you get the story. Butts in chairs, sound on tape, and evidence in hand is the only way to come home. It's not the kind of work-life balance that breeds a healthy family dynamic or even high job satisfaction. But it does give you job security and street cred with the other producers.

After five years of flying across the country on a dime, pulling off exclusive interviews, and securing evidence ahead of the competition, I had street cred to spare. Even though I knew that going to jail for a story would really only help my profile in the national media, I wasn't keen to add "time behind bars" to my list of producer accomplishments.

The lunch recess was over, and I was back in court. I was still waiting for an update from my attorney and trying to keep up with the testimony while my mind was everywhere but on the case in front of me.

I saw my phone silently alerting with an unknown Austin area code on the screen. I slipped out of my pew, winked at my shadow, and pointed to my glowing phone. Surprisingly, she didn't follow me this time. Was she losing interest already?

I ducked into the hallway and picked up the call. There was a Travis County judge on the other end of the line. It was Julie Kocurek, the head district judge in Austin, who also happened to be a survivor of a 2015 assassination attempt. I'd been patiently trying to book her for three years, first sending flowers to her hospital bed and then letters to her office once she returned to the bench. She was a total badass and had quickly become one of my personal heroes. Not only had she survived a brutal shooting, she'd filed for reelection from the intensive care unit. She was easily the most coveted story on my wish list—and had been for practically the whole time I'd been at CBS.

Judge Kocurek told me she'd been thinking really hard about doing an interview, and she wanted to talk to me in person about it. I was thrilled, and for the first time all week, thankful that I was in Austin and not three hours down the road at my house in Dallas.

I told her I was covering the Shawn Gant-Benalcazar trial in Judge Crain's court but that I could meet her during lunch hours or before or after court. She opted for a lunch date, and we set it for the following day. Not even the looming threat of wrongful imprisonment could dampen my spirits now.

As I was getting ready to head back inside, my phone rang again, and this time it was my attorney.

"Do you have good news for me, Sam?" I asked optimistically.

He let out a sigh that said he did not, in fact, have good news at all.

"So I've seen the video from the courtroom security camera. And it does not look good."

Again with the not-looking-good comment! Were they all reading from the same script?

"I need you to tell me exactly what happened when the sheriff's deputy left y'all alone in the courtroom. In your own words, to the best of your ability, I need you to remember it and to describe it to me."

I felt like I was a witness on the stand. I sat back down on the bench in the hallway and let out a sigh of my own.

"There was really nothing to write home about. I don't even remember what we did. We were grabbing all our gear, trying to get out of there before GI Joe realized we'd been in the courtroom two hours longer than we told him it would take to set up."

I laughed as the memory started to come back to me.

"It's actually kind of a funny story. Turns out the cop was a returned Peace Corps Volunteer, like me, and we ended up swapping stories for hours, which was totally unexpected because he seemed like he hated my guts when he first met me."

"Keep talking," my attorney instructed.

"We carried on for so long that the crew had ample time to set up everything they needed, plus all the bells and whistles. When he left us alone in the room, we were so proud of ourselves that I think we high-fived. We definitely had a few laughs at his expense."

This was getting good, but Sam wanted more. I wracked my brain trying to replay the scene.

"I think at one point, Dave asked me to talk into the mic at the attorney table, and Steve listened to the audio levels. I remember there was a wire that wasn't taped down and we thought it would be a tripping hazard. Since I was right there and smaller than both of them, I crawled under the table and gaffed it."

Sam was clearly pleased with this explanation. And then he clued me in as to why everyone kept saying that it "didn't look good for us."

The video from the security camera in the courtroom didn't have an audio feed. So all the investigators were going on was a three-person pantomime and a missing flash drive. And the picture that painted, without my innocent explanation of laughing at the deputy and taping down an errant wire, was one of subterfuge and coordinated criminal activity.

In the eyes of the state of Texas, the moment the deputy left the room, we had sprung into action, searching the prosecution table high and low for the flash drive containing the evidence, and then promptly loading it into our gear bag. As soon as the deputy returned, we bolted with the stolen goods.

It was a surreal experience to hear a completely false, albeit plausible, explanation for all of our actions.

Sam told me he thought everything was probably going to work out now. "You have a very reasonable and innocent story that accounts for everything they are accusing you of. Just remember to say it exactly like that when you make a statement about what happened."

Oh boy. I did not like the sound of that.

"Do I have to make a statement at all? Can my statement be no statement?"

Sam was perplexed. He thought I'd be eager to put something on the record explaining myself. But as a true crime producer, I've seen way too many cases where a defendant's own words are picked apart line by line and become the biggest evidence against them at trial. I wasn't giving them a single syllable to analyze, if I could help it.

"They expect you to give a statement," Sam told me. "It doesn't have to be a big deal. But if you refuse to make one, it might signal to them that you are scared."

Well, they were right about one thing at least.

I told Sam I would think about it but that I was leaning very heavily to the side of not talking at all. He told me he would try to implant the idea that I had a rock-solid alibi and lay some traps for doubt on the DA's case.

That sounded like a much better plan to me than voluntarily going down to the sheriff's office and making a statement that would be scrutinized by the brightest minds in Travis County.

Sam promised not to make any commitments about my statement until we talked again, and I headed back into court. I tried to focus on the positives. If the truth couldn't save me, maybe staying silent would.

The day had been eventful enough already, and it was barely 2 PM. I dutifully took notes in court, grateful for the distraction and some normalcy in my workday routine. Then came the afternoon recess, the last one of the day. As I popped out to stretch my legs, I noticed I had a missed call from my attorney and a text message instructing me to call him as soon as possible. I braced for more bad news and dialed him up.

"Well, they found the flash drive," he told me.

"Thank God! So this is over now?"

Sam regretfully told me no, it was not over at all. The prosecution had found the flash drive in a most peculiar way. It was sitting on top of a trash can, in the breezeway between the DA's office and the courthouse. Slightly damaged and placed askew, the flash drive appeared to have been put there intentionally. Can you guess who they thought was responsible?

A new chapter of the investigation was just beginning, based on the theory that we had not only stolen the flash drive as originally alleged, but now I had dumped it, after getting spooked by the threat of a search warrant.

I didn't even know where the breezeway between the DA's office and the courthouse was. I told Sam as much and asked him if it was in a secure area of the building, one that would need a key card to access it. Unfortunately, the breezeway was open to the public, but Sam agreed I had brought up a good point. I wasn't from Austin or overly familiar with the inner workings of the Travis County courthouse.

What was really crazy to me was the idea that I would ever choose such a location to "dump" a stolen item. Let's imagine for a moment that I did steal their flash drive and I got spooked, like they are alleging. There is no way in the world that I am bringing that item back into the courthouse. I would throw it away at a dumpster downtown or flush it down the toilet at my hotel. There are about a dozen other places I could choose that make way more sense than placing it on top of a trash can right by the DA's office.

I asked Sam if there were security cameras in that hallway, and if they could review them to prove that I had never been there. Or, even better, could they see who had actually placed the flash drive on the trash can lid? I had zero hesitation about suggesting this course of action because I knew for a fact it wasn't going to be me, Dave, or Steve on that camera.

Sam said he would try to find out, but in his experience, a lot of those security cameras didn't actually work. Isn't that how it goes? The camera in the courtroom was used to condemn me, but the camera that could prove my innocence isn't functional.

I laughed at the increasing absurdity of the situation and headed back into court, where I updated Dave and Steve on the latest development. The rest of the afternoon passed without incident, and it was finally time to be dismissed for the day. I looked around to see if there were signs that I was going to be detained again, but the investigator two rows back just smiled and stayed seated as I gathered my things and made my way to the doors.

I was holding them open for Dave and Steve when I saw some attorneys coming up behind them. My Southern politeness kicked in, and I kept holding the door as the prosecution team pushed a metal cart down the center aisle. It was a haphazard-looking scene. The cart was loaded up with binders, file folders, cardboard boxes, and Tupperware containers. As they turned the corner, several items fell off the cart and a trailing assistant stopped to grab them.

Dave, Steve, and I locked eyes and immediately had a hive-mind experience. What were the odds that this was how the evidence had disappeared? I could see the flash drive falling off the cart on the eve of the trial, only this time the prosecution's assistant hadn't spotted it. A few days later, someone stepped on it in the breezeway between the DA's offices and the courthouse, and they'd picked it up and placed it atop the first surface they found: a trash can.

Seemed way more likely than the theory that had been concocted to include our involvement. We got out of the building and called our attorney from the crew van. He thought our logic was sound, and he said he'd keep working back channels to indicate confidence in the strength of our case.

"They'll never believe you are innocent. But I think I am gaining ground on them believing that it's not a winnable case."

This was a window into the world of criminal prosecution that I never expected to have. Even when evidence appeared to contradict my involvement, the state found a way to shoehorn it in on me. There was nothing I could say to defend myself. They had already made up their minds that I was guilty. The best thing I could do was stay silent and let my attorney do his job.

I had a newfound empathy for all those suspects who had said they were being railroaded for crimes they didn't commit. I wasn't being falsely accused of murder or facing life in prison, but I was the victim of tunnel vision and an overzealous investigation that seemed to delight in targeting me. And let's not forget this was no small thing they were accusing us of—they were pushing a felony case.

I parted ways with Dave and Steve for the night, and I counted my blessings that the week was coming to an end. Tomorrow, I would get to meet with Judge Kocurek, a welcome distraction from the insanity of the other courtroom I was frequenting, and I would get to go home to Dallas. Or at least I hoped I would.

I realized I had never told my attorney that I had planned to fly home on Friday afternoon, spend the weekend with my family in Dallas, and come back to Austin Monday morning. Was I free to leave Travis County? I'd never imagined asking that question to anyone, but suddenly it felt like a pressing matter. I dialed Sam back immediately.

"Ah, that might be tricky," he said when I told him I wanted to fly home for the weekend. "We should probably give them a heads-up, so they don't think you are fleeing the jurisdiction."

The drama of this week just wouldn't let up.

My general mode of operating falls under asking for forgiveness, not permission, but I was no longer in ordinary times. I was in a situation that required constant legal counsel, and the last thing I wanted to do was give the investigator tailing me an excuse to move in for the arrest. She looked like she really wanted to slap the cuffs on me herself. I wouldn't give her the satisfaction if I could help it.

"Okay," I told my attorney. "I trust you."

Friday morning, I got to the courthouse with pep in my step. My attorney had alerted the DA's office about my travel plans, and they acted unconcerned. He told me there was still a chance they would "pick me up" at the airport but said he didn't think they had enough of a case to arrest me yet. Sam had also requested a courtesy heads-up if I was going to be charged, so I could turn myself in.

"What a treat that would be," I thought out loud.

"Beats being booked at the Austin Airport," Sam quipped back.

He did have a point.

As excited as I was about getting out of Austin, I still had an important matter to attend to before my flight. During the lunch recess, I headed over to a different courtroom and knocked on the door for the chambers of Judge Julie Kocurek. It was unlike any door I had seen at a courthouse before. Stainless steel, with a camera and doorbell security system, it looked more like it belonged at a bank safe. But I couldn't blame Judge Kocurek one bit.

In November 2015, Judge Kocurek was ambushed by a masked gunman outside her own home. It was a chilling scene. The night had been cold and rainy, and the Kocurek family had attended a high school football game.

The judge left early with her son, who was driving the SUV when it pulled up to the driveway of their suburban Austin home. He noticed a bag of leaves was blocking his direct path into the garage, so he got out of the car to move them. That's when the gunman popped out of the bushes and approached them.

Her son, only fifteen, blocked the gunman from shooting his mom directly by standing in between them. Instead, the gunman had to shoot through the window, giving Judge Kocurek precious seconds to dive on the floor of the vehicle and shield her head with her hands. The killer unloaded the entire clip into the car and fled down the street into a waiting vehicle.

Her son called 911 and the fight to save Judge Kocurek's life was on. She would spend a month in the ICU, battling life-threatening infections and complications, and undergo more than thirty surgeries to repair injuries to her face, head, and hands. Four months after the shooting, Judge Kocurek was back on the bench. Since then, she had advocated for Texas legislation that strengthened courthouse security and privacy for judges.

Her attacker, a career criminal named Chimene Onyeri, had found her home address online and stalked her for weeks before the shooting. He was convicted and sentenced to life in prison earlier this year, at a federal trial I had also attended. Judge Kocurek had always been kind but firm with me about not going on camera.

Never one to give up, I had sensed the timing might finally be right, now that the federal sentencing hearing was complete. I had given a handwritten note to Judge Kocurek's bailiff on the first day I was in Austin, which already felt like a lifetime ago. And now she was taking me up on my request to meet in person and privately discuss the possibility of an interview, at long last.

I identified myself on the security camera and was buzzed through the steel door. It opened and closed with a heft that made me feel safe, and I hurried inside.

Her chambers were like a museum. Cards, posters, and letters adorned every wall. There were signed photos from celebrities, newspaper clippings, and pictures and drawings from children across the country. I had never wanted to do a story on someone more in my life. She was a living hero who continued to inspire people and defy the odds. In my line of work, I rarely got to tell stories with a happy ending.

After the week I'd had, it was a welcomed reminder of the best of true crime journalism. As I took in the room, I noticed a treadmill in the corner, collecting dust. Judge Kocurek told me she was a runner before the shooting.

"My family bought me that because they don't want me running outside anymore," she said with a sympathetic smile. "But I rarely use it because I hate treadmills."

We were kindred spirits already.

We chatted easily for the next half hour, and at the end she agreed to do an interview for a *48 Hours* special series called *Live to Tell*, which were first-person stories of survival. The series was the brainchild of senior producer Judy Tygard, who'd created the concept in 2009. At this point in my career, I had only worked with Judy once, when she'd been the senior producer on a story I'd developed on an unsolved murder in Fort Worth. It had been a memorable experience for all the wrong reasons. Namely, I'd gotten crossways with Judy over an editorial decision that she hadn't asked for my opinion on, but I went ahead and gave it to her anyway. She cut me down to size, lecturing me on the chain of command and reducing my role on the episode.

It was, at the time, the strongest reprimand I'd gotten at 48, and as a result, I expected pushback on my role on Judy's *Live to Tell* series. That was ironic given that I had nursed the Judge Kocurek story for three years, and I was hand delivering it on a silver platter. But I knew, coming from me, it wasn't going to be seen as a peace offering. More like a shot across the bow. I would have been better off getting "assigned" the story from Judy, but where's the fun in that?

These thoughts were swirling in my head as I thanked Judge Kocurek for her time and told her I'd be in touch about the production schedule.

I was flying high after that meeting, and I didn't want to come back down. I decided to head to the airport early rather than attend any more of the trial, where I had begun to feel like an inmate rather than an observer.

I'm pretty sure I skipped down the hallway and out the door that Friday afternoon. If I was on borrowed time, at least I was going to enjoy it. But my lighthearted mood was short-lived. When I got to the airport, I had that queasy feeling that something wasn't right.

Since joining CBS, I'd become quite the frequent flier, racking up miles by the thousands and making air travel seem routine. But today, the TSA agents made me nervous. And it seemed like there were more Travis County sheriff's deputies than usual in the terminal. Was I being paranoid or was something about to go down?

As I made my way through security and headed to my gate, I had the distinct feeling that someone was chasing me. I tried to shake it off and not look behind me like a nutcase. But then I felt a tap on my shoulder.

"Excuse me, you left this in the bin," said a man holding my laptop.

I've never been more relieved to see a stranger—and not a cop—in my whole life.

When we landed in Dallas, I could finally breathe. I was free of the watchful eye of Austin authorities for the first time all week, and it felt great. I took an Uber and relished a peaceful evening at home with my husband and son. We had already put the kiddo to bed and were lounging in the hot tub when I saw my phone lighting up. Why was Susan Zirinsky calling me at 10 PM on a Friday night? Was I about to be arrested in a bikini?

I turned off the jets and answered my phone.

"Good news," she said immediately. God, I loved people who led with that disclaimer.

"The DA agreed to drop their investigation. The information they got off the flash drive said that no one had opened the files since the Sunday before the trial started, so their case for felony evidence tampering is pretty much dead in the water."

Waves of relief washed over me.

I told her it was the best news I'd heard all week.

Zirinsky agreed and said she never had a doubt. "I think they were a bunch of liars and just didn't want to admit that they lost the damn thing themselves."

We laughed and exchanged a few more choice words at their expense.

"You're good to go back there on Monday, right?" she asked in a way that wasn't really a question.

"Sure. What's the worst that could happen?"

Over the weekend, I got a call from Detective Derek Israel. I figured he was going to congratulate me on avoiding arrest and prosecution. But that was only half of it.

Now that the case had been dropped, he could give me a full peek behind the scenes of the investigation. And it was a doozy. Way crazier than I had even known. I hadn't been paranoid to think I might be arrested at any moment. Apparently, that was the plan, on several occasions, but cooler heads prevailed.

The very first night, when we were detained, the whole purpose was to buy enough time to get a judge to sign off on a probable cause affidavit against us. But Judge Julie Kocurek, the head district judge of Travis County, wasn't convinced the state had met their burden of proof. I always knew I liked that woman. The topic had never come up during our meeting, and I'd had no idea she was even privy to the details at the time, let alone that she was the one who held my fate in her hands.

Derek told me that when Judge Kocurek refused to sign off on the affidavit, the DA investigators still tried to strong-arm an arrest by referencing a statute that says you don't need to establish probable cause if you have reasonable belief that a felony is being committed. The case against me checked all the boxes, but at the end of the day, they decided it would create a media firestorm to arrest a journalist on a trumped-up evidence tampering charge in the middle of a capital murder trial.

Derek told me that the DA's office was so convinced that I still had the stolen flash drive in my possession that they had an investigator tailing me to see if I'd do something stupid like try to dump it somewhere. And according to her reports on my behavior, I was acting increasingly nervous and flighty. They referenced how I frequently ducked out of the courtroom midtrial, suspicious behavior in their book, but in reality, I was fielding calls from Judge Kocurek and my own attorney. It's amazing how people see what they want to see.

After they'd recovered the flash drive, on top of a trash can of all places, the DA's office once again poised for an arrest. Derek said they were trying to get me to come in and make a statement at the sheriff's office, and they planned to arrest me right afterward. Good thing I had followed my intuition about staying silent.

Derek also had the inside track on my Friday flight plans. He said they knew what flight I was on and had seriously debated picking me up at the airport to prevent me from leaving Travis County. In the final hour, they decided to let me fly home and give me the feeling that I was out of their reach for the weekend. In reality, they were still trying to get data from the flash drive to make a case against me.

If they had discovered that the files had been accessed in the period of time when the flash drive was missing, then they would have put together a case and arrested me at my home in Dallas. They had my address from my driver's license, the one they'd taken a picture of when they first detained me in the courtroom.

In a weird way, it was actually comforting to know I hadn't imagined the intensity of the situation. Given the option, I think I'd rather be arrested on false charges than be a head case with paranoia.

No longer the target of a felony investigation, I returned to Austin the next week, footloose and fancy-free. I suddenly had ample time and energy on my hands. And it was a good thing, too, because the capital murder trial was really getting interesting.

The state had wrapped up their methodical case against Shawn Gant-Benalcazar, proving his connection to the disgruntled landscaper Timothy Parlin, as well as tying him to the crime scene with physical evidence found at his home. And then there was the fact that he'd confessed to two Austin police detectives, including Derek Israel, and promptly fell asleep right there in the interview room.

"If they sleep, they're guilty," Derek told me. "I've seen it loads of times."

The case had baffled investigators for months before they'd made an arrest, but now it was laid out so clearly it didn't seem like there were any surprises left. Then Shawn announced he'd be taking the stand.

It's always an interesting day in court when a defendant testifies, and especially so when there's a recorded confession to counter. The state had opted to play the interview in full, so we'd heard hours and hours of conversation between Shawn and the detectives, culminating in a description of the murder, including the specifics of where the victim was stabbed and how many times.

When I'd talked to Shawn myself, months earlier in the Travis County jail, he'd told me to watch the videotape carefully.

"It's been altered," he said as he glanced furtively around. "I don't know how they did it, or what government software they used, but they spliced the video to make it look like I confessed. I never confessed."

No matter what your opinion was of the case against Shawn, you had to admit he was one disturbed individual. Although, given what I had just been through, I had a glimmer of empathy.

Back in the courtroom, he was about to take the stand in his own defense. Wearing a gray suit, no tie, and with his dark hair pulled back into a low ponytail, Shawn looked more like a bartender or a nineties sitcom actor than a cold-blooded murderer. That was the magic of the courtroom. By design, everything was so professional and cordial that no one ever really looked guilty on sight. The mug shots, interrogation videos, and crime scene photos told a different story, but it was always interesting to see suspects all cleaned up and on their best behavior, politely answering questions while their lives hung in the balance.

Presumably, they were innocent. And they deserved the benefit of the doubt that the American legal system affords to all accused criminals. But someone had stabbed poor Kathy Blair, a children's choir director, in her own home. And Shawn had a lot of explaining to do if it wasn't him.

On the stand, he put forth a different theory than the one he'd given me from jail. No longer claiming the video had been "spliced" together with a secret government software, Shawn now alleged that he'd been tricked into confessing due to exhaustion.

"I made it all up. It never happened."

The state had a field day with that defense, going back over the details of the crime scene that matched Shawn's confession, details that had never been released publicly.

It took less than three hours of deliberating for the jury to return a guilty verdict, and Shawn was automatically sentenced to life in prison. It was a huge victory for the prosecution, who was trying the case for the second time this year, after the first trial ended in a hung jury.

Dave and Steve were in position with a camera in the courtroom for the verdict, and now I was signaling them to cover the hallway so I could get reaction interviews. The post-trial action moves fast, and if you miss it, you never get it on camera again. People clear out and that in-the-moment energy is gone. You can interview the same people the next day, but it won't feel like it does when the verdict first comes down.

After everything we'd been through in this trial, I wasn't going to miss the grand finale. I hustled out the door and blocked the hallway to the DA's office. Turnaround is fair play.

"Hold on a minute there, can I talk to y'all real quick?" I said in my best cop impersonation.

DA Margaret Moore gave me a sheepish smile.

"Of course, ask me anything you want," she said.

"In that case . . . ," I countered.

We laughed in that funny-not-funny way, and then something happened that I never expected. The DA actually apologized to me.

"I'm sorry about all that. It kind of got out of hand. But we were just doing our job. No hard feelings?"

What could I say? I definitely still had feelings about being tailed by investigators and threatened with felony prosecution. But I also had a job to do, so I put on a big bullshit smile.

"No hard feelings," I lied. "Now how about that interview?"

10

PULLING A FAST ONE

So much of the producer's life is about rolling with the punches. One day, you're the target of a felony investigation. The next, you're chasing down your own leads on suspected criminals.

Tonight, I'm in a corner booth in a quiet Italian restaurant in Houston, sitting across from a man who was once hired to kill two people.

"All a big misunderstanding," he says, lifting his hands in surrender. "I'm not that guy."

I want to believe him, but I'm a natural skeptic. *48 Hours* producer Ryan Smith is by my side, and I'm grateful for the backup. The case has been the talk of the true crime world for weeks, and we're trying to find our own angle on the sensational murder-for-hire story.

We've spent the last couple days running and gunning on the streets of Houston to track down this alleged hit man, and he is finally right in front of us.

Moataz Azzeh is a young man in his twenties of Middle Eastern descent. He's a US Army veteran who served in Afghanistan with distinction, interpreting for his squad and earning a Purple Heart, among other commendations.

He survived a roadside bombing that killed several in his unit before being medically discharged, and he has the scars to show for it. I want to see him for the American hero he was, but it's complicated.

In documents that were recently unsealed, Moataz was named as the original hit man hired by Dr. Leon Jacob, the up-and-coming transplant surgeon whose lawyer smuggled me into that clandestine courtroom hearing in Houston at the beginning of this book, and his girlfriend, Dr. Valerie McDaniel, a prominent veterinarian.

Moataz had allegedly accepted thousands of dollars to kidnap and kill Leon's and Valerie's exes, and was the one who ultimately became the whistleblower on the whole operation. There are reports that Moataz was given immunity in exchange for his cooperation, and that he might not be entirely innocent, though he would tell us differently.

Ryan and I tracked Moataz down through his own criminal record, following a theft case to a bail bondsman, whose records listed Moataz's cell phone number. We were as surprised as anyone when he picked up the call and agreed to meet us for dinner that same night.

The story was highly competitive, with all three major TV networks vying for characters to use in their coverage. Our boss, Nancy Kramer, was thrilled we had set up the first meeting with the alleged hit man, but it wasn't without its own risks. We shared all the details of our location and agreed to a specific time for a check-in call.

Moataz had suggested an Italian restaurant on the outskirts of Houston, and Ryan and I got there early to scope it out. We found a quiet spot in the back section, an almost basement-like room with brick walls and roomy leather booths. It looked perfect, and we claimed a spot while we waited for our hit man to show himself.

We already knew what to expect because the local news had shown up on his doorstep and stuck a camera in his face the day the court documents were unsealed. With that kind of introduction to the media, we figured Moataz would be a cautious customer, and we were right.

He arrived and immediately laid out the ground rules.

"No cameras. No recording of any kind until I give the go-ahead."

We told him we weren't looking to surprise him. "If and when you go on camera with CBS, it will be your decision."

We took it slowly, ordering appetizers and filling the space with small talk. There was no reason to rush Moataz, and we figured the longer we kept him talking, the better our chances were to book him for an actual interview.

There was still a lot of mystery in the story, including the detail of how Moataz and Leon had actually met. It's not like the two men, nearly twenty years apart in age, had much in common. Their only connection seemed to be that they shared the same bail bondsman.

Moataz would later agree to say that he'd been introduced to Dr. Jacob through a "mutual acquaintance." As much as we wanted to fill in all the holes, we knew we couldn't get every question answered. We'd have to settle for the big ones and leave the rest to our audience's imagination.

The story that Moataz told us over a leisurely dinner was full of intrigue. He'd used a fake name, worn a wire, and surreptitiously recorded dozens of phone calls with Leon Jacob. For the first few months, he'd worked alone, gathering details about Leon's motives and the target of the operation. He collected around nine thousand dollars in the process, and he happily spent it.

"If this guy was crazy enough to give me his money, why wouldn't I use it?"

But as time went on, Leon was growing impatient with the lack of results. And Moataz wasn't about to do anything to harm Leon's former girlfriend. "I saw an opportunity to help someone, and to protect them, and I took it."

Moataz went to the Houston Police Department and revealed the whole plot, including the fact that he'd taken Leon's money under the guise of being a hit man. HPD got their undercover unit involved, and Moataz agreed to introduce a disguised detective to Drs. Leon Jacob and Valerie McDaniel.

By then, the plot had grown from threats and kidnapping to torture and murder. There were disturbing conversations about how to handle all the hypothetical complications of the assignment, including Dr. Jacob at one point suggesting an injection of potassium chloride to trigger cardiac arrest.

"He said it wouldn't leave a trace."

The story was so engrossing that we'd lost track of time. We were huddled close over the table, talking in hushed tones when a waiter approached us.

"Excuse me for interrupting, but are you Ryan Smith with CBS News?"

"Yes," Ryan replied suspiciously.

"There's a call for you at the front. They insisted we come get you."

Moataz jumped up from his seat and scanned the restaurant. "What's going on? Is this a setup? I told you no cameras!"

We were equally confused by the call, and I assured him we hadn't brought a crew, and that we didn't know what this was all about.

"I don't know who is on the phone, but I promise you there are no CBS cameras coming."

I thought Moataz was going to storm out of the room right then and there, and I was doing everything I could to keep him calm.

"An ambush interview like this would not do us any good. That's how the local news operates, not us."

The truth is the only people we ambush interview are hostile characters: suspected killers, cagey attorneys, and alleged co-conspirators. But it wasn't the time to get into the nuances of our reporting strategy. I just needed to keep him in the room until Ryan got back and not reveal all our secrets in the process.

Mercifully, Ryan reappeared alone. Moataz sat back down, and we all waited eagerly for the download.

"So that was our boss in New York," Ryan said, and I knew it was the truth. "She gets a little nervous sometimes when she doesn't hear from us. But it's all good now."

The check-in call! We had completely missed our agreed-upon time, and Kramer had assumed the worst. She'd been trying to call and text us for the past hour, but we didn't have service in this area of the restaurant. All of her missives had gone straight to voicemail.

We shared a collective laugh of relief as Moataz scanned the room one more time before taking his seat.

"Sorry guys," he said. "With what I've been through, it's hard for me to trust the media."

We'd weathered the storm and come out stronger. To celebrate, we ordered another round of drinks. Then we got back down to business.

"How would you like to come to New York, all expenses paid, and tell your story exclusively to *48 Hours*?" we asked, full of liquid courage.

"Let's do it," Moataz said, and we raised our glasses in victory.

11

UNDER THE GUN

It's the middle of the night, and I'm tiptoeing through an ice-cold hotel room to find the bathroom in the dark. My work at CBS sends me to so many locations that I regularly wake up in unfamiliar surroundings and lie there for a minute before my memory jogs. This time, I'm inching next to the wall, feeling for an opening to indicate the hallway, when my fingers land on a Pack n' Play. My son's. I'm not halfway across the country or even the state. I'm in a hotel ten minutes from my house, with my husband and child.

It wasn't how we'd planned to spend this summer night. We'd fled only a few hours earlier, grabbing supplies for a last-minute overnight trip born of necessity. We had finished dinner and were getting ready to start the familiar bedtime choreography (bath, book, rocking; repeat as needed), when it happened. There was a stillness in the air, and as we ascended the stairs, a heat wave enveloped us. I know there are parts of the country where you can get by with a cracked window or a box fan, but Texas in July isn't one of them. And certainly not with an infant. We instantly realized that the air-conditioning was broken and there would be no sleeping here tonight.

My frequent CBS travels afforded me a few secret weapons for disasters such as this, including a prepacked go-bag and enough hotel points to put us up on a whim. I've stayed in so many Marriott hotels that it actually smells like a version of home to me. I know where they keep the extra blankets in the closet and that I can borrow workout clothes through the fitness center if I forget mine.

I've traveled so much without my family that traveling with them feels exotic and novel, and I lean over my son's makeshift crib and kiss his forehead. I spy 1 AM on the clock and crawl back into bed, snuggling next to Riley and burying my head under the down comforter, totally unaware of the terror unfolding down the road.

For every highlight-reel moment of true crime producing, there are plenty more that send you straight to your knees. One of the hardest stories of my career went down on familiar territory, right in the heart of Dallas.

The summer of 2016 was marked by a number of high-profile police shootings of Black men in the US. On July 5, Alton Sterling was shot and killed by two police officers outside a convenience store in Baton Rouge, Louisiana. On July 6, Philando Castile was shot and killed during a traffic stop outside St. Paul, Minnesota. And on July 7, there were organized protests against the shootings across the country, including one in downtown Dallas. There were a thousand people in the streets, including a hundred Dallas police officers, when gunfire erupted shortly before 9 PM.

Like so many mass casualty events, initial information was chaotic and indicated that there could be multiple shooters. When the dust settled, authorities learned that only one man was responsible for the attack: Micah Xavier Johnson, a twenty-five-year-old Black man and US Army veteran.

Using his tactical training, Johnson drew the officers out and ambushed them, taking strategic positions on the street before eventually retreating to a second-story window where he picked off more officers with a semiautomatic rifle. He killed five police officers and injured nine others. The fatalities were Lorne Ahrens, Michael Krol, Patrick Zamarripa, Brent Thompson, and Michael Smith. It was the deadliest day for US law enforcement since September 11.

Johnson's own demise was a coordinated event as well, with police tracking him to his final location by following a trail of blood up a stairwell at El Centro College. A SWAT team exchanged hundreds of rounds of gunfire with Johnson and spent hours attempting to negotiate a surrender. Ultimately, the officers settled on a novel approach. They used a robotic, remote detonation device to deliver a fatal explosion of C4 at 2:30 AM, killing the shooter instantly.

I didn't know any of that when I woke up on the morning of July 8, 2016, in a hotel room, but I was about to get a rude awakening. My phone had a series of missed calls and my inbox had ballooned with unread messages. I wiped my eyes and wondered if I'd slept through the entire day. But the clock said 7 AM, and no one in New York usually calls me before nine. Something had to be terribly wrong.

I pulled up my voicemails and listened to the oldest ones first. They had started coming in around 11 PM. The unmistakable voice of senior producer Patti Aronofsky bellowed through my ear. "Can you get to downtown Dallas? There's an active shooter and we're trying to get information on it." Next message: "There are reports of a sniper picking off protesters, so if you go to Dallas, be careful."

Then the text messages started, from Patti and others across the CBS ecosystem. Everyone wanted to know how fast I could launch into producing a story about an active mass shooting in my hometown, but I was still numb from the news.

I turned on the TV in the hotel room and saw every station was already covering the disaster, from local outlets all the way up to CNN and Fox News. When Riley popped back in the room with the ice bucket, I broke the news to him. We both knew this would be a huge story for CBS and *48 Hours*. Good thing I already had a bag packed.

As any journalist will tell you, the best way to report out a story is with boots on the ground. I had scanned the local newspaper at the hotel and saw there was a vigil planned for noon at Thanks-Giving Square downtown. A sculpture and fountain garden, it was normally such a peaceful space. Back when I'd worked at People Newspapers, our office had been right around the corner, and I'd often wandered into Thanks-Giving Square to eat my lunch or sip a coffee.

Considering how quickly everything had happened, there was no time to get a *48 Hours* camera crew assigned to the vigil. If we wanted any of our own footage, I would have to shoot it myself, on my iPhone. Most people think the national media is more coordinated than that, but the truth is, we are frequently running and gunning with limited supplies and manpower. What makes the national media work are the people who improvise and wear multiple hats until backup can arrive. I knew we'd eventually have a crew in Dallas, but in the meantime, I wasn't going to miss the action.

An English major and former print journalist, I'd had precisely three days of professional camera training from a camera class for field producers *48 Hours* hosted at the broadcast center in New York. It was my first and only time ever operating a professional camera, and the last day had included some instruction on how to shoot high-quality video on a smartphone.

After we'd gotten the basics in a conference room presentation, we were handed gear and told to go practice what we'd just learned in Midtown Manhattan. We were supposed to shoot a series, which is three shots at varying angles to introduce a new subject. A wide, establishing shot; a close-up of some detail; and a third shot at midrange with some action. For example, the instructor told us, if your story is about a coffee shop, you might shoot the signage outside, steam coming off a cup, and a customer sipping on the finished product.

It was a helpful explanation, but I knew I wouldn't be doing much future filming at Starbucks. I wanted to get some real-life experience, the kind that would help me in my new career as a true crime producer. I had noticed that one of the staple shots for courtroom footage was "the perp walk," when the defendant is escorted in and out of the courthouse or jail. I figured that was a shot I might actually need to film one day, so I went to a street corner to practice keeping pace with pedestrians at the crosswalk.

As you might imagine, most New Yorkers were not pleased with me throwing a camera in their faces as they made their way down Tenth Avenue. It was actually pretty realistic conditions for the years ahead, when I'd have to jockey for a camera position on murder suspects. I grabbed a series of walking shots, a wide image of the crowded crosswalk, a close-up on feet shuffling past, and then, I saw something that caught my eye. A man with an artificial leg.

Ever the reporter, I had so many questions for him. And thanks to the professional camera in my hand, I had an excuse to ask them. I approached him and made my pitch.

It started out like any interview, where he gave his name and what he did for a living. I learned he was an usher at one of the theaters in town. Then there was a great reveal that he only had one leg. I had all these dramatic, artsy shots of his artificial leg, and he explained that most people thought of him as disabled, but he didn't see himself that way at all. He explained he'd lost his leg in a motorcycle accident when he was teenager. He still did everything he used to, including riding motorcycles. "It's all in how you see yourself. You are the only one who puts limits on your potential."

When we returned to the broadcast center an hour later to share our footage with the class, I quickly realized that I'd done a completely different assignment than anyone else. There were a lot of coffee shops, fruit stands, and flower stores. But there was only one heart-to-heart with a peg-legged man.

"How did you find a one-legged man to interview in under an hour?" another producer asked me.

The truth was, I didn't go looking for an amputee in the Big Apple. I just stood at the corner and let the story unfold in front of me.

I got to Thanks-Giving Square around 11 AM, and it was already buzzing with people. There were hugs, tears, and a general feeling of disbelief in the air. Most people walked around in a daze, and I was one of them. There were police everywhere, and I couldn't imagine what it must feel like to be protecting a city while mourning the death of your colleagues who died doing the same thing.

I went back to the lessons from my CBS camera class, and I filmed a series of shots with different groups of mourners. One in particular, a young man dressed in white and holding a cardboard sign that said "Love > Hate" stood out to me. The handmade sign and the emotion on his face made me want to ask him questions, maybe even snag an interview on the fly. But the official program had just begun, and the timing didn't feel right. I stood back and filmed another series. The close-ups on his sign, a flickering votive candle, and a wide shot of the crowd would eventually make it past the editors and into the episode, "Bringing a Nation Together," earning me my first credit as a producer and camera operator.

A handmade sign at the Thanks-Giving Square vigil in Dallas, 2016.

As the vigil ended, I realized I needed to take off my crew hat and put on my producing one. Correspondent Maureen Maher was on a flight from Chicago to Dallas, and when she landed, she'd need someone to interview. I scanned the crowd for a friendly face and located a familiar-looking man in a cowboy hat. He had spoken during the vigil, though I hadn't caught his name. *When in doubt, go with the guy in the big white hat,* I told myself, knowing New York would instantly approve on optics alone.

David Thibodeaux and his wife, Karen, were Dallas pastors and police chaplains, and as African Americans, they had a nuanced understanding of the challenges facing the Black community and law enforcement. I shook their hands and held on for dear life. They agreed to be interviewed, and I immediately got their cell phone numbers and called senior producer Patti Aronofsky in New York to update her on my bookings.

Patti is a classic New York personality. She barks orders and doesn't take shit from anyone. I respect that about her, but we've never really gotten along. Our communication styles and life experiences are pretty much diametrically opposed. One time, I was in Patti's office while she was on the phone, and she was really laying into someone. After she abruptly ended the call, I must have had a stunned look on my face that told Patti she should probably explain herself. Patti said it was her nanny on the phone, and it seemed to me she was proud of how she'd behaved on the call. She looked me square in the eyes as she launched into a story about how this nanny "owes her" and can never quit.

She told me plainly that a while back, her nanny had gotten herself into a scrape and called Patti to bail her out. While most parents might reconsider employing such a caregiver, Patti saw this as an opportunity for leverage. Before she helped her, Patti gave her bad-girl nanny an ultimatum: "If I do this favor for you, I own you. You can never say no to me again or I'll tell every family you try to work for what you did." And that's how she ended up with the most loyal nanny in NYC. I was shocked by her admission, but it also felt like a warning from a senior producer. Why else would she have this conversation in front of a subordinate, much less go the added length to explain it to me? In my opinion, the reason seemed clear. I felt like Patti wanted me to know that she would use damaging information against anyone, if it made her life easier. I made a mental note to be extra mindful of my tongue around Patti, a habit that would serve me well for years to come.

I've been on the receiving end of many of Patti's rants about one thing or another, but I can't really remember the specifics. When people start yelling, I tend to tune them out and wait for cooler heads to prevail. Turns out that means I miss about 90 percent of what Patti says to me. It doesn't make for the best working relationship, but I'd always figure out a way to get through the conversation using context clues.

Patti was happy enough with my bookings, but I could also tell she was still mad at me for not picking up the phone at 11 PM and inserting myself in an active shooting. Good thing I don't owe her anything.

Patti told me we were officially "crashing" an episode on the shooting, and we'd been given our regular Saturday-night time slot for the special. My head was spinning. We had twenty-four hours to turn around a special on the deadly attack.

The game plan was to divide and conquer, and CBS had teams in all three cities where the recent shootings had taken place: Baton Rouge, Louisiana; St. Paul, Minnesota; and Dallas, Texas. Because Dallas had suffered the most casualties, it would serve as home base for the episode, which would be carried live through the studio in New York. In addition to the team from *48 Hours*, we would be working with producers across the network to put the special together.

CBS snagged a block of hotel rooms downtown so we could work more efficiently, and I called Riley to let him know he could check out of one hotel and move to another one for the weekend while our A/C issues got sorted out. At least we'd be together for a few hours in between shoots.

As a parent, you want to be there for all those milestone moments—the first words, laughs, and steps. But you never know when they're coming, and you could just as easily miss it on a trip to the grocery store as you could on a breaking news story. I'll always be grateful that I got to witness my son's first steps on the hotel lawn that weekend. Timing, as they say, is everything. And when he toddled over to me after a marathon day of field producing, I felt like the luckiest working mom in the world.

Correspondent Maureen Maher was due in Dallas any minute now, and I headed over to the lobby bar to meet her and veteran producer Lucy Scott. Lucy had worked for CBS in New York for over a decade before making the transition to Texas and part-time producing gigs. A midwesterner with an easy smile and boundless energy, Lucy and I were fast friends.

Before *48 Hours*, she'd worked on nearly every show at CBS, including the morning and evening news, plus a stint at *60 Minutes*. It was well known that Lucy had been fired from *60*, though she never wanted to talk about it. Not that I could blame her. Lucy had been one of the research producers on the infamous "Killian Documents" controversy about George W. Bush's military record in 2004 that led to the end of Dan Rather's career at CBS News.[7] The whole sordid affair had recently been made into a movie (called *Truth*, of all things) with Elisabeth Moss playing the part of Lucy Scott. If you're gonna go down, that's not a bad way to do it. After being unceremoniously ousted from CBS, Lucy had worked in the private sector for a spell and taught journalism classes at Southern Methodist University in Dallas. She'd found her way back to CBS through freelance assignments, primarily for *48 Hours*.

I'd been paired with Lucy before, but it was my first time working with Maureen Maher. Arguably the most recognizable of the *48 Hours* correspondents, Maureen had the role of "fronting" all the rerun episodes that aired on the Investigation Discovery network. If you watched *48 Hours* as it aired for the first time on CBS, you'd see a revolving carousel of correspondents reporting on each episode. But if you caught the reruns months later on cable, you'd see Maureen in the studio, introducing each show in a fierce-looking leather jacket. It was common knowledge that she had a closet of leather jackets that she maintained for her on-camera persona. She didn't wear much leather in real life, but she needed a tough, recognizable image to present the gritty murder mystery of the day. When she retired from CBS in 2021, she donated all her leather jackets to charity.

Although she was now based in Chicago, Maureen had lived in Dallas before and had a good handle on the city. She'd been launched into the story out of a cannon, like the rest of us, and she wasn't slowing down anytime soon. We ordered a pot of coffee and started strategizing. I told her about the Thibodeauxs, and she was grateful for a solid booking that could show the community impact. But she also had her eye on public officials and put Dallas police chief David Brown and Mayor Mike Rawlings at the top of her wish list. It was a tall order for the next twenty-four hours, but we were up to the challenge.

I had no time to process the complicated emotions that I was feeling because this particular true crime story was happening in my community. It wasn't some far-flung tragedy that I was parachuting in and out of. Long after the camera crews would leave, I would still be reminded of the downtown shoot-out that killed five police officers. For years afterward, as I passed the

---

7 Jarrett Murphy, "CBS Ousts 4 for Bush Guard Story," CBS News, January 10, 2005, https://www.cbsnews.com/news/cbs-ousts-4-for-bush-guard-story-10-01-2005/.

community college campus that became a war zone, images and quotes from officers' body cams played in my head. Was there an off switch for this trauma playlist? And would I ever find it?

Back in the restaurant, the bill for the coffee came, and Maureen threw down her CBS card first. Imagine our surprise when the waiter came back and sheepishly said it had been declined. Maureen let out a big laugh and said, "That figures. I'm in the middle of a contract negotiation." CBS Business Affairs plays to win, always. Even when it means cutting off the card of your on-air talent while filming a breaking news story. Lucy picked up the tab with a wink, and we raised our coffee mugs in solidarity, clinking out cheers to the craziness of TV news.

The next day was a blur of door knocks, phone calls, and film sets. We managed to land an interview with the mayor, but the chief of police was slammed. We'd have to rely on public statements and press conferences if we wanted to go to air that night, and there was no changing anyone's mind on that.

Lucy and I tag teamed shifts staking out the house where the shooter had lived with his parents in Mesquite, a suburb east of Dallas. It was an exercise in futility, but we had to check the box for the corporate execs, and we left notes and business cards on the front door when our knocks went unanswered. We shuttled back and forth from staking out the suburbs to our home base downtown, using the travel time to catch up on phone calls. I was chugging coffee and popping Advil to stave off the inevitable stress headache that I knew was lurking in the shadows.

In a normal production process, there is an entire week dedicated to fact-checking the scripts. Associate producers run through every line, confirming dates, numbers, and anything else we could possibly get wrong by going directly to the source. The scripts are then annotated like a bibliography and sent to the legal department for bulletproofing. But when you are crashing an episode in a matter of days, you don't have that luxury. The shooting took place on Thursday evening, and our special report was going to air at 10 PM Eastern on Saturday.

Our fact-checking process would have to be accomplished like everything else in this crash, on the fly. The public information officer for Dallas Police was being inundated with requests from all over the country, and his voice-mail was completely full and couldn't accept new messages. I realized we both followed each other on Twitter, and I could slip into his DMs. It wasn't the most traditional way to fact-check a script, but he actually responded, and our attorneys gave it their stamp of approval.

The clock was ticking for our time slot, and everything was going down to the wire. We had a satellite truck taking the interview feeds from Dallas to New York, where editors were scrambling to find the right time codes and sound bites to plug in from the scripts. We were running on fumes, but the finish line was in sight. My final interview finished feeding with an hour until airtime. I had been running all over town since Friday morning, and I couldn't wait to get to my hotel room and watch the episode with Riley.

Our son was already asleep, so we kept all the lights off and the volume low as we snuggled up in bed to take in the show. We flipped the channel to CBS right as the local news was ending, and then the screen went black. Pitch-black. Dead air. At first, I thought it had to be a problem with hotel TV, but no other channel was affected. It was definitely an error on the CBS end of things. It felt like an eternity as fifteen seconds of blackness dominated the screen, and then, our episode began.

No one had planned that level of drama, but when you are dealing with live television, there is very little margin for human error. Someone in the control room hadn't switched the feed fast enough and the result was dead air on national television. Technical blunder notwithstanding, the episode was critically acclaimed, earning a 2017 New York Press Club award for special event reporting and an Emmy nomination for outstanding coverage of a breaking news story in a newsmagazine show.

We ultimately lost the Emmy to the folks across the street: Lara Logan in a flak jacket, reporting from Iraq in a piece for *60 Minutes* called "The Battle for Mosul."[8] It would turn out to be something of a swan song for the war correspondent, who exited CBS News the following year for far-right

---

8 *60 Minutes*, season 49, episode 7, "The Battle for Mosul," aired November 6, 2016, CBS, https://www.cbsnews .com/news/60-minutes-battle-for-mosul-iraq-lara-logan/.

pastures. Her journey at the network and for *60 Minutes* had been arduous. In 2011 while on assignment in Egypt, Logan was viciously attacked and sexually assaulted by a street mob. She'd bravely continued to work at *60* and cover the Arab Spring, but those close to her wondered if she'd ever truly processed the trauma.

Award night glory notwithstanding, Logan no longer felt proud to work at CBS. Her career choices since then have grown increasingly fringe in nature, resulting in headlines such as "Lara Logan's Break with Reality."[9] That's a high price to pay for a golden statue.

But no one gets out of network television without some battle scars paving the way. Logan's harrowing ordeal affected her in complicated ways. And while my own experience with CBS paled in comparison, the secondary trauma I was dealing with as a career true crime producer had started to take its toll.

The smallest thing could send my heart racing. A bright yellow ribbon, peeking out from my son's knapsack, put images of crime scene tape in my head. As I loaded groceries into my trunk, the sight of jumper cables reminded me of a death scene where the victim was hung by his own safety equipment. As much as I tried to compartmentalize my work, there were hidden land mines at every turn of my seemingly safe suburban life. How much longer could I keep the darkness at bay?

9   Elaina Plott Calabro, "A Star Reporter's Break with Reality," *The Atlantic*, June 12, 2023, https://www.theatlantic .com/magazine/archive/2023/07/lara-logan-60-minutes-correspondent-conspiracy-theories/674168/.

12

CRIME OF OPPORTUNITY

As a true crime journalist, I get a lot of tips from the public. Strangers on social media, not to mention friends and family, often bend my ear about a case that's close to them. Working leads and finding stories to develop into potential episodes is a big part of my job, and when I'm not actively involved in a production, it's what I spend the most time doing. But truth be told, most of the tips I get from the public are dead ends.

It's not that they aren't interesting stories. These leads almost always have attention-grabbing details and elements of intrigue that send me down a brief rabbit hole. But in order to sustain an hour of television, you need more than just one bend in the road, and generally speaking, you also need an ending. Unsolved mysteries have their place in the pantheon of true crime television, but *48 Hours* isn't really the home for them. For more than thirty years, our audience has been conditioned for us to provide a satisfying conclusion, and switching up the formula is a recipe for low ratings.

But the stories that haven't been tied up in a nice little bow are also exactly the ones that everyone is dying to divulge to a true crime television producer.

If the story is really intriguing, I'll set a Google Alert for the missing person's name, or that of the murder suspect, so I won't miss any public developments. I've come to rely on these alerts so much that I even have a few set up for personal interests, like estranged relatives and friends who I suspect may make the news one day.

There are a few tips, however, that have broken through the mold and ended up on national television. I still remember sitting at my desk when a particular Facebook message came through. It was in my "Other" inbox, and I reflexively winced before clicking into it.

If you're not familiar with the Other inbox, it can be a real mixed bag of communication, especially as a female journalist. It's where messages land from people who aren't directly connected to you but have managed to track down your social media profile. I've gotten every kind of insult and threat you can imagine zipped into my digital mailboxes from strangers across the globe. But every once in a while, someone actually says something of value. It's these rare occurrences that keep me checking the mysterious Other inbox, just in case.

The message was brief and included an attachment of a missing person flyer. A desperate-sounding woman said her cousin had disappeared during Hurricane Harvey, and they couldn't get ahold of the local sheriff's department to report it because the phone lines were still down. Then she asked for my help. My heart went out to her, and I sprang into action. I figured at the very least, I could find a working phone number for the Chambers County Sheriff's Office so she could make an official missing person report.

The woman on the flyer staring back at me was named Crystal McDowell. She was a mother of two, recently divorced, and working in real estate in Baytown, Texas. She'd disappeared after leaving her boyfriend's house, and her car was also missing. I'd grown up not far from Baytown and was familiar with the low-lying coastal area near Galveston. I also knew that Hurricane Harvey was in full force, causing massive flooding and power outages across the region. A number of people were considered "missing" at the time simply because they were out of communication. But the details surrounding Crystal's disappearance were suspicious, because she was supposed to pick up her kids from her ex-husband on the morning she vanished. It definitely sounded like there was a high potential for foul play.

I called the main number for the Chambers County Sheriff's Office, and sure enough, the number was not in service. I tried several department extensions and got the same ominous message. I would have to dig deeper, and I zeroed in on the elected sheriff, Brian Hawthorne. Using the CBS subscription to LexisNexis, I got a hit for his cell phone number. He answered on the first ring.

As it turned out, his office was already aware and investigating the missing person's case of Crystal McDowell, but he was happy to have some help from the national media. He explained authorities had recently found Crystal's car abandoned in a hotel parking lot, but they were still looking for witnesses from the day she disappeared. Sheriff Hawthorne said he'd be willing to give an on-camera interview about the status of the case and plead for the public's help in finding Crystal.

Investigators who will openly work with the media while a case is still in progress are few and far between, and I couldn't wait to get Sheriff Hawthorne on camera. But there was just a slight problem with that plan. A missing woman isn't nearly enough to get a green light on a 48 Hours production budget. We had no way of knowing how the story would unfold, or if there had even been a crime committed at all. There could be untold weeks, months, or even years of investigation ahead, with no guarantee of any resolution. And while the ideal scenario for everyone involved would be for Crystal to be found safe and reunited with her family, that storyline wouldn't carry an episode either. There were just too many unknowns to launch a 48 Hours production at this stage.

But I couldn't shake the feeling that this was a story that needed to be told, and I knew there was real public service in getting the word out about a missing woman in the middle of a hurricane. It may not have been a fit for 48 Hours yet, but I wondered if the story could find a home on another show at CBS. I called my boss, Nancy Kramer, and filled her in on the case of Crystal McDowell, then I offered an unconventional plan to cover the story for the morning show now, with the potential for a 48 episode later.

"The sheriff is willing to go on camera, and I know CBS News has crews in the area covering the hurricane. Could CBS divert some personnel to do a story on this missing woman and the fact that the sheriff's department is literally underwater?"

Kramer's appetite for my unorthodox reporting style can come and go, and I didn't know which way she was leaning this time around. She seemed distracted, and I quickly learned she was working on the Queen's special yet again. "We're interviewing Paul McCartney next," she told me before giving me her blessing to pitch the morning show on the Crystal McDowell case.

I fired off an email to producer Kaci Sokoloff, the morning show booker who I'd worked with on the Chris Kyle story. She liked the idea and wanted me on the ground to report it out with her team, but I was five hours away from the Gulf Coast in Dallas, and the hurricane meant flights were out of the question.

For the time being, I'd have to settle for working the phones and coordinating the interviews remotely. It was coming up on 5 PM, and instead of wrapping up for the day, I was just getting started. I texted Riley to let him know I was going to be pulling an all-nighter for the morning show, but the good news was that for once I didn't have to leave my home office to do it.

We were still several years away from the 2020 pandemic, and the idea of remote work was a fringe concept. I called Crystal's cousin to update her on the latest, and she was grateful that the sheriff's office was going on camera and asking for the public's help. Like so many families searching for a loved one, Crystal's relatives were desperate for information and had started their own investigation. When adults go missing, it's a challenging situation because it's not a crime to disappear of your own free will. In order for the police to take their investigation to the next level, they need indications of foul play. Without any signs of distress at Crystal's house, the case was seemingly at a standstill.

Her cousin told me that Crystal's last known location was her boyfriend Paul Hargrave's house, where she'd spent the night and left at 7:10 AM to pick up her children from her ex-husband. The timeline was exact because Paul had security cameras at his house, and they captured Crystal walking through the living room and driving away in her black Mercedes. This was a made-for-TV development, and I knew I needed to get ahold of Paul—and hopefully that footage—for the morning show. I found a cell phone number online and punched it in.

"This is Paul, how can I help you?" came through the line.

It was an odd way to answer a personal cell phone, but who was I to judge? I got right down to business, introducing myself and listing several ways that he could help me, such as providing a copy of his security camera footage and giving an on-camera interview. He agreed to both, and I couldn't wait to share the good news with producer Kaci Sokoloff.

Between the sheriff, Crystal's boyfriend, and the camera footage, we had all the elements we needed for a winning morning show segment. I worked the phones to coordinate the interview locations with the CBS crew on the ground in Baytown and kept trying to reach Crystal's ex-husband, Steve McDowell, for an interview as well. Off the record, Sheriff Hawthorne told me that they had three suspects in Crystal's disappearance: her boyfriend, Paul; her ex-husband, Steve; and her uncle, Jeff.

As an insurance policy for a future *48 Hours* episode, I really wanted to get all three men on camera now, while she was still a missing person. It was a lot to ask for in time to make the cut for the morning show, but it couldn't hurt to try. Plus, I already had Paul giving me the green light. My repeated texts, calls, and social media messages to ex-husband Steve went unanswered, but I did get a response from Crystal's uncle Jeff on Facebook. I quickly got him on the phone and gave him my pitch for an interview, while carefully avoiding that I knew he was a suspect in the case.

Uncle Jeff had been the one to report Crystal missing; they worked together in local real estate. He agreed to an interview, and in just a few short hours, a CBS crew was at his doorstep. Everyone knew that we were working toward a potential 48, and it wasn't just a quick hit morning show piece that would never see the light of day again.

The crew was following the 48 and 60 protocol of never turning the camera off once the subject entered the frame. We roll on everything, even when the little red light goes off, we are still up and running. You never know what you might capture in those unguarded moments. Plus the set-up shots, swigs of water, and handshakes offer "behind the scenes" glimpses to our audience, and we like to sprinkle them in when we can.

The interview with Uncle Jeff was a TV gold mine for several reasons: He was a suspect, a witness, and emotionally wrecked by his niece's disappearance. He sobbed on camera, fulfilling the role that every hardened true crime producer looks to cast for an episode: a crying relative.

The story ran on August 31, 2017, and included the breaking news that Crystal's black Mercedes had been found in a flooded Motel 6 parking lot. It was unlocked, and there was cash sitting on the console. Two people were ransacking the car when the authorities arrived, but police determined they were unrelated to Crystal's disappearance.

"We are very, very confident that she is not a victim of the storm," the sheriff told CBS. The camera lingered on his enigmatic expression for a few more seconds, giving the perfect segue to talk about the "persons of interest" in Crystal's disappearance. While the sheriff had shared his unguarded feelings off camera that three men in Crystal's life were suspects, he was playing things close to the vest on national television. We peppered in sound bites from Uncle Jeff and boyfriend Paul but had to settle for Facebook photos of ex-husband Steve, because he still wasn't responding to our interview requests.

The piece was a hit, and Gayle King even opined live from the studio that it "sounded like an episode of *48 Hours*." I couldn't have agreed more. Using the momentum from the morning show, I asked the sheriff if we could keep a crew with him during the investigation to cover any developments. It's the kind of request that I try my best to throw out with an air of confidence, but one that I never actually expect to get approved.

Most law enforcement agencies use the press sparingly and give access only at strategic moments. But I sensed an opening from Sheriff Hawthorne, and I could tell he was really considering the outlandish idea. I was grateful this was a phone call and not an in-person meeting, because I don't think I could have hidden the incredulous look on my face when he suggested I come down to the sheriff's office to talk about it.

One of the biggest differences between television jobs and other media gigs is the kind of contract you sign. In newspapers and magazines, you typically have an open-ended employment arrangement, meaning that you get hired once and are on the job until you quit or get fired. But in television, you are always on a limited time frame. Most deals are for two or three years, with new hires getting only six months or a year to prove themselves worthy of another contract. Veteran on-air talent might get a five-year deal, but even that is pushing it.

My first *48* contract was for six months, and I'd graduated to annual deals after that. At the time of the Crystal McDowell story, I was up for a new contract, and I was pushing for a two-year commitment. Because of the length of negotiations, an annual contract meant you were fighting for your position every nine months, which is a pretty exhausting way to earn a living. I never wanted to feel like I was on the bubble to lose my position in Texas, which didn't actually appear on any organization chart, so I made sure I had more stories make air than any other producer on the show. If you ever wonder what New York media types think of the rest of the country, just remember that they call anywhere that isn't NYC "the field." That pretty much tells you everything you need to know.

I figured the best way to create job security was to deliver original episodes. You might not like my feisty personality, my penchant for rule breaking, or my Texas twang, but you can't argue with cold, hard numbers. Most producers have two or three episodes a season. I was averaging five. What can I say? I like a little wiggle room.

Fresh off Maureen Maher's credit card debacle during the crash production of the Dallas police shooting, I was keenly aware that CBS Business Affairs would not take it easy on me just because I was in the field during negotiations. If anything, they would use it to their advantage as leverage over me.

The ironic thing was that I was actually dying to be in the middle of the action on the Crystal McDowell case, and I would have launched on the story in a heartbeat if I wasn't in the middle of contract negotiations.

Nothing would have made me happier than to have gotten out of the land of paperwork and into the thick of production. But instead, Kramer was yanking my chain. They were offering me a new contract, sure, but they wanted to pay me less to do the same amount of work. I was both insulted and confused. I was coming off my most productive season ever at *48*, with five credits to my name, and I had several other shows in development. I was rocking and rolling with more work than I knew what to do with, and apparently that was a sign they needed to take me down a peg.

"Every department is having to make cuts," Kramer told me. "This is the best we can do."

I guess they had to make up the costs of all those celebrity interviews for the Queen's special somehow.

"If you're making cuts, why not start with producers who've only worked on one or two shows that made air all season? I'm doing the work of two people, and you want to pay me less?" I asked her incredulously.

Kramer told me it wasn't personal. The cuts started with the least seasoned producers. I was just coming up on three years at CBS, while most other producers had a decade or more experience. I couldn't argue with the dates, but that didn't mean I was going to play nice either. If they wanted to cut my salary, they were going to get a decrease in production as well. And I'd prove I was serious by refusing to travel on the McDowell case until I had a reasonable offer on the table.

It's Labor Day weekend, and I'm at the park with my son, pushing him on the swings as he giggles with delight. While I'm happy to have this time with him, it's hard not to think about what's happening down on the Gulf Coast. There's a full-scale search for Crystal McDowell, complete with the Chambers County Sheriff's Department and assistance from the Texas Rangers. My colleague Ryan Smith is in the middle of the action, embedded with a camera crew in the heart of the investigation. After I set the whole thing in motion for CBS, it was killing me to skip out of the filming. But I know it's the right decision for my contract negotiation. No pain, no gain.

Ryan keeps me updated on the shoot, and the details are almost too good to be true. The sheriff is giving us access to the actual war room as investigators go through the case. We are allowed to film their unguarded conversations and strategy sessions in real time, and we can even ask the district attorney and the sheriff questions in the hallway between interviews with suspects. This is the holy grail of true crime television: unfettered access, a live investigation, and a ticking clock with a missing woman. I wonder how long I can hold out.

Ryan is trying to be understanding, but I know my strategy is hurting him, too. "Wish you were here," he says as he fills me in on the day's developments. A pair of Texas Rangers have come down to work the case with the sheriff's department, and they are handling the interrogations. Multiple suspects failed polygraph exams, which doesn't make their job any easier, but it sure is going to make our episode more exciting.

Uncle Jeff has effectively been ruled out as a suspect, and boyfriend Paul isn't being asked to come in for questioning anymore. The only person who is still getting interviewed is Crystal's ex-husband, Steve. And he's getting interviewed a lot. He comes to the sheriff's office in the morning and doesn't leave for seven or eight hours. The Texas Rangers end up telling him to go home and come back the next day so they can get some rest. And this has been going on all week.

Ryan has been hanging out with the district attorney and the sheriff, but the Texas Rangers won't let him—or the cameras—anywhere near them.

"It feels like something big is about to happen. There's major tension in the air," Ryan says.

He isn't the only one feeling the heat. I've been fighting with CBS Business Affairs all week, countering their offer with some new terms of my own, including a release from the exclusivity clause. If they want to pay me less, then they shouldn't have a problem with me finding work elsewhere to make up the difference. Of course, I know they will have a problem with this, but it's all part of the game. And I have to show them I'm willing to walk away before they'll give me anything resembling a fair shake.

Meanwhile, the days keep ticking by, and the investigation is barreling down on the coast. On Saturday afternoon, I get a text from Ryan. The investigators are going on a field trip, and it looks a whole lot like a body recovery mission. The sheriff himself tipped Ryan to the off-campus excursion, and the camera crew followed the county vehicles out to a swampy area in the middle of nowhere. The Texas Rangers were furious and told the crew they couldn't enter the woods. It's just as well, because footage of the sheriff's deputies getting ready to search will set up the scene, and we can't air images of a dead body anyway.

As a crime show on a major network, we have very specific CBS News standards that dictate what we can and cannot show in an episode. Crime scene photos and video are allowed, including images of blood spatter, as long as they are on inanimate objects and not body parts. The actual victim can be shown only in blurred form, to depict body positioning if necessary for the storytelling, for example in cases where there's a question of murder, suicide, or an accident. Autopsy photos are not allowed, but we can use the diagrams and drawings that accompany the medical examiner's report. If any of the above exceptions grace your screen, you're watching cable crime, not network coverage.

The search continues for hours, and Ryan is texting me updates as more and more county vehicles arrive at the scene. I'm flipping quesadillas in the kitchen when I see Ryan's call coming through.

"The county coroner just pulled up. They must have finally found her."

It's been two weeks since Crystal disappeared without a trace, and the thought of her body sitting out in the elements that long is enough to make me lose my appetite. I turn off the griddle and close my eyes.

Her poor family. This is going to devastate them.

I've been texting with Crystal's cousin, aunt, and uncle ever since the morning show story. But I know I can't be the one to tell them this news. I don't have official confirmation, and it's not my place anyway. But I still feel guilty, like I'm holding out on them when they've been so open with me. I slide down to the kitchen floor and put my head in my hands.

Even though I love my job in true crime television, the weight of working murder story after murder story is starting to add up. And it's spilling out into my life in unexpected ways. There's a heaviness that's settling into my bones, and it feels foreign. When my husband asks what I feel like watching on TV these days, I always say the same thing: "something lighthearted."

The week after Crystal's body was discovered and her ex-husband was charged with first-degree murder, I reached terms on a new two-year contract with CBS. It wasn't a perfect deal, but it was so much better than their initial offer that it felt like a big win. Those business affairs execs are no dummies.

Hurricane Harvey was long gone from the Texas coast, but the damage from the Category 4 storm would take years to repair. When I got out to Baytown to start filming sit-down interviews on the story a few weeks later, there were still road closures and flooding hampering our efforts. We needed locations to film interviews, and we were having trouble finding a suitable space.

As a field producer, a big part of my job was to scout locations and book venues ahead of the production team coming to town. Oddly, I've found that the best place to interview someone about a murder case is at a wedding venue. The locations are beautiful and spacious, and they generally have availability during the week. While it might cost ten thousand dollars to rent for a wedding on a Saturday, you could get the same space for a fraction of the cost during business hours. And because the locations were heavily used, they had all the trappings that a film set needed, including bathrooms on-site and plenty of decorative items to build out the shot.

The wedding venues around Baytown had all been flooded and were in no shape to host us. We ended up filming down the road in College Station, Texas, where Steve McDowell's daughter from a previous relationship was attending Texas A&M University. Krysta McDowell agreed to do an interview with *48 Hours* correspondent Maureen Maher.

I had spoken with Krysta on the phone a few times and taken her to lunch once before the interview, but we hadn't really gotten into the details of what she knew about the case and when she learned it. As the defendant's daughter, she would have been a valuable interview no matter what. There's always extra tension in the air when you interview a member of the defendant's family. Typically, the people speaking on behalf of the accused are the parents. And they believe in their loved one's innocence wholeheartedly. TV interviews, however, have a way of revealing more information than most people intend to share. And when Krysta sat down on camera, we discovered just how much she had to offer our story.

A petite blonde with an easy smile, Krysta was a natural on camera. Although nervous at first, she warmed up quickly as Maureen ticked through the background questions. Krysta had lived with her dad and stepmom, Crystal, for a few years in high school, and she witnessed their volatile relationship firsthand. She remembered lots of arguments and described their love as "toxic," so she wasn't surprised when her dad told her about the divorce. But even though they'd legally separated, there were signs they might reconcile. At the time of her disappearance, Crystal still lived with Steve, though they no longer shared a bedroom. There was talk of Crystal organizing a family cruise in a few months, and Steve was invited. He told his daughter he was planning to propose again, and he'd bought his ex-wife a new white dress.

But then Crystal started dating Paul Hargrave and spending the night at his house. In fact, in the days leading up to her disappearance, Crystal had told Steve that he was no longer welcome on the family cruise, and that she'd be taking Paul instead. As Krysta shared this crucial news on camera, it sounded an awful lot like a motive for murder. And Krysta was only getting started.

CBS correspondent Maureen Maher interviews Krysta McDowell.

Maureen asked her about the last time she spoke to her dad, and Krysta teared up. He'd called her late one night and told her to come to Baytown "as soon as she could." It was after 2 AM, and Krysta didn't understand why she couldn't wait until the morning to make the trip. "He told me that if I wanted to see him, I better come right now." She jumped in the car in the middle of the night and headed straight to her dad's doorstep.

They talked through the night, and slowly but surely, Steve McDowell started to reveal his secrets to his oldest daughter. The conversation turned to Crystal's disappearance and the search for her body. Steve told his daughter that if he led authorities to the remains, they'd lessen his punishment. Krysta was confused, asking him how he could possibly do that.

"And he just said, 'What if it's true?'" Krysta told us through tears.

After that, her father broke down and sobbed. And a few minutes later, the Texas Rangers were at the door. It was the last time she talked to her dad as a free man.

We were stunned. We had no idea Steve had effectively confessed to his daughter. What a thing for a parent to do to a child. Maureen handed Krysta a tissue, and we all took a moment to absorb the information. Steve had entered a not-guilty plea, and Krysta would probably be called as a witness against her own dad at trial. Depending on what she said, our raw interview tapes could be subpoenaed by the prosecution. This story was getting more complicated by the minute.

After we finished the sit-down interview, we still needed to grab B-roll with Krysta. We headed over to the Texas A&M campus to get some shots of her walking around. The crew asked me if I got a film permit. I smiled back at them. "Don't ask questions you don't want the answers to."

We did a quick camera spray on campus, grabbing as many shots as rapidly as we could and hightailing it out of there before anyone had time to check for pesky permits. Technically, because we are a news crew, we shouldn't need a permit to film on public land, and Texas A&M is a public university. But the story we were doing isn't actually a news piece about the college, so it's a bit of a gray area, or at least that's my story and I'm sticking to it.

As we were leaving, I noticed Krysta's car, a blue Shelby Mustang. I knew I'd seen it before but couldn't place it.

"It's my dad's," Krysta offered. "He gave me the keys before he got arrested."

We knocked out the rest of the interviews in a week flat, filming with the sheriff and the district attorney at their offices. It was a bland shot, but at least there was no longer standing water in the building. We got the ticktock of the investigation straight from the sheriff himself, and I still can't believe how much he was willing to reveal before the trial.

When Crystal left her boyfriend's house, authorities believe she went straight to Steve's, and a tragic confrontation ensued. Steve told the Texas Rangers that he snapped, and he even acted out how he choked Crystal from behind. He needed to get her body out of the house, and he used her own vehicle to do it: first dumping her in a low-lying, wooded area before taking her Mercedes to the Motel 6 parking lot and leaving it unlocked with the keys on the dash.

But how had he gotten home after abandoning Crystal's car? Surveillance video from nearby businesses offered a clue, with a man looking an awful lot like Steve McDowell paying cash for a bicycle at Walmart the same day that Crystal went missing. Twenty-four hours later, Hurricane Harvey made landfall. It really was the perfect storm.

In all the chaos and confusion, Steve might have even gotten away with murder if the Texas Rangers hadn't come to town. I learned that Texas Ranger James Holland interviewed Steve for over forty hours in the week after Crystal's disappearance, and Holland was the one who convinced Steve to lead authorities to her body. I put in a request to interview Holland and his partner, Texas Ranger Steve Jeter, with the Texas State Police, but it was shot down because the investigation was still ongoing. Guess nobody told the sheriff and the DA.

Our episode aired a few months later, before ABC's *20/20* or NBC's *Dateline* had even managed to find Baytown on a map. I had pulled off a major coup, getting our story way ahead of the competition and the trial, which was still years away from the courtroom. By the time Steve McDowell went on trial in June 2019, I'd practically forgotten about the case.

It was my way of coping. Once a story aired, I'd push the dark details and images away to make room for the next case, emotionally and physically. I'd take every document on the story from my desk and file it away. Then I'd clear all the related documents from my desktop, archive the emails, and try to forget every horrible thing I'd once committed to memory. I'd go on an extra-long run, take a really hot shower, and tell myself that it was over, and I was safe.

After a dozen stories, I'd gotten pretty good at it. So much so that I didn't even remember the significance of the Texas Ranger at the heart of the McDowell interrogation, James Holland. But as you'll see, his testimony would change that, along with the course of my career at CBS News.

13

IN COLD BLOOD

It's a rainy February afternoon, and the whole house smells of deliciousness. This is a rarity in my world, and I'm savoring the scene of domestic mastery. Hours earlier, I'd chopped and sliced a variety of vegetables and thrown them in a Crock-Pot with a couple pounds of brisket. It's been slow cooking all morning and appears to be properly simmering.

I'm not a natural chef, but I can make a handful of meals with predictable quality. I'm trying to expand my repertoire as a romantic surprise for Valentine's Day, and I'm double-checking the recipe list when I see Kramer's call coming through. I stare at the screen and debate picking up.

Because I'm the only *48 Hours* producer who lives in Texas, I do most of my work from home. I do have a desk at the CBS News Southwest Bureau, but when I go there, I'm often the only one in the building. Any good newsroom is a touchdown point, a place to file expenses, make phone calls, and log tape. The real reporting happens everywhere else.

I do my best work in the field anyway. My office might as well be a hotel room, a courthouse, the police station, or an attorney's office. That's where the real action is for a crime producer. When I'm not on the road, I spend most of my time reading the crime sections of Texas newspapers and crafting pitches on the more promising cases.

To keep everyone on staff up to speed, there's a daily email that goes out compiling all the major crime stories in the US. In the early-morning hours, production secretaries scour the headlines to highlight compelling stories. The email hits our inboxes around 10 AM, and we're all supposed to scan it for stories in our coverage area that we might have missed in our daily paper coverage.

Working from home means I can start my day at 6 AM, reading through emails and writing up pitches in my pajamas for an hour or so before my son wakes up. Once he's at daycare, I'll go for a run, clear my head, and be back at my desk in time for the morning murder headlines to roll in.

I remember when I first started working at *48 Hours*, I couldn't believe the volume of crime stories taking place every single day, in every city in America. A sampling includes:

"Texas man gets life for paying to have fiancée murdered a week before wedding."

"Man charged with murder in stabbing death of runner."

"Ex-student found guilty of helping friend plot the murder of his secret girlfriend."

"Newlywed sailor accused of drowning his wife is caught on camera in a heated argument."

"Woman charged with murder of her 65-year-old husband after 'new information' emerges."

Four years in, it's commonplace for me to scroll through a dozen or more murder cases while I sip my morning coffee.

Like any creative person, I work best in spurts of activity. All morning, I'd been working on a cold case murder story, my first one to pitch at *48*, and I was stuck. I was writing and rewriting the pitch for the unsolved murder of Jennifer Harris when I realized I needed to step away from my desk if I was going to get anywhere. Crock-Pot concoction to the rescue.

My phone is still ringing, and I grab the call before it sends Kramer to voicemail, a big no-no in her world.

Without much of a greeting, my boss asks me, "How fast can you get to Parkland, Florida?"

My Valentine's Day meal won't be set at a table for two this year. I lower the heat and scribble down instructions for when Riley gets home from work later. Then I Google "Parkland, Florida."

The mass shooting at Marjory Stoneman Douglas High School in Parkland, Florida, was the worst such casualty in years. The shooter, nineteen-year-old Nikolas Cruz, had waited until classes were about to be dismissed that afternoon to terrorize campus. Using an automatic rifle, he'd callously picked off his former classmates and teachers as they ran for their lives.

Then he'd stowed his gun in a backpack and casually walked to a McDonald's and ate a hamburger. He was taken into custody a short time later without incident. The security camera footage laid out the case against him, as did his own words to students just moments before the shooting began.

"You might wanna get outta here," Cruz said as he entered the building. "It's about to get messy."

I grabbed a seat on the last direct flight from Dallas to Fort Lauderdale on February 14, 2018. Winter storms kept the plane on the tarmac for hours, and I used the time to read through the latest developments on my phone.

I started compiling a document with all the strongest articles on the story and tried to commit the new names and locations to memory. I was parachuting into another disaster zone, and the more information I took with me, the better my chances would be for bringing home the story.

I noticed several other CBS staffers from the bureau on the plane as well. I nodded to correspondent Omar Villafranca and his producer Rodney Hawkins. Omar and Rodney were my favorite bureau people to work with. They were both Texans, a rarity in this business, and they shared the quintessential friendliness and tireless work ethic that I'd come to recognize as a state attribute. I knew they wouldn't shy away from long hours or tough questions, and they'd have a positive attitude to boot. When you're working a horrific story like a school shooting, you have to fight to keep the light alive. I was grateful to have at least a few friendly faces to help the effort.

When we landed in Fort Lauderdale, the sun-drenched billboards and tourists wearing "vacation vibes" T-shirts seemed awfully out of place. This day was not turning out at all like expected. A few hours ago, I had been planning a Valentine's Day dinner and watching the sleet come down in Texas. The second that thought entered my mind, I had a wave of guilt for the victims and survivors of the shooting. My day might have been upended, but their lives would never be the same. I tried to tell myself that while this was a tragedy, it wasn't *my tragedy*. I'd always been so good at separating myself from my job.

But something about this one felt different, even from the airport.

Seventeen people had died, and now news crews from across the country were descending into their community to report on the tragedy. It was nearing midnight by the time I reached my hotel. I fell into the bed and scanned my ever-growing inbox for instructions. The morning show was going to report live outside Parkland High School, and they wanted to use that as the rendezvous point for all CBS personnel. I set my alarm for 4 AM and hit the lights.

The site of the Parkland school shooting, February 16, 2018.

One of the best things you can do as a producer is make sure everyone on set has food, water, and a way to use the bathroom. These basic needs seem like luxuries when you're running on little sleep and less patience. I always stock up on granola bars, bottled water, energy drinks, and ibuprofen when I'm heading to a shoot. I've yet to find anyone who isn't happy to see me roll up with this supplies.

Finding a bathroom is harder, but I can usually manage it by sweet-talking a nearby establishment. If it's a restaurant or a gas station, it's easy enough to make a purchase and use the facilities. But my real wins are when I get us into office bathrooms or other private businesses.

This was admittedly a lot easier before Donald Trump was elected president in 2016 and declared the media "the enemy of the people." I always believed in the public service component of journalism. We are quite literally working *for* the people. I remember one of my college media advisers had a bumper sticker that said "Have you read the news today? Thank a journalist."

Like any industry, there are bad apples, but the vast majority of journalists work hard, for little pay, and in dangerous and stressful settings to bring the news to your fingertips. Our work is on public display, and our successes and failures play out for all to see. It's a pretty unusual work environment if you think about it. But most people don't.

When I reached the live shot location, my backpack was brimming with energy drinks, power bars, and fresh fruit. It was still pitch-black outside, and as I approached the streets outside Marjory Stoneman Douglas High School, I could see a glow of red and blue lights. The sea of law enforcement was dotted with media vans and satellite trucks. Without the sirens blaring, the lights had an ominous effect, bathing everything in silent flashes of color. I showed my CBS ID to an officer directing traffic, and he let me past the barricades. I inched down the street, scanning the eerie scene for signs of CBS. I spotted the black-and-white eye on an antenna and snaked around the block until I found it. The Dallas bureau chief had rented an RV for the occasion. That was one way to solve the on-site bathroom problem.

Jeff Glor, the newly minted anchor of the *CBS Evening News*, was somberly reporting outside the school in jeans and light-blue button-down. He was pulling double duty for the morning show, and his stoic expression was in stark contrast to the usual jovial demeanor of the early broadcast. Networks only fly in anchors to report live for the really big stories. Mass shootings, terroristic attacks, assassinations, and major political events like elections and impeachment are a few examples. In four years at CBS, this was my first story where an anchor had flown in from New York.

As I watched Jeff run through his piece and prepare to go live, I looked around for other producers. The best way to spot one is through the process of elimination. The best-dressed person is always the on-camera talent. They are also the only person who pays any real attention to their hair and makeup. Anyone wearing a T-shirt and cargo pants is with the crew, and that means the remaining people are producers.

They'll typically be wearing black, something akin to business casual but dirtier than you'd see in an actual office. They will also have a giant thermos of coffee at the ready at all hours of the day and night. It didn't take me long to locate a pair of suspected producers from the morning show, camped out on the curb with their laptops open. I walked up to them and introduced myself.

"Oh great, *48 Hours*!" one said enthusiastically. "You must see this kind of stuff all the time."

I smiled weakly and tried to think of an appropriate response. This was actually my first school shooting, though my third mass shooting. Even though I worked the murder beat, I usually didn't speak to families in the early days of their grief. We have a general rule of thumb that says wait until one week after the funeral before making contact. But this was hours after the shooting itself, and in some cases, families were still waiting to see if their injured children would survive.

All this was swimming in my head, and I realized I still hadn't answered. But was it even a question? By the time I looked back at them, they were glued to their laptops again. I took a seat on the curb and followed suit.

"Our targets are anyone who was at the school during the shooting and their families," one producer said out loud. "We made some good inroads yesterday and have a student headed here this morning." In the TV booking world, anyone you want to get on camera is called a "target." It's the lingo we always use no matter what the story is. It never occurs to anyone how tone deaf it is for a mass shooting.

Stoneman Douglas student David Hogg arrived a few minutes later, and I was assigned to be his "handler," meaning I would get him coffee and snacks, show him where he could use the bathroom, and generally "hold his hand" until he went on camera.

Polite and clearly exhausted, David looked like a traumatized teenager. Considering his last twenty-four hours, I couldn't believe we were about to put him on live television. It seemed morally questionable at best, and I also wondered about the legality of engaging a minor for an interview. These concerns couldn't have been further from the official parameters of my job. I was supposed to get him on camera, not question his fitness to be there. But I couldn't help myself.

"Do your parents know you are here?" I asked him as I handed over a cup of coffee.

"Yeah, they know," David said as he took a sip.

I guess that was as good for parental consent as I was going to get for putting a kid on national television. Soon after that I learned David was a senior, not actually a minor at all, and a journalist to boot. And I exhaled. A teacher from Stoneman Douglas arrived next and was going to be interviewed alongside him. As I watched the segment go live, I knew I was witnessing history.

David wasn't just some terrified kid who'd survived an unbelievable tragedy, although he'd definitely fit those descriptors as well. Anyone could see that this was not merely a "man on the street" interview like so many morning show segments.

David was well spoken, on message, and action oriented. I was impressed, and I could see his journalistic DNA shining through. He was a natural-born storyteller. The teacher being interviewed alongside him was fading into the background. I knew the morning show producers had booked the teacher as a safeguard in case "the kid" froze up and couldn't carry the interview. But David was clearly in command of the situation, and my fears about him were unfounded. He was in his element, and I sat back and took in his passion.

David and some of his classmates, including Emma González and Cameron Kasky, would come together two days after the shooting with the simple idea to do something about mass shootings in America. They had a clear and bold goal: that no students would ever have to go through what they were facing right now. Just six months later, David and his younger sister Lauren Hogg would write a bestselling book together: #NeverAgain.

I didn't know any of that then, but I could see something special was happening. And when David told me they'd already begun documenting their experience on camera themselves, I encouraged him to keep going. "You are doing all the right things," I told him. "This is your story, and you should be the one to tell it."

I'm standing in the lobby of the Broward County jail. Visitation hours are about to begin, and a small group of people are waiting on little plastic chairs. A jailer comes into the room with a clipboard and asks us each who we are there to see. When it's my turn, I say, "Nikolas Cruz." He looks up from his clipboard and makes eye contact with me.

I'm expecting more questions, lots more questions, starting with "Who are you and what is the nature of your visit?" But they don't come. He just stares silently at me, and I return his gaze. "ID," he says finally. I hand him my Texas driver's license. I'm toeing the line again. Following his instructions but not offering up any extraneous information, like I'm a producer with CBS News. I could have handed him my CBS ID, but he didn't ask for a press pass.

He marks down my information and hands back my ID, then he moves on to the next person. I'm genuinely curious how this is going to shake out. My official assignment for the morning show is still students and survivors. But I've already called and texted every number I could find, plus FedExed letters to their doorsteps. I have their addresses, but I'm not door knocking mass shooting victims two days after the massacre. I draw the line there.

My expertise is the court system, and it took me all of ten minutes to find Nikolas Cruz's booking information. I have his inmate number, his cell block, and his physical address. I was going to write him a letter, like I usually do for 48, when I realized I should check visiting hours. Turns out, it was today. Thirty more minutes pass before the guard returns and calls my name. I try not to look too surprised and head to the door.

"You'll need to put your cell phone and keys and any other personal belongings in a locker before going to the visitation room," he says.

I dutifully empty my pockets into the secure locker.

"Follow me," he says.

It is a really weird feeling to be completely possession-free in the modern world, and I'm instantly uneasy. Never mind the fact that we're in jail, and I'm about to visit a mass murderer. I stick my hands in my pockets and shuffle down the tile hallway. We're about ten yards away from a glass-lined room where I can see other people are visiting inmates. My heart is pounding, and for the first time, I start thinking about what I'll actually say to Nikolas Cruz. I hadn't planned any further than getting past the guards.

"How are you?" is usually a safe opener. Considerate but not overly familiar.

"Do you know what you did?" might be next. Why would I pull punches? I should ask him flat out, "What were you thinking?"

I'm lost in thought, and it barely registers that the guard is on his walkie-talkie, then he turns to me. "Are you a member of the media?" he asks.

Oh shit.

"Yes," I say matter-of-factly.

A string of expletives flies out of his mouth, and he barks back over the walkie-talkie to return Nikolas Cruz to his cell. Then he grabs my arm with the authority that only law enforcement has and speed walks me back to the lockers. I say nothing. Because there's nothing to say.

When we get to the end of the hallway, he cuts me loose. I make eye contact and he breaks the silence.

"Why didn't you tell me you were a member of the media before now?" he questions me.

"You never asked," I reply.

I didn't know the term "secondary trauma" when I was working this mass casualty event, but I was definitely living proof of the concept. I walked around in a daze during the day, and at night I curled into the fetal position and cried. It felt like the only human reaction to the horror I was witnessing. Children murdered in their school hallways. Teachers shot to death while trying to shield students from gunfire.

I was still on the booking team, trying to find "voices" for CBS News reporting. I felt like we had already found the best ones in David Hogg,

Emma González, and Cameron Kasky. But the powers that be wanted more. I remember a special request for someone who had been injured in the shooting and was still recovering. These are the kinds of ideas that pop into the heads of corporate execs in corner offices. And it takes people like me, on the ground at whatever tragedy we are covering, to make them happen.

I have a vague memory of sitting in a hospital waiting room, trying to suss out if anyone near me was related to a victim. We knew the right hospital from press releases about the victims, but HIPAA laws prevented any further disclosures. I felt like a media vulture, but I was in that waiting room on direct orders from my bosses. I shifted in my seat and tried to think of anywhere else I could justify being dispatched.

I got back on the Broward County website and learned there was an initial hearing for Nikolas Cruz set for that afternoon. It was just a magistrate hearing and would most likely be shown to the media via a camera feed, with Cruz in a remote location in the jail. But his attorneys would be at the courthouse in person, and I could try to get an interview with them. The hearing would probably last thirty minutes, and I'd need something else to fill the rest of my day.

I scrolled through the latest coverage in the local media and learned there was a vigil planned for that evening at a park in town. Bingo. I'd had success at the last mass shooting vigil I'd covered; maybe this would prove to be my niche. I shuddered at the thought. But at least it got me out of hospital duty.

I was driving up to the courthouse when I saw my son's preschool calling my cell phone. A ball of nerves, I picked up immediately.

"There's been an accident," the woman said to me in a serious tone. My mind was flooded with images of a mass shooting, and I immediately went to a worst-case scenario. I almost fell apart right there on the other line.

"What kind of an accident?" I asked, my voice breaking.

The woman told me that my son, who was all of two years old, needed a change of clothes.

"Good lord, is that all?" I said. "You scared me half to death."

I texted Riley the request. Then I emailed the school with instructions that going forward, my husband should be the first parent called "in case of emergency."

The magistrate hearing for Nikolas Cruz was attended by every media outlet in the country, and I had a full CBS News crew with me at the courthouse. As the attorneys filed out of the hearing, I was part of the media gaggle approaching them for comment.

"He's a broken child," public defender Melisa McNeill said.

She also described the nineteen-year-old boy as "sad, mournful, and remorseful," but I knew "broken child" was the sound bite everyone would run with on the evening news.

Considering the evidence, Cruz was being held without bail. Authorities were already running down a ticktock of his activities. The ATF learned Cruz had purchased his guns legally about a year before the shooting.

Police were working to meet with every witness, and they'd already conducted over two thousand interviews. Using the school's surveillance cameras and Cruz's own phone, they'd learned that he'd been dropped off outside the school by an Uber driver at 2:19 PM. The entire attack lasted less than forty-five minutes. Cruz fled the scene alongside students seeking shelter, eventually ending up at McDonald's before being detained by local police a few blocks away.

Cruz's appointed defense attorney was clearly dealing with a lot. "I had to have the exact same conversation as every parent in Broward County, and then I had to go meet with my client," McNeill said to the throngs of press gathered outside the courtroom.

The vigil is a blur of candles and crying children. There's music, and speakers on a stage, and groups of people handing out bottled water. I wasn't prepared for the level of grieving I encountered. The Dallas police shooting vigil had been somber and sad, sure, but those were all grown men, killed in the line of duty. They had signed up for a job that put their lives on the line, and in the end, they gave the ultimate sacrifice. But in Parkland, the victims were innocent students and teachers. Their untimely deaths hit so much harder.

I feel like an intruder, a voyeur. I take out my phone to try to capture some footage like I'd done in Dallas, but nothing I do seems to work. The nighttime lighting is all wrong, or maybe it's my shaking hands and the pounding in my chest that messes up my shots. Either way, I don't last long. I can't describe it other than to say that I knew I had to get out of there. I don't have another hotel room booked. My luggage is all packed up in my car. I had half hoped that maybe CBS would send me home today, and I could just head straight for the airport.

But that isn't happening. It's nearing 9 PM, and I don't have a clue where I am going to sleep tonight. Sleep is not something I figure I'll be able to do at all, so I just start driving. I need the peace and solace of waves, and I point my car east until I hit the coast. I get a room and dump my stuff. Then I sit out on the beach on a dark, moonless night and ponder my life choices.

In later years, I stopped waiting for permission to go home. And when I felt that familiar pang of an anxiety attack, I'd book my own ticket. But I was still dozens of murder stories away from that awareness—and the courage to act on it.

The next-day overnight letters I had FedExed to shooting victims were starting to arrive, and my phone was blowing up with unknown numbers. I tend to cast a wide net, because you never know if the first listed address or phone number is accurate. If you're already sending one letter or text, why not send it to every possible location? Give yourself a greater chance you'll hear something back. Sometimes, okay most of the time, that response is "wrong number," but even then, at least you can cross something off the list.

In the midst of all the errant contacts, I managed to hit on a couple of winners. My best booking was a teacher who hadn't talked to the media yet. He was gracious and kind to me on the phone and thanked me for sending a letter and not showing up on his doorstep, like the local media had. I did the pre-interview questions, asking him where he'd been when the gunfire broke out and how he'd kept everyone calm while sheltering inside the building. It was harrowing stuff, and I was honored that he shared it with me.

I wrote up a quick note and called the morning show bullpen in New York, where there's always someone on the desk to answer calls from the field, day or night.

I explained my booking to the producer on the other end of the line, but he didn't seem too interested. "We already have enough students and teachers who were sheltering and unharmed," he said. "We need injured people."

When I look back at Parkland, I see it as the beginning of the end for my career at *48 Hours*. Witnessing that raw trauma and seeing so many young lives cut short or forever altered affected me deeply. While other producers seemed to easily jump from tragedy to tragedy, I was still reeling from the last one, despite my best efforts otherwise. Visions of sobbing children and crime scene tape played in a loop I couldn't turn off.

A month after the shooting, *48 Hours* ran a special on Parkland called "39 Days." It won numerous accolades, including an Emmy and the Edward R. Murrow Award for best network news documentary. I couldn't bring myself to put my name on the credits. It felt like what the students were doing themselves was the story, and we inserted ourselves into it in a way that I'm still not entirely comfortable with.

After returning from Parkland, I remember half joking to my colleagues that I needed therapy. Much truth is said in jest. It would take three more years before I could admit I did need help processing all the trauma I'd witnessed. And once I opened that door of self-reflection, my days in true crime TV were numbered.

I'm kneeling on a brightly colored carpet, holding my cell phone in landscape mode and using the camera function.

"As much as possible, you want to be down on their level," I tell the small group of people assembled in front of me.

"Hold the phone steady and let them move in and out of the shot. Ten seconds is a good target length."

I'm at my son's preschool, talking to a handful of teachers and administrators about best practices for cell phone videos and pictures. Then I send them out into the playground to practice what they've learned. It's nice to think that their images are all going to be happy ones.

Not long after I got back from reporting on the tragedy at Parkland, it was Teacher Appreciation Week. The school director asked for parents to sign up for volunteer slots, and I felt bad about snapping at her when she'd called me in the middle of an intense workday. I wanted to redeem myself.

I figured a crash course in cell phone photography would be more valuable than handing out donuts. Plus, I was tired of the blurry photos and jumpy videos that the preschool usually sent of my son and his friends. Turns out, chasing down criminals is good practice for filming toddlers, who can be equally as elusive on camera.

It's a crisp fall morning, and I'm running through Arbor Hills Nature Preserve in Plano, Texas. It's only a ten-minute drive from our house, and I love how wild and unkempt the area is, compared to the rest of the suburban landscape.

As I round a corner, a woman passes me going in the other direction. I lock eyes with her for a moment and feel like I know her. We both keep running, but her face stays with me as I try to place it in the proper context. Big brown eyes, a warm smile with a slight tilt of her head.

It hits me. She looks like Christina Morris. Only, how would I know that? Christina's dead and I've never even met her.

I rack my brain for the details. Christina was last seen at a Plano shopping center. She was kidnapped and murdered in 2014. I'd looked at her photograph so many times as part of my job at *48 Hours* that her facial features are still swimming around in my head as someone I actually know.

The realization is jarring, and I stop at an overlook to catch my breath. How many more of these images had been imprinted on me? I close my eyes as a slideshow of murder victims and their killers starts to play. Too many to count.

When people asked me how I dealt with the emotional toll of working in true crime, it always felt like a trick question. Did they really want to know about the nightmares, where I'd see crime scene video playing in my head? Or hear that I couldn't go into a crowded mall, movie theater, church, or concert without planning an exit strategy in case of a shooting? Probably not. So instead, I'd wave them off with a line about compartmentalization, and I'd do my best to convince myself it was true.

Admitting that the trauma was seeping into my life seemed like a weakness and a burden too heavy to bear. It was much simpler to steel my nerves, put on a brave face, and go find our next murder story. I think that on some level, I could sense that my career clock at CBS was ticking faster, but I wasn't ready to face the music just yet. I told myself that every job is a beatdown in its own way, and mine just happened to be an emotional roller coaster through murder and mayhem.

I was searching for meaning and a case where I could have an impact. The next time I got on a conference call with the planning department, I decided to pitch a slew of potential wrongful conviction cases based in Texas. I'd been talking to defense attorneys, the Innocence Project, and private investigators who all had great intel on under-the-radar cases with big plot twists and alternate suspects.

I know that in the past, *48 Hours* would have championed one of these cases. They'd done it before with great success. But with shrinking budgets and rising episode counts, I was told wrongful convictions no longer fit the company bill.

"Getting someone out of prison takes a lot of time and money, and we just don't have the resources to do that right now," an executive said. "We need to get back to basics. Find some cases where the husband did it. Those work so well."

14

DODGING A BULLET

It's a chilly winter morning in Austin, and I wake up with a crick in my neck. I swing my legs over a futon and look around at the unfamiliar surroundings. A decade ago, this would have been more fun, but in your thirties, the appeal of crashing on your friend's couch is fading fast.

There is no shortage of great hotels in Austin. The Westin has the best rooftop pool, but the InterContinental has the coolest lobby bar and restaurant. In a pinch, I'll stay at the Courtyard Marriott by the lake. And yet, here I am, brushing my teeth in my friend's kitchen sink. Just another day in the glamorous life of a network television producer.

The truth is, I could be waking up in a real-life bed this morning, my own, three hours up the road in Dallas. But I wasn't going to miss this day of filming in exchange for a good night's sleep. I'd worked on booking the key character for this episode for four years: Judge Julie Kocurek. At that point, I'd stayed on this story for longer than any other in my career. Nothing would keep me from her interview, not even my bosses in New York who told me they didn't have room in the budget for my flight and hotel room. Good thing they couldn't see my eye roll over the phone.

In 2018, the budget for an episode of *48 Hours* was around $150,000. I knew my local travel expenses weren't breaking the bank, and this faux thriftiness was really just a way to keep me at arm's length from the story. What can I say? Sometimes I'm too much for people. Considering my history with Judy Tygard, the creator and executive producer of the *Live to Tell* series that Judge Kocurek was appearing on, I wasn't surprised.

But I also wasn't going to be bigfooted out of my own story and miss out on seeing Judge Kocurek under the lights. I'd been through the wringer with deeply disturbing and tragic stories back-to-back. I needed a win, and as horrific as Judge Kocurek's ordeal had been, she'd survived it. So when Judy and other high-ranking producers on the story said "Sorry, kiddo. We'll get you next time," I bit my lip and pretended to believe them. "That's okay," I said. "I'm just glad we got the story. That's the important thing."

I wasn't going to miss our interview with Judge Kocurek . . . even if CBS had other ideas.

And while that sentiment was true, it wasn't going to stop me from producing Judge Kocurek's interview. They kept me on the phone while they ran down the plan for the shoot, and I switched the call over to my earbuds so I could start packing. If I was going to drive to Austin, I needed a head start.

Correspondent Peter Van Sant has a saying about difficult people at *48 Hours*. He calls them death islands, a la World War II. "You don't go through a death island. You go around them."

With Peter's words ringing in my ears, I hit the road to Austin and called one of my old college roommates along the way. Sarah Viesca, aka Sarah Fiesta, was happy to play host and relive our glory days. You gotta love a friend who only needs a few hours' notice that you're coming to town.

"So why won't CBS put you up in a hotel this time?" she asked me over margaritas later that night.

"Well, they didn't actually want me to come to this interview," I tell her, and we both crack up. "Isn't it cute that they thought they could stop me?"

You'd think after five years they'd know me just a little bit better than that. If it was that easy to dissuade me, I'd never have booked Judge Kocurek in the first place. So perhaps it's fitting that I had to finagle my way into the filming.

I dust the Tex-Mex off my hands and pull out my cell phone: Twelve hours 'til the crew call. Time to alert the boss that I'm in town.

I fire off a breezy-sounding text. "Hey, since there's no money in the budget for my travel expenses, I'm crashing with a friend in Austin. Couldn't miss Judge Kocurek's CBS debut. See you in the morning."

Every job has office politics, and network television is no exception. The difference is that many of our workplace dramas play out in living rooms across the country. If you know what to look for, you might even catch some of the action. For example, ever notice how often the title of CBS's morning show changes? It's because they're constantly rebranding in an attempt to place higher than third in the rankings. *Good Morning America* doesn't have this problem.

My best sources of information about behind-the-scenes drama are the crews themselves. Back in the golden age of TV, each network had its own crew on staff, and they saw everything. But these days, camera operators and sound technicians who only work for one set of call letters are an endangered species.

And if you thought TV producers were cutthroat, you wouldn't believe the sabotage I've seen with competing crews. There's one in particular whose head games are legendary. They operate outside of New York, but they definitely have an Empire State of mind. Their nickname is Bigfoot, for their ability to squash smaller crews and steal their contracts. The evil genius part of it is that they've actually convinced the corporate execs in New York that they are trying to train new crews to help them. But gosh darn it, good help is hard to find. Especially when you are actively sabotaging the process.

I've seen it firsthand, on multiple occasions. The Bigfoot crew will ask for recommendations of young, up-and-coming crews in local markets. Then they will "train" them on how to shoot a *48 Hours*–style interview. They will give them just terrible advice, blowing out the shot, oversaturating color levels, using the wrong focus length, you name it. Then they will report back to New York that they've given the new crew all the correct specs and they should be good to go for the interview. But just in case, they are going to set up an additional camera of their own. And when the footage comes back all kinds of messed up from the local crew, it's Bigfoot to the rescue. The local crew is then blacklisted, further cementing Bigfoot's outsized imprint in the market.

Because freelance crews work for every network, they are very disciplined about not revealing the competitive stories they cover (which would be career suicide). But they can't help themselves from engaging in a little gossip from time to time.

Can you blame them? They easily spend sixteen or more hours on set, getting to the shoots early to set up and always leaving last. The generally accepted protocol at the end of filming is for the highest-ranking producer to declare it's time to play "screw the crew."

This is a not-so-secret code for producers to hit the road so the crew can tear down the set. We could stick around until they wrapped up, but union rules dictate that we can't actually touch the equipment, so we'd only be offering moral support. The crews that really like each other will keep an ice chest of beer in their van and crack them open once the suits have vacated the premises. It's also when they share the best stories about "the talent," as on-air personalities are known, and I like to hang around for it when I can.

One of my favorite gems came from a sound technician who shall not be named. He regularly works with all three networks and clued me in to a little thing at ABC called "the Double David."

As the anchor of *ABC World News Tonight*, David Muir has a lot of latitude. Anchors are the top of the food chain, sitting above correspondents and reporters. In addition to his sign-on and sign-off phrases, David Muir has engineered another way to get his name on the air twice as often. Every time the story is thrown to another on-air talent, they are required to double tag him, saying his name at the beginning and end of their segment.

That's right, David.

Back to you, David.

As a casual viewer, you might not even notice all the Davids flying around, but to those in the biz, it's called "the Double David." As in, "On a scale from one to Double David, how egotistical is this guy?"

I know what it might sound like coming from a CBS alum, but I'm not trying to pick on ABC. The truth is, David Muir wasn't the only one with a reputation that precedes him. NBC's Brian Williams was known as the "rock star." The only evening news anchor to regularly get guest spots on late-night television, is it any wonder that Brian had trouble distinguishing reality from fiction? In 2015, when he was ousted from the anchor chair at NBC over an exaggerated story about his own wartime reporting, television producers everywhere exchanged a knowing look.

It's a common problem for correspondents to enhance their reporting stories to make them sound more exciting. While trading tall tales at cocktail parties is one thing, it's the producer's job to make sure the talent keeps their feet on the ground when they go on the air. And the higher the anchor's star rises, the harder it is to talk them down.

At *48 Hours*, there were certain correspondents who you could give direction to like a normal person, simply flagging them on a misstatement and offering an easy fix. But there were others who required a careful dance for any corrections. Richard Schlesinger, for example, wanted any additional questions or clarifications written down and handed to him on a slip of paper. Toward the end of the interview, he'd ask "the peanut gallery" if they had anything to add. This was the producer's cue to hand him any notes on the interview. He'd review them in his chair, still under the lights, and decide which ones to actually verbalize. On the scale of correspondent quirks, it was a small idiosyncrasy. And I could understand the logic behind it.

Andrea Canning on NBC's *Dateline* was the only correspondent from another network that I'd gone toe-to-toe with in the field. We were attending a hearing on Dr. Leon Jacob's attempted-murder-for-hire case in Houston, where the courthouse and the jail are just a few blocks apart. When it ended, it was a mad dash to the jail for visiting hours. Because she's on air, Andrea Canning was dressed to impress, and she popped off her heels to beat me to the jail lobby. I knew right then she was a worthy competitor.

When I got inside, there was already a line to check in, and I wondered who else was in town to talk to Dr. Jacob. Inmates are typically allowed only one visitor per day, unless it's a family visit. If more than one person came to visiting hours, the inmate had to choose between them. I filled out the paperwork to speak with Dr. Jacob and waited to learn my fate. Andrea had made it through the line as well, and I spotted a producer from ABC's *20/20*.

"Can you believe ABC sent a guy?" I said as I exchanged a glance with Andrea. "Strategic mistake."

The jailer called out Leon Jacob's name and said that he had three visitors to choose from. CBS, NBC, and ABC lined up against the glass and Dr. Jacob looked us over. I'm a confident person, but I knew I had very little chance of getting picked over the blonde celebrity. When Andrea's name was called, I reached out my hand.

"Good game. Until next time." She smiled and shook my hand before heading into the visiting area.

Dateline got the win with Dr. Jacob that day at the jail. But our *48 Hours* episode aired before theirs, and that's what really counts in television. But while everyone in television fights over first place, there is such a thing as airing too early, when a network jumps the gun and puts out a story before the real facts have shaken out. Also known as the Cautious Broadcasting System, CBS lives in fear of this scenario, which is why it was all the more surprising when the Queen's special aired twice before she died—and zero times afterward.

The first iteration, "The Queen Carries On: A Gayle King Special," came out in May 2021, and by that time, it was already a long-running joke among producers. The special had been in production for over five years, draining network resources and busting budgets. And everyone watched and waited for Queen Elizabeth to just die already so we could air the damn thing and move on with our lives.

But she just carried on. And on. And on. So long, in fact, that network executives finally threw in the towel and aired the final installment, "Her Majesty the Queen: A Gayle King Special," in June 2022. Three months later, Queen Elizabeth died at the age of ninety-six. Despite millions of dollars and thousands of crew hours invested in the project, there was no CBS special on her death. ABC, meanwhile, aired a three-hour live event, "A Celebration of Queen Elizabeth II's Life," the day after she passed away. Score one for ABC.

For most of my career at CBS, Scott Pelley was the evening news anchor. An extremely fit, silver-fox type, Pelley works out religiously and snacks judiciously. Although he's a Texan, born in San Antonio and raised in Lubbock, he doesn't eat like one. He stashes raw cashews in his pockets and pops them into his mouth between meals, which largely consist of chopped salads and

Scott Pelley, left, making a signature on-screen move.

very little dressing. His chiseled frame lasted six years in the chair, ending his run in 2017. His signature move, taking off his glasses, crossing his arms, and pondering a question, gave him a professorial air, and a sense that he was above the celebrity fray of the other two networks.

While that may have been true, it didn't help the ratings. ABC and NBC regularly jockeyed for first place in the evenings, with CBS left to claim third year after year. Still, Pelley was beloved at CBS, and the whole network was shocked when his contract wasn't renewed. The ratings gave management an easy out, but rumors swirled among the rank and file that Pelley had done something during negotiations to turn the tide against him.

Probably the most self-serving rumor I heard was that he'd led with such an enormously high salary increase that they'd opted to let his contract lapse rather than counter it. Gee, wonder who started that one? It's exactly the kind of folktale management would love circulating in the bullpen.

In 2019, Pelley told Brian Stelter on CNN's *Reliable Sources* that he was ousted over repeated complaints about a "hostile work environment."[10] But complaints aside, Pelley didn't go far, landing across the street from the CBS Broadcast Center at *60 Minutes*, where he'd already had a side contract for years, pulling double duty with the *Evening News*. It definitely raised some eyebrows when Pelley labeled CBS News writ large as a hostile workplace and then retreated to *60 Minutes*, the show with the most brutal reputation in television.

---

10 Hilary Lewis, "Scott Pelley claims he lost 'CBS Evening News' job over 'hostile work environment' complaints," *The Hollywood Reporter*, May 26, 2019, https://www.hollywoodreporter.com/news/general-news/scott-pelley-fired-cbs-evening-news-hostile-workplace-claims-1213757/.

15

FACING THE FIRING SQUAD

I'm sitting in a dark, windowless screening room in Midtown Manhattan. Before going inside, veteran *60 Minutes* producer Draggan Mihailovich gives me the rookie ground rules: "Don't speak unless spoken to. If anyone has a question for you, they will address you by name."

I nod silently to indicate my clear understanding of the pecking order and duck in to find a seat.

Led by executive producer Bill Owens, a galley of senior producers sit in a raised row of chairs to screen the first cut of our piece "The Ranger and The Serial Killer." I'd been to dozens of CBS News screenings by then, but they had all been for *48 Hours* episodes. I'm beginning to see that while the two shows were on the same network, they were worlds apart.

The CBS Broadcast Center was located at 524 W. 57th Street, and it's where all the hard news shows, including *48 Hours*, were made. *60 Minutes*, meanwhile, was across the street at 555 W. 57th. This was not merely a coincidence or a logistical decision. It was indicative of the entire ethos at *60*. We are better. We are different. You don't belong here.

What's wild to me is how this singular *60* attitude goes against the grain of the overall CBS News culture, which is welcoming, collegial, and regularly feels like a team sport. But at *60*, it's more like *Lord of the Flies*. Not only does no one have your back, but they are probably sharpening a tool to impale you with at an opportune moment.

The feeling of being on the same CBS team was the first thing to fly out the window when I walked in the door at *60*. My ID badge didn't even work at the security desk.

At *48*, the screenings were celebratory occasions. We'd worked for months or even years on an hour of television, and now we were all in the same room to watch it together on a big screen. It was almost like a mini movie premiere, complete with popcorn and a festive dress code.

Before the screening, our executive team had closely followed the scripts, given us notes, and watched rough cuts of the show. In other words, there were very few surprises in the *48* screening room. It was actually the policy of all the senior producers at the show that if you had a major script issue, you had to bring it up with them before the screening. No one likes to be put on the spot in front of the boss.

But screenings were not just rubber-stamp events. We had to watch with a careful eye for consistency, legal issues, and overall accuracy. Typically, the biggest problems in screenings would be narration lines that we'd written—and rewritten—a million times. Inevitably, we'd insert some incorrect detail, improperly state an opinion as fact, or misattribute a quote. Unlike sound bites from an interview, narration lines were entirely our own inventions, and it was just too easy to get it wrong.

We watched them like hawks, along with dates and anything that had to do with math. It sounds silly, but maintaining an accurate timeline and keeping up with the ever-changing figures (people's ages and the amount of time that passed since the crime) was always a challenge.

The only other concerns that I really remember coming up in *48* screenings were about special arrangements we'd made with characters. In one episode, we worked with an alleged hit man and agreed to shoot him in shadow, obscuring his identity and changing his voice. But we ended up including a shot that showed a specific tattoo on his hand, which would have immediately identified him to anyone who mattered. I caught it in the screening, and our editors were able to push in on the shot and keep his hand off camera. Another time, on the Crystal McDowell case, we had left a phone number unblurred on a shot of the whiteboard in the war room footage.

These little details were often the biggest issues in a 48 screening. But in 60 land, the screenings were far more explosive. And it was by design. No one on the senior staff, including executive producer Bill Owens, had ever seen so much as a rough draft of the script before the screening. It was a true reveal of the entire piece, one week before it was supposed to air. For the life of me, I cannot understand why anyone would think this was a good idea. But no one questions 60 protocols, and I certainly wasn't going to step in front of the firing squad as a rookie producer who had snuck over from 48.

I never expected to end up across the street at 60. Unlike so many people who worked at other CBS shows, I had not been pining for a spot on the marquee program. I'd never even watched an episode of 60 Minutes until I started working there. It wasn't personal; it was generational. 60 Minutes was the show my grandparents watched, along with Wheel of Fortune, Jeopardy, and PGA tournaments. I didn't see the appeal, and for my first five years at CBS, I barely gave 60 a passing thought. I never imagined it would one day be my saving grace and lead to one of the biggest stories of my career.

I first heard Texas Ranger James Holland's name echoing through the halls of the Galveston County courthouse during the murder trial of Steven Wayne McDowell—the ex-husband of slain and buried Crystal McDowell. The defense had asked for a change of venue due to all the media attention—i.e., me—and it had been granted. So instead of having the trial in Chambers County, where the murder took place, it was moved to the next county over, on the Gulf Coast of Texas.

I was chatting with Steve's daughter, Krysta, and feeling like I was taking something of a victory lap. We'd already aired our episode "Storm of Suspicion" on the case twice before the trial. That was a new record for me.

ABC and NBC were running around with their pants on fire, trying to book everyone I'd already interviewed, plus locking down their own exclusives to justify a new episode on what was, thanks to CBS, an old story. I'll admit I was enjoying watching them sweat. I didn't have to book a single new interview for our episode. All we were going to do was update Act 6 with the verdict. The way I saw it, I didn't even really need to be at the trial every day, but my boss had a different opinion.

Getting to Galveston had been an adventure in itself, and I almost didn't make it. I sat at the Dallas airport for five hours with delays from a tropical storm before my flight was canceled. Dejected, I'd driven back home around midnight and tried to rebook a new flight for the morning. But there was no guarantee that we'd be able to take off.

My only real option was to drive more than three hundred miles from Dallas to Galveston, a journey that could take up to six hours, depending on traffic. The trial started at 9 AM. The stress headache was already coming on strong, and I massaged my temples and calculated how much sleep I could reasonably get before hitting the road.

At 3 AM, I was behind the wheel of a rental car, with a large thermos of coffee as my copilot. I punched in the address for the Galveston County courthouse. The glamorous life of a television producer.

There were no cameras allowed in the courtroom at the opening of the Steven Wayne McDowell murder trial. I squeaked in the door just as the bailiff was signaling the start of the trial, and if it hadn't been for the unmistakable image of Chambers County district attorney Cheryl Lieck, I would've thought I was in the wrong place.

The man sitting in the defendant's chair looked nothing like the Steve McDowell who had been arrested for the murder of his ex-wife, Crystal, two years prior. Back in 2017, Steve had been fit, clean shaven, and casually dressed. In his booking photo, he scarcely had a wisp of hair on his body. But today, Steve McDowell had a gray, scraggly beard down to his chest. He was wearing a suit and had gotten thicker in the middle, with a small belly rounding over his belt buckle. He was almost like a deranged Santa, minus the red stocking cap.

I wasn't the least bit sorry about the lack of cameras in the courtroom. It was my preference, considering we already had enough content to fill an entire episode and then some. The last thing I wanted was my boss getting the wild idea that we should scrap the first cut of the story and start from scratch with a true trial hour. I'd be stuck in Galveston for a month if that were the case. I shuddered at the thought.

By the time of his trial, Steven Wayne McDowell's appearance had changed dramatically.

It's not that Galveston isn't a nice enough town, but it's not home. And while I enjoy a couple nights away here and there, the appeal of traveling for days on end fades fast when you have a toddler at home. Especially because I know how hard it is on my husband to function as a single dad when I'm on the road. Most people can't believe that I continued to work in more or less the same fashion after having a baby. I remember the slack-jawed comments of well-meaning strangers upon learning that I was a new mom.

"Who's taking care of your baby?" they'd ask, horrified.

"My husband, the baby's father, the one who cocreated him with me," I'd reply.

For some reason, when Riley went on a ten-day business trip to India three months after our son was born, no one asked him the same question.

Back in the courtroom, I settled in for opening arguments. I didn't really have to take court notes, but it gave me something to pass the time. And I'm a sucker for a good sound bite, even if I'm the only one who gets to hear it.

"Crystal had a tragic beginning to her life, and it ended the same way it began," District Attorney Lieck said. "She was born to drug-addicted parents. She was sexually abused. She was abducted, and she was raped and kept in a cage."

It was harrowing stuff, and the jam-packed courtroom was silently taking it all in. I knew Crystal had been named after crystal meth, but the rest of the details were a shock to me as well. And I'm grateful the state didn't use any visuals for this portion of their case.

At this point in my career, I'd stopped looking at crime scene photos in detail, ditto that for autopsy ones. I'd confirm that the files were there, and then I'd copy them over to our shared company hard drive and tell the associate producer to label and log them. I wish I had thought of this tactic years earlier, but I still saved my brain from countless grisly images by adopting it when I did.

Back in the courtroom, the state took only three minutes for its opening argument, wasting no time in implicating Steve McDowell for the murder.

"He choked his ex-wife to death in front of their five-year-old daughter," Lieck said, pointing to Steve.

The defense didn't even give an opening statement, opting instead to let testimony begin straightaway. It was an odd choice, but then again, Steve had already confessed to the Texas Rangers and led authorities to the body. What exactly would an opening statement look like in light of those facts?

Crystal's boyfriend Paul Hargrave took the stand first for the state and explained that the couple met when she came into his jewelry store. They'd been dating less than two months when she disappeared.

"She kept quiet about a lot of things," Paul said, speaking in a whisper.

The next witness was Texas Ranger Steven Jeter, who'd been called out on the missing person case when Hurricane Harvey was in full force.

When the Texas Rangers get involved in a case, everyone sits up a little straighter and takes notice. The institution of the Rangers is as old as Texas and dates back to the frontier days, when their main job was protecting settlers from Native American attacks. Of course, that's a politically loaded statement in itself, considering our idea of "settling" Texas involved supplanting the community of indigenous people who had made their home here for generations.

Today, the Texas Rangers are an elite unit of the Texas Department of Public Safety, our state police agency. Rangers are called into the toughest cases in Texas, when other agencies are in over their heads. Unlike other agencies, their jurisdiction spans the entire state, and they generally walk around like they own the place. It's easy to spot a ranger in their distinctive uniform: cowboy boots and hat, khaki pants, white shirt and tie, with a silver star badge pinned to their chest. Thanks to rigorous fitness standards, they look like Texas's version of a superhero, and they act like it, too.

"This part of the world was upside down," Jeter said on the stand, clutching his white cowboy hat in his hands.

Jeter had conducted the initial interview with Steve McDowell as a witness, not a suspect.

"When I walked out of that first interview, I had a very strong feeling that he had something to do with the disappearance of his wife."

For the second interview, Jeter brought along another Texas Ranger who specialized in interrogation methods: James Holland.

Before Holland would take the stand, the court went into its morning recess. I jumped at the chance to stretch my legs after six hours in the car and two more on a wooden court bench. I was walking the halls, happy to be free of the constraints of court attendance when I spotted Krysta McDowell.

Krysta's life was another tragedy in this sad, complicated story, and my heart went out to her, practically an orphan at twenty-one. I went over to say hi and noticed she had textbooks in tow. She was taking summer classes and trying to keep up with the coursework while attending her dad's murder trial. We chatted easily, and I realized that court had probably started back up again, but I didn't really care. What was another Texas Ranger going to say that I hadn't basically heard already?

We'd been talking for a while when Sheriff Brian Hawthorne tapped me on the shoulder. "You really should go in there," he said, gun belt glistening.

I looked back at him quizzically. He knew better than anyone that I'd already had a pretty thorough sneak peek of the case against McDowell.

"You won't want to miss Ranger Holland's testimony. He's one of a kind," the sheriff said as he opened the courtroom door for me.

Well, hell. I couldn't very well turn him down. I grabbed my bag and told Krysta I'd catch her later. The courtroom was packed, and if it wasn't for the sheriff next to me, I'm not sure I would have gotten a seat. But he cleared out some space in the front row for us, and I sat down feeling like a kid who'd been caught skipping class.

Ranger Holland was in the middle of his testimony, and I was playing catch-up. I scrawled details down in my notebook. "Holland says they talked for 12 HRS." This was definitely not a typical police interview, the kind that ran forty-five minutes and miraculously cut off when it was time for dinner.

"We bonded over the fact that we both had an affinity for Ford Mustangs," Holland said with a smirk, adding that he'd lived in Chambers County twenty years ago and still had friends here, some of whom McDowell knew.

Why was this guy making himself sound like besties with a murderer?

Holland explained that after several days of marathon interviews, McDowell said he wanted to tell him "about the hell he'd been through" with Crystal.

They went for a drive and ended up on a park bench, where McDowell spilled his guts.

Holland said McDowell told him about ten different men who he was aware his wife had slept with during their marriage.

"He said she had affairs all the time, all over the country, and the kids weren't even his. What really bothered him was that she was screwing all these douchebags, and he just couldn't deal with it."

Wow. Screwing? Douchebags? This was not your average police officer testimony. I turned to the sheriff and raised my eyebrows as a sign of thanks for pulling me out of the hallway. This was definitely TV material.

Holland's unusual testimony had the courtroom captivated and hanging on his every word. Now we were moving into the actual confession, and the crucial information that allowed investigators to recover Crystal's body.

"He said he was ready to get this over with," Holland recalled.

They left the park and drove back to the sheriff's office, where Holland closed the deal with methodical precision. In video footage of the interrogation, McDowell appeared every bit a broken man. He was hunched over, arms crossed, and practically sinking into the chair.

The ranger, meanwhile, was in his prime. He moved with purpose across the room, setting up his backup digital recorder and striding over to a chair that he pulled up close to McDowell. They sat knee to knee, and McDowell confessed his sins.

"We got into an argument," McDowell said.

Holland testified about what he identified as the breaking point for McDowell.

"She told him that she never loved him."

McDowell snapped and choked her down in the bedroom. Her last words to her husband allegedly were: "You're scaring me."

While these intimate details were haunting, there was no guarantee that it could ever be confirmed with physical evidence, because Crystal's body had been missing for two weeks.

Holland kept pressing, asking McDowell to put himself back in that room, in that moment after she stopped breathing.

"What did you do next?" Holland prompted him.

McDowell said he put a Target shopping bag over her face, so he didn't have to look at her anymore. Then he zip-tied her hands and feet in a fetal position and covered the body in multiple industrial trash bags before placing it in the trunk of her Mercedes.

This information would later be confirmed with the discovery of Crystal's remains. Her decomposing body was in the fetal position, with zip ties and the Target bag still in place.

It was a lot to take in, this graphic and horrific description given in a sterile courtroom. Holland was clearly a professional, and while the rest of the room was reeling, he appeared calm and at ease. The district attorney asked Holland if he frequently worked murder cases. Holland said yes, and then shared that he was currently involved in a serial killer case with ninety-three victims. I jotted this number down with disbelief in my reporter's notebook.

How in the world had I not heard of a serial killer with ninety-three victims?

I'm standing in the hallway outside the courtroom, staking out my position to approach Ranger Holland. Since he first testified, I've done a deep dive on his cases. Turns out, this guy's been all over the place, involved in practically every high-profile murder investigation in Texas for the last twenty years. As head of the Rangers' unsolved crime investigation team, he's been quietly closing cold cases with hard-fought confessions that often lead to digging up a body—or what's left of it. He was even named Texas Police Officer of the Year for 2019. The only people he hasn't been talking to are the press, and that's exactly why I've never heard of him until now.

As a journalist you never want to become part of the story, but sometimes it's unavoidable. *48 Hours* was so entrenched in the McDowell case that we even became part of the trial, with a copy of our episode introduced into evidence. We were reporting on Crystal as a missing person, and the case turned into a murder investigation in real time as our cameras were rolling. The sheriff was the one who let us in the war room. What's a producer to do?

The trial judge clearly disapproved of *48 Hours'* involvement in the case, and he regularly referred to the "media sideshow" that had been allowed to operate in Chambers County. I stared at the floor and tried to sink into the wooden bench when the topic came up in open court. It was more than a little awkward to take notes as the judge lambasted your employer. The Texas Rangers, however, had been the exception to media cooperation in Chambers County. The sheriff's department and district attorney had opened their doors wide to us, but no interviews or evidence access was granted with the rangers. They wouldn't even talk to us off the record, and the steely glares they shot in our direction during filming left little room for interpretation. But with the trial underway, I figure it's time for a fresh start.

The courtroom door swings open, and Rangers Holland and Jeter march into the hallway. They look like a couple of Old West action figures, complete with braided leather gun belts. They are holding their white cowboy hats, because while it's part of the official Texas Ranger uniform, no real cowboy ever wears his hat indoors.

I approach them both and extend my hand as I introduce myself as a producer with *48 Hours* on CBS. They are polite and engage in a little small talk, but I see Holland eyeing the exit at the end of the hallway. I can tell my time is growing short, so I go for the kill.

"It would be an honor to interview the master interviewer. Our audience would be hanging on your every word."

Holland smiles back and then lets loose a dagger. "I don't give interviews, but maybe Jeter will talk to you."

Holland slaps his partner on the back, and we all laugh. I get Jeter's card and learn that he's retired from the rangers now and is working for the campus police at Sam Houston State University.

I don't give up that easily, though, so I keep talking to Holland. For any journalist worth a damn, saying you don't give interviews is not a deterrent. It's more like catnip. I hand them both my CBS News business card, and Holland is intrigued by the address.

"You don't sound like you're from New York."

"That's because I'm not. I'm a Texan, born and raised."

He asks me where I went to college, and I'm all too happy to drop the name of my alma mater, Baylor University. His eyes light up.

"My wife went to Baylor," he tells me, clearly surprised that I'm not some East Coast elite.

"All the best ones do," I quip back.

I try to use this newfound connection to nudge Holland and Jeter toward having lunch with me, but they shoot it down immediately. Still, there's enough encouragement that I know I'm not leaving this meeting empty-handed. I have Jeter's contact information, now I just need Holland's.

I ask if they are sticking around for the rest of the trial and they say no, they have to get back to work and are leaving in the morning.

"Well in that case, I should get your number so I can keep you updated if anything exciting happens."

And just like that, Holland is giving me his cell.

It's not an interview, but it's a foot in the door. I'll take what I can get.

I'm sitting by the hotel pool in Galveston, and it's getting pretty rowdy. I look at my watch and wonder how much longer until I can call an Uber. I've been partying with the district attorney's office and the sheriff's department all evening, and I'm having trouble keeping up. The trial has been the culmination of two years' worth of dinners, drinks, and after-hours hang outs. Ever since I first got the Crystal McDowell story on the CBS morning show, it's been a nonstop parade of leisurely lunches, late-night dinners, and more texts and phone calls than I can count. I've been in their offices. I've been to the Chambers County Jail, and I think I've memorized their favorite after-hours drinks. And it's not that I haven't enjoyed myself in the process, but it has been a job for me.

I pull out my flash drive and a handwritten wish list of exhibit numbers from the trial. There are lots of ways to obtain official evidence in a criminal trial, if you know the right person to ask. Although it's unorthodox to get files copied over at a hotel pool party, it's not illegal. I was a member of the press, asking the prosecution team for something that they had the power to release to me, if they saw fit. Of course, they could always deny my request if they wanted to cite any number of statutes available to them, including the ongoing investigation. But that's a judgment call for them, not me.

I request an Uber on my phone as the sheriff swims by my table. As the files copy over, I tell myself there are worse ways to earn a living. And that this unconventional night at the office will all be worth it if by midnight, I have copies of the evidence in my possession before any other network. That said, while I like to have a good time as much as the next TV producer, I really don't appreciate anything messing with my workout routine. I just want to go to bed so I can sleep this off and still get in a run along the beach before court in the morning.

It's approaching 9 AM, and I hustle up the steps at the Galveston County Courthouse. I pass the prosecution team in the hallway, and we acknowledge each other professionally. Scenes from the last twelve hours play in my head. The poolside drinks and smokes appear all but impossible now, under the fluorescent lights and business attire. The difference between night and day in true crime TV.

I find a seat in the courtroom and wait for the morning testimony to start. The state has already rested, and no one knows for sure who the defense is planning to call as witnesses. The biggest question is whether or not the defendant will testify. If he does, the trial will probably last several more days.

Prosecutors can't help themselves when a murder defendant goes on the stand. They will ask every question they can think of, twice. But if he declines to testify, the trial could go into closing arguments today.

There's a feeling of anticipation in the air, and lots of whispering and sidebar conferences between attorneys. And then it happens, the judge orders Steven Wayne McDowell to rise. He says he's going to testify in his own defense.

Now I'm the one who can't help myself, and I slip my phone out of my bag and text Ranger Holland.

"Your boy Steve is about to take the stand," I write.

A few minutes later he replies, "All the best ones do."

With his long gray beard and soft features, the Steve McDowell in the witness chair bears little resemblance to the man who once confessed to killing Crystal McDowell, and I know it's by design. I've seen too many murder trials where the defendant drastically alters his appearance by the time he enters the courtroom. It's a not-so-subtle way of trying to distance themselves from the person who stands accused of a heinous crime. That guy in the mug shot? He's not me. The one on camera confessing to the murder? Never seen him in my life.

The latest version of Steve McDowell takes the stand and adjusts his suit jacket.

"Are you ready to tell your story?" the defense attorney asks.

"Yes, sir. I am," he replies.

Steve McDowell runs through the highlights of the last decade with Crystal. There are happy memories from the early years, their dating days, getting engaged, and then a wedding on the beach. Soon enough, they had two kids and were taking vacations and trips as much as possible. She was working as a flight attendant, so there were a lot of travel opportunities.

"It meant a lot to her to start family traditions."

But we weren't here to discuss their highlight reel. Or else we wouldn't be in a courtroom. The defense attorney starts asking about affairs, and Steve lists so many men's names that I lose count. Steve says he found out about his wife's dalliances by looking at her email.

"We shared passwords."

The defense introduces Crystal's emails with a half dozen men as exhibits. I'm surprised the judge lets it in, but the state isn't objecting, so I guess there's no reason not to allow them. There are a shocking number of lurid text messages. I remember Steve's daughter comparing them to *50 Shades of Grey*, and I realize it wasn't an exaggeration. These texts span the length of their marriage.

"I loved her, and I still wanted to be with her."

In the spring of 2017, after ten years together, Crystal filed for divorce. Steve didn't contest it, but they told almost no one. That summer, they continued to live together and take family vacations together.

"It was like nothing changed. She said it was just a piece of paper, and it didn't really mean anything."

But as the summer came to a close, Crystal started acting differently. Steve said she was no longer affectionate with him, and she started spending nights away. Crystal was dating someone new, Paul Hargrave, and now she wanted to take him on a cruise with the kids, and not Steve, just as his daughter had told us.

This was devastating news.

"We had talked about getting married again on the cruise."

The defense attorney steers Steve toward the morning of August 25, 2017, calling it the date of "the incident."

Steve shifts in his seat and leans in close on the mic.

"I was in the shower, and I heard knocking on the bedroom door."

He'd locked it for privacy from the children, who were sleeping on the couch.

According to Steve, Crystal came in and went to the bathroom. Then she took off her dress and sat on the bed.

"She asked if I missed her, and I said yes," Steve tells the packed courtroom. "Then she told me that she needed a hug."

He hugged her, but Steve says Crystal wanted more.

"She wanted me to lie down in bed with her and talk to her."

They ended up having sex, which Steve says Crystal initiated.

"She reached around and grabbed me. I knew she was in a good mood because she called me 'Daddy.'"

But the good mood wouldn't last. They ended up arguing over plans for the cruise, and it got heated.

The courtroom is dead silent as Steve repeats the same breaking point that he'd shared with Ranger Holland in the interrogation room.

"She said she didn't love me anymore, and that she hadn't loved me for a long time."

Steve is choking up now, his voice breaking.

"I told her to stop, and I begged her to quit being mean to me."

You'd almost think he was the victim, and not the other way around. But he's not the one who ended up hog-tied in a garbage bag.

His description gets increasingly bizarre as he tries to talk his way out of a premeditated murder charge.

"I put my arms around her. I didn't want to fight anymore. I just wanted to hug her."

Now that was a new one. He's actually claiming he hugged her to death? I took down his words as fast as I could.

"She became limp, and she fell. I realized she wasn't moving anymore."

After disposing of his wife's body in a garbage bag, he put her in the trunk of her car. And then he took the kids out to breakfast while he secretly plotted how to get rid of their mom's body.

"I just tried to figure out what I was going to do next."

The rest of Steve McDowell's testimony seemed to go in slow motion. I wanted to fast-forward to closing arguments and get this case in the hands of the jury, but the wheels of justice can't be rushed. Steve was on the stand for two days going over every dirty detail. When the body recovery photos were on display, I directed my eyes to the space between my feet. I counted the flecks in the carpet and tapped out silent rhythms with my toes until it was taken off the screens.

Hearing a killer describe their dark deeds is something I never got used to, even though it became a regular feature of my work life. The hardest part about covering murder is that in the end, it never makes sense. There's this misconception that we can "understand" violent crime and put the pieces together in a logical sequence of events. But in my experience, it's always haphazard chaos at the end.

Outside of a war zone, killing someone is inherently illogical to me. There are so many cleaner, smarter, safer ways to solve your so-called problems than taking a life and effectively ending your own. But once a person goes to that dark place in their mind, there's no talking sense to them. Their world is upside down, and it'll never be right again.

After Steve McDowell was found guilty and sentenced to fifty years in prison for murdering his wife, I ran through my *48 Hours* checklist of post-verdict tasks:

1. Hand a letter with twelve business cards to the bailiff and ask him to deliver it to the jury.
2. Get reaction interviews from the prosecution and defense as soon as possible, preferably while still on courthouse grounds.
3. Request a copy of all the exhibits from the court reporter.

It was all muscle memory for me at that point, and I couldn't wait to reach the finish line and hand the story baton to the production team in New York. I'm not superstitious, but I do believe in the power of positive thinking. My suitcase was already packed in my car, and I'd checked out of the hotel that morning. I was all too happy to be able to hit the road straight from the courthouse.

I had a long drive home ahead of me, and I wanted to make good use of it. I dialed up Texas Ranger James Holland. In many ways, he was still a mystery to me. But I knew one thing for sure: that guy could talk to a tree.

16

GOING FOR BROKE

I've never been one to shy away from a challenge. What's life without a little risk? But even I know a lost cause when I see one. And it was clear to me that Ranger Holland had no interest in giving an interview on the Steve McDowell case. He was instantly dismissive of the idea. And, confusingly, also willing to stay on the phone with me. I'd told him I was driving from Galveston to Dallas, and he seemed content to keep me company on my road trip. He asked me all sorts of questions about my career in journalism and how I ended up at CBS. Somewhere down the highway, I started to realize *I* was the one being interviewed, and I tried to steer the conversation back to him and his "no media" policy.

But he deftly maneuvered around my questions and was in clear command of the conversation. I was just along for the ride. I joked that I was going to get pulled over by a state trooper and keep him on the line to talk me out of the ticket.

After a while, Holland brought the conversation back around to McDowell. He said even though he wasn't interested in discussing that case, he did have a pitch of his own. I rolled my eyes, and I clenched the steering wheel.

The typical cases that cops pitch me are ones I could never put on television. They are the most disturbing cases imaginable. Child abductions and torture cases, dismemberments, and ritualistic killings. The stuff of nightmares that haunt even the most hardened investigators. They can't get those cases out of their heads and so they want to offload them into mine. I have cut off more cops than I can count in the middle of horrific crime scene descriptions.

Knowing I needed to let Holland speak his piece, I braced myself for the carnage. To my surprise, he didn't launch into a story that was gratuitously violent and or otherwise unfit for network television.

He started telling me about a serial killer named Samuel Little, a onetime boxer turned drifter and con man who had confessed to ninety-three murders, spread across the country over the last thirty years. Yes, it was horrific, but it was the cold, clinical kind of horror that works well on TV. I realized this was the same case he'd mentioned offhand on the witness stand to show his bona fides in effective interview and interrogation methods.

The volume of victims was hard to fathom, and I wondered how I hadn't heard of this before. Holland explained that the story originated in California and hadn't hit the national radar yet. But the FBI, the Department of Justice, and the Texas Rangers were about to change that. They wanted to release a statement in August declaring Samuel Little the most prolific serial killer in US history, and they were looking for an exclusive TV partner to make the announcement.

Had I heard him right? This was a huge scoop, from a cop who had never given an interview in twenty-five years. I needed to think clearly, so I pulled off at the next exit and got out my notebook. If I didn't write this down now, word for word, I'd never believe it myself.

Motivated by a desire to match up victims from decades-old cold cases, Holland was finally willing to break his cardinal rule about talking to the press. Working with the FBI, Holland had identified a handful of victim descriptions to bring to the public for the first time. Most of Little's kills had been prostitutes, and all were down on their luck by the time they'd crossed paths with him. It was proving impossible to find family members and friends to corroborate all the victims.

I'd gotten inside scoops from sources before, but none had been this tantalizing. I was being given the chance to break the story of the most prolific serial killer in the country and help solve some of the remaining cases. But even though I worked at CBS News, I was an obscure field producer based in Texas. The kind of story Holland was talking about belonged at the forefront of our national coverage. How in the world was I going to pull this off?

I spent the weekend after the McDowell trial reading every article I could find about Samuel Little. There wasn't a ton to go on, but the best reporting by far was in the *Los Angeles Times*. I told Riley about my latest and greatest story idea, and he was excited for me. He could tell I had that new-story energy, and I wasn't going to be able to focus on much else until I got it on the page. Thankfully, our son was still taking naps, so I got in a few power hours of uninterrupted research before Monday morning rolled around.

A common courtesy at *48* is to let you take a few days to recover during the week after a trial wraps and you've returned home. I was grateful for the quiet inbox and cell phone, but my personal workload was on full blast. There's nothing like the fear of losing a huge exclusive story to motivate a journalist. Holland had given me the heads-up on Samuel Little and the impending August deadline with the feds, but I knew the story wouldn't hold for long. If I didn't have CBS on board in a big way, Holland would go somewhere else. In fact, he probably already had feelers out with other networks.

I started to write the bluesheet for the pitch on the Samuel Little story in my head on the drive home from Galveston. Holland had so many rich details about the killer and his victims that I could see the story playing out in my mind before I ever got the chance to start typing. Still, there were so many ways to present it. With a story this big, spanning thirty years, where do you begin? It definitely wasn't a traditional *48 Hours* murder mystery, with a cheating spouse who was probably a doctor—or married to one.

After a few phone calls, I felt comfortable enough with Holland to let him in on my dilemma. I was beginning to see he was something of a walking contradiction. A serious lawman, yes, but with a rebel spirit. He commanded respect, but he also told me to call him Jim almost immediately. It didn't exactly roll off my tongue at first.

I told Jim that I was struggling with the best way to pitch the Samuel Little story to *48*.

"It's not our bread-and-butter kind of story, which should be a good thing, but it makes getting past the initial pitch phase more difficult."

Jim's reply surprised me.

"Actually, I was thinking it would be a perfect story for *60 Minutes*."

I tried to stifle a laugh, not because he was all wrong, but because I was.

"Well, there's just one problem with that. I don't work there."

60 Minutes has been called the most exclusive hour on television, and they pride themselves on the fact that they have no true competition. All the other CBS News programs have counterparts at ABC and NBC. I was intimately familiar with the battle royale between *48 Hours*, *Dateline*, and *20/20*. But the morning show wars between *Good Morning America*, *Today*, and *CBS Mornings* are probably the most well known. Still, every major network time slot has a nemesis. The big three evening news programs all fight for first place in the rankings, along with the political power hour on Sunday mornings: *Face the Nation* on CBS, *Meet the Press* on NBC, and *This Week* on ABC.

But *60 Minutes* stands alone on Sunday evenings, and they like it that way. Once upon a time in 2011, NBC tried and failed with a hard news program of their own, *Rock Center with Brian Williams*. But even then, it was airing on Monday night, so it wasn't a head-to-head challenger.

I never fully realized the value of a common enemy until I worked for the national media. To get a job in network news, you have to naturally be a competitive person. Many of my colleagues were former college athletes, and I don't think that's a coincidence. The drive to compete and win is part of what makes a great journalist, and the biggest media companies are the hardest ones to work for because they are the most desirable. They have the biggest audiences, and they can afford to pay higher salaries than local news.

At *48 Hours*, we had a healthy way to channel our competitive energy. We knew exactly who our enemies were: *Dateline* and *20/20*, and we fought like mad to beat them on every story. But at *60 Minutes*, a funny thing happens. There's no other show to target, so the competition turns inward. They fight each other for stories, for airtime, and for correspondents. Some producers are so paranoid (or, one might say, realistic) that they refuse to throw scripts away in the office trash cans. They will actually carry the older versions home to dispose of them securely.

Jim's hopes and dreams for the story aside, I knew my first stop on the pitch circuit had to be 48. It's bad office politics to send a story outside before you've made the rounds with it internally. And although I don't mind rocking the boat when I need to, I try not to create waves unnecessarily.

In 2019, Susan Zirinsky had been tapped as the president of CBS News and was no longer the executive producer at 48. When Judy Tygard was named her successor, I hoped my previous hijinks wouldn't come back to haunt me. Since getting crossways with Judy early in my career, I had mostly tried to correct my course. She was a veteran of the program and an extremely well-respected senior producer. I could understand why she'd been hard on me in the past, and I'd come to admire her. While I couldn't relate to it, I respected that Judy was a straight arrow, through and through. And that's exactly why I was fretting about how to pitch this unconventional story to her.

I looked for any serial killer stories that 48 had covered in the past and tried to find something familiar that I could use as a building block for my Samuel Little pitch. I came up empty, making me even more fatalistic about my chances.

Nevertheless, I put together the most compelling 48-esque bluesheet that I could on Samuel Little. Our episodes typically focused on the victims' families and law enforcement. I had the lawman box checked, and I knew with ninety-three victims that I could find a family or two to represent that side of the story. The politically correct term we use to describe palatable victims is "sympathetic." This is code for non–drug users from middle-class to upper-class backgrounds. With Little preying primarily on prostitutes, I knew this was my biggest challenge for 48 sensibilities.

For me, looking at the sketches of Jane Doe victims was haunting. There had been ninety-three lives ended and countless others deeply affected and changed forever, all because of the actions of one man. Years later, I'd still be able to see the images in my mind, sometimes unbidden. The names and details scrawled next to the portraits come back to me when someone mentions a place where Little preyed on victims, like Tupelo, Mississippi. And if I'm driving over swamplands, I'll steal a glance at the murky water and look for a hand or a dirty mop of hair. Many of Little's victims have never been found.

Jim told me about several of Little's victims who had worked in traditional settings, including a schoolteacher and a nurse. My best chance to win Judy over would be to highlight these "sympathetic" victims who could be "the girl next door," to use another tried-and-true 48 formula. Normally, I would need to go through my immediate supervisor before pitching a story directly to the executive producer. But it was the dead of summer, and my boss, Nancy Kramer, was in the middle of a three-week vacation.

I was torn. If I waited for her to return, I knew I'd miss the window of opportunity for Jim's exclusive. But if I pinged Kramer on vacation for her opinion, she'd almost certainly shoot it down. Getting the green light from her is hard enough under normal circumstances; double it for vacation mode. And if she gave the story the axe, I'd really be in trouble if I went against her and sent it up the chain to Judy anyway. What's a renegade field producer to do? I reasoned that I had to go straight to the top. At least I'd know I took my shot.

I bit my lip and fired off an email to Judy Tygard with my Samuel Little bluesheet attached. I laid out everything I could think of to make it compelling for her, including the exclusive announcement with the FBI and Texas Ranger James Holland's first-ever interview. One of the oldest news values in the book is timeliness, and this story had a ticking clock. Judy recognized the urgency and told me she would review the pitch overnight and give me a call in the morning. I was grateful she was giving it her full consideration, especially considering everything else she had on her executive producer plate.

I'm an eternal optimist, and I always think every story I pitch is going to get greenlit. Why else would I put in the work? But with this one, I was questioning myself the whole time, and when Judy called me before 8 AM the next day, I had a feeling it wasn't going to be good news. I picked up the phone and stepped out on our back patio so my son's cartoons wouldn't be playing in the background. Judy let me down nice and easy, complimenting the thoroughness of the pitch and the unique opportunity but passing on the story nonetheless.

"It's just not the right story for 48."

I knew there was no point in trying to convince her otherwise. It was clear her mind was made up and she was giving me a call to share the news, not debate the merits. Lesson learned, I put my finger to my lips to physically stop myself from arguing with her. The Samuel Little story wasn't going to be on *48 Hours*, but maybe it could still find a home somewhere on CBS. The next pitch was where I should channel my efforts now, not attempting to resurrect the one that just got buried.

I wanted to start writing my *60* pitch right away, but it would have to wait. I looked at the clock and realized if I didn't leave now, I might miss opening arguments. My grace period from covering the McDowell trial had come and gone, and I was due in court on a new case: the capital murder-for-hire trial of Chacey Poynter.

I'm driving to the Hunt County Courthouse on a blistering summer morning. It's already ninety degrees out, and the sun has barely made it over the horizon. My ten-year-old Toyota Corolla is like a tin can, and the A/C is whizzing with effort. I call Jim Holland from the road to give him the bad news. Ever the investigator, he can tell right away that something is wrong based on my voice inflection. When I tell him that *48* passed on the story, he almost sounds relieved.

"Gosh, Claire, I thought somebody died. Chin up. There's still *60 Minutes*." I shake my head and let out an exasperated sigh.

"I'm going to try to get an introduction at *60*, but I don't know a soul over there. Just getting in the door is going to be a long shot."

Jim tells me not to sweat it, and then turns up the heat by saying he's also talking to a producer at NBC.

"Promise me you won't agree to an exclusive with NBC before talking to me again," I plead as I punch the gas and push my tin can to its upper limit.

Chacey Poynter looked like she had it all: an adorable daughter, a doting husband, and a spacious house in the country. She was just twenty-two when she married Bob Poynter, a burly firefighter almost twice her age. It was his second marriage, and even though he already had a pair of adult daughters, he was delighted to welcome a new baby with Chacey.

The trappings of their happily married life, however, were just a mirage. Chacey had been seeing other men on the side while her husband worked two-day shifts as a fire captain in a Dallas suburb. Chacey, a dental hygienist, went online to find dates while her husband was working, and it wasn't long before she had fallen in love with a truck driver named Michael Garza.

The two carried on a torrid affair, brazenly meeting for sex at Chacey and Bob's own home, always after her baby had gone to sleep. Chacey told Michael that she and Bob were getting divorced, and that he was physically and emotionally abusive. Still, she worried that his connections as a fireman would give him the upper hand in the divorce, possibly even allowing him to gain custody of their child.

By September 2016, Chacey and Michael were dreaming of a life together and planning ways to get Bob out of the picture—for good. In a series of texts just days before Bob's murder, Chacey wrote to Michael, "I do love you and I'm grateful to have you in my life. I can't wait to get this behind us and see how great life can be."

Chacey went on to say, "I've made my decision . . . I'm just scared you will look at me different."

Michael responded, "It won't be any different . . . I will take care of him."

According to authorities, on September 9, 2016, Chacey was playing two roles: affectionate girlfriend to Garza—and estranged wife of Bob, looking to reconcile. After arranging a babysitter, Chacey sent Bob a hopeful text: "I think we will get through this, but I do want to talk."

Bob quickly responded, "Okay baby, me too."

The loving texts continued for hours, with Chacey eventually suggesting that they meet for tacos around 10 PM. But they'd never make it to the restaurant. After taking a dirt road "shortcut," Chacey told Bob she'd gotten stuck in the mud. A dedicated first responder, Bob rushed to her aid. Little did he know, he was walking into an ambush.

Police say Michael Garza was lying in wait with a camo hunting rifle and took aim as Bob arrived on the scene to help his wife. He was shot once in the head and died instantly. But the story doesn't end there. Chacey told police that she never expected Michael to kill Bob. She only wanted him to scare her husband. It was Michael, she claimed, who took it a step further and showed up to the meeting with a gun.

Chacey said she tried to call 911, but Michael grabbed her cell phone and threw it in the mud. Frantic, Chacey ran into the street and waved down cars until someone finally stopped. She tried to tell police about the misunderstanding, but all they heard was a cheating wife, a jealous boyfriend, and a lure for murder. Chacey was taken into custody at the scene, and her boyfriend Michael Garza was arrested two days later.

Michael went on trial in 2018 and was found guilty and sentenced to life in prison. Now it was Chacey's turn to face a jury of her peers.

I'd been following the case ever since the night of the murder in 2016. It was initially reported as a roadside shooting, and there was speculation that it could be a random act of violence or an extreme case of road rage. But after taking Chacey into custody at the scene, it didn't take long for the Royse City Police Department to put the pieces of the murderous puzzle together.

While the investigation had been swift, the journey to trial took nearly three years. The district attorney ultimately decided to waive the death penalty, so Chacey would either go free or be automatically sentenced to life in prison. There was no in-between.

Chacey's trial marked just the fourth time I'd covered an alleged femme fatale. The vast majority of murders are committed by men, and so the minority cases are all the more intriguing to a journalist.

I tried to size up Chacey from my position in the courtroom gallery. Dressed conservatively, with light-brown hair and a deferential demeanor, Chacey looked almost nothing like the woman who had called 911 from the scene of her husband's murder.

Back then, Chacey was a blonde bombshell, sporting Daisy Duke cutoff shorts, a T-shirt, and a ponytail. She was tan and lean like a summer camp counselor, with the energy to match. In court, Chacey looked more like a school librarian. Wearing a cardigan, she kept her head down and occasionally tucked her light-brown hair behind her ear as she whispered to her defense attorney.

Because I'd popped in to Michael Garza's trial in 2018, I had a pretty good preview of what would be revealed in Chacey's case. The lurid messages between the secret lovers amounted to a text-by-text plan for murder, geolocated to the scene with cell phone towers. In my mind, it really wasn't a question of if Chacey was guilty, but how guilty?

Her defense team was working hard to get lesser charges included in the jury instructions. This is a common—and often effective—strategy for shrewd attorneys who know their client has the deck stacked against them. Given the evidence, they understand that a jury, especially a Texas one, will want to find the defendant guilty of *something*. And if they are given more options than just capital murder, it increases the odds of a lesser conviction. Manslaughter, negligent homicide, and even aggravated assault are all options that I've seen defense attorneys successfully add to a jury charge.

While my body was in court covering a murder-for-hire trial for *48 Hours*, my mind was humming on how to get a serial killer story on *60 Minutes*. I racked my brain for any connections I could leverage at the show. But all I'd ever heard from *48* was how much *60* producers turned their noses up at true crime.

Correspondent Maureen Maher shared that she once had a conversation with Jeff Fager, then the executive producer at *60*, in his Manhattan office. Jeff had the audacity to tell Maureen, a seasoned investigative journalist, that she "couldn't handle *60*." It was a comment Maureen repeated often and with as much amusement as skepticism.

Having worked with correspondents on both shows, I can attest to the fact that Maureen would more than hold her own at *60*. But that kind of exclusionary attitude comes standard in network news. Media is the only industry experience I have, so I can't say if this kind of hubris is true of other workplaces. To give you an idea of the egos in national TV, consider the fact that the two most common analogies at CBS were to brain surgery and rocket science, and it wasn't presented with any irony.

Producing television, managing characters, and writing scripts were frequently compared to operating rooms and mission control. This is how seriously TV people take themselves. When I was working in newspapers, magazines, and digital media, I never heard these kinds of comments. Print journalists actually look down on TV, calling it "the dark side" and "the lowest form of the medium." I think there's a bit of jealousy behind those insults, especially because television has bigger budgets and audiences than print. Personally, I'm a fan of both. I appreciate the art form of television as well as the purity of the written word.

While I was closest to the correspondents at *48*, I didn't think any of them could help me get a foot in the door at *60*. Maureen's experience with Jeff Fager wasn't exactly encouraging. So I branched out in two directions that I thought had the most promise.

First, I fired off a text to Chuck "Hollywood" Stevenson. He was the most well-connected producer I knew at CBS, and I figured if anyone at *48* had intel on *60*, it would be Chuck. Next, I reached out to national correspondent Omar Villafranca, who was based in Dallas. We were friendly and had worked together on a few mass shooting stories in Florida, as one does.

The Parkland school shooting was actually the second time in as many years that I was dispatched to the Sunshine State to cover a mass casualty event for CBS. In January 2017, there was a shooting at the Fort Lauderdale Airport that killed five people. *48 Hours* was interested in the story when they thought it was a terrorist attack, but when it turned out to be just your garden-variety lone-wolf shooting, they pulled me off the story.

I was there for a hot minute, maybe two days. While working with Omar on pieces for the morning and evening news, I briefly spoke with Governor Rick Scott. I probably wouldn't have remembered the meeting, if not for a bizarre piece of mail that turned up the following week. It was a handwritten note alleged to be from Governor Scott, thanking me for visiting Florida and wishing me the best on my future travels. The fact that I was there for a mass shooting, and not a vacation, didn't appear to register for him.

Chuck got back to me right away, calling me on my cell while I was filming B-roll for the Chacey Poynter episode of *48 Hours*. Crouching in some bushes so I wouldn't end up on camera, I took the call alongside the dirt road where Bob Poynter had been murdered.

"*60 Minutes*, huh?" Chuck said with all the intrigue in the world. "What kind of story are you trying to pitch them?"

I gave him the short version, leading with the fact that Judy had passed on the story for *48*. Chuck told me there was a top player at *60* who had started her career at *48*: Tanya Simon, who was now the number two at *60* as the executive editor under executive producer Bill Owens. Her father, Bob Simon, had been a legendary *60* correspondent up until his tragic death in a car accident in 2015.

Tanya left *48* in 2000, well before my time at the show, so we didn't have a real connection. But maybe she would be more open to hearing a pitch from a *48* producer than other *60* brass. I thanked Chuck and filed away the information for later use. Then I ducked back onto the main road to pick up where I left off on the B-roll shoot for Poynter.

The detective who'd interrogated Chacey had just arrived at the scene, and I jumped in the car with him. I was juggling multiple murder stories, and I hoped I could keep the details straight. Pushing thoughts of serial killers and Texas Rangers out of my mind for the moment, I turned to the detective and asked him to tell me about the night he met Chacey Poynter.

The TV world runs on a seasonal schedule, with new episodes coming out in the fall and reruns airing all summer. There are exceptions to this, and sometimes the network will order a "summer six-pack" of new *48* episodes. But most of the time, producers spend the summer stockpiling stories for the fall. It's a great time for "evergreen episodes," cases that can air any time because they've either already been adjudicated or are unsolved.

Even though the Chacey Poynter trial was in June, her case didn't check any of the summer boxes and worst of all, it was now competitive. The summer is especially problematic for competitive stories because you can't beat another network to air unless you are willing to change your season premiere. And even then, you are at the mercy of network schedules.

NBC's *Dateline* had sent two producers to the Hunt County Courthouse, and they were peacocking all over town. I gave senior producer Anthony Batson a heads-up that we were no longer alone on the story. He agreed to send me backup so we could work the courtroom and the hallway during the trial. If *Dateline* had two producers on the ground, so would we.

In theory, this sounded like a good thing, and I was already imagining what it would be like to have someone to split booking duties with and bounce ideas off of during breaks. What I hadn't counted on was that the producer they sent didn't actually want the story to succeed.

Ten years my senior, this producer, who I'll call Brenda, was hell-bent on killing the Poynter story. I'd been paired with Brenda before, and she always seemed to find some reason to get the story I was working on scrapped. Back then, I hadn't realized her whole game plan was to fail. She was one of those producers who had built a successful career on killing stories, and it would have been impressive if it wasn't so maddening.

Brenda's goal was to spend as much time as possible researching stories from the comfort of her own home. After literal years of this "research," she'd go on one or two field trips and return home with a slew of reasons why the story was unworkable for CBS.

More than once, Brenda had even fooled me with these little field trips to Texas, but I was not about to let her get away with it again. I had spent years nursing the Poynter story along, checking in with the victim's family and wining and dining the attorneys. If Brenda wanted to waste her own time, that was fine by me. But I drew the line at wasting mine.

How to play it, though? I knew Brenda wasn't going to suddenly grow a conscience and a work ethic. It occurred to me that I had to find a way to beat her at her own game. The sooner she thought the story was dead, the sooner she'd go home, and I could actually get back to work.

There's a saying in true crime television for when a story is too big to fail. It's called "interviewing the janitor," and it means that no matter who you have to interview to tell the story, you aren't walking away from it.

Crime cases that captivate the public interest and have compelling plot points simply won't be abandoned no matter the booking obstacles. A modern-day example is Gabby Petito, the social media–savvy Gen Z who went missing in the summer of 2021 while documenting a cross-country road trip with her boyfriend. Historic cases include Laci Peterson, Caylee Anthony, and JonBenét Ramsey. All three networks cover stories when they're that big, with cable shows piling on for years, even decades, afterward.

For all my faith in the Chacey Poynter case, I knew it wasn't a landmark crime story. If we didn't have the bookings, CBS would be willing to walk away from it. They wouldn't go after the janitor on this one. I had to deliver the principal voice, and in this case, that meant Chacey herself.

Getting suspected killers to go on camera was becoming something of my specialty, but this case presented some novel challenges. For starters, I was going to have to work my magic behind Brenda's back. If she caught wind of my plan to bulletproof the story, Brenda would stop at nothing to drop a bomb on it. I knew the safest course of action was to keep Brenda far away from my real target, and so I came up with as many tasks as I could that I "needed her help with." They all involved copious amounts of writing, which served the dual purpose of keeping her busy and satisfying New York's need for constant information from the ground.

While she typed up "pros and cons" lists of the story's merits, I was camped out in the defense attorney's office, bending their ear on why Chacey was their best witness. Most of the defendants who agree to an interview are not on great terms with their attorneys. But Chacey was in lockstep with hers, which meant I had to be, too. Playing to their egos, I filmed with them as much as possible. Getting little bits of business in their office, walking to and from the courtroom, you name it. I had no idea how much of it would actually end up in the episode, but it gave me a reason to be in their orbit. Plus, I was literally blocking *Dateline* producers from coming through the door.

The week was winding down, and Brenda was itching to get back home. She'd stayed glued to her computer and was fully convinced that she'd sunk the story with her keystrokes. Hey, it'd worked before. I was counting down the hours until I could send her on her merry way to the airport. She'd made no secret of the fact that she thought the story was a lost cause, and that we'd get beat to air by *Dateline*. I pretended to agree with her. "Can't win 'em all," I said with a sly grin on my face as I bid her adieu during the lunch recess, praising her wisdom for getting on the road early to beat the Friday traffic.

With Brenda's dust disappearing over the horizon, I drove straight to the Hunt County jail. Moments like this were so professionally fulfilling that they almost made me forget the tragic circumstances that made the story possible.

I'm face-to-face with Chacey Poynter. She's sitting in a small plastic chair just inches from me as I apply a makeup sponge to her face. It's a new role for me to play, makeup artist for an alleged murderer, but I'm not complaining. The novelty of it all is actually pretty entertaining.

Normally, we'd have a professional makeup artist, but this interview came together so quickly that we didn't have time to find one. And our request to have Chacey uncuffed was denied, so she's stuck with me, a woman who wears makeup so infrequently that I can't remember the last time I bought any that wasn't for an accused killer.

I peel the plastic wrapper off a new mascara wand and go to town on her lashes.

I wonder how she's going to get this gunk off her face when she goes back to her cell?

"Do you have any other lipstick?" a man's voice says from the dark void behind us. It's one of her attorneys, weighing in on the optics. I riffle through my stage makeup bag and produce a fresh tube.

The day I added "makeup artist" to my resume.

I notice there's a growing crowd in the background. The sheriff has apparently invited his entire staff to watch our interview. They all stand guard around the perimeter of the room, in full uniform with weapons at the ready, as I trace the outline of Chacey's lips. This is one weird day at the office.

I smile and apologize for the slow pace. "Sorry, I'm not used to putting makeup on someone else," I tell her.

"Except for that one time in college, right, Claire?" correspondent Peter Van Sant says with perfect comedic timing.

The deputies burst out laughing as Chacey and I are left speechless. Most people don't know that before Peter started working in television, he was a stand-up comedian. The instinct to crack a joke has never left him.

I take a breath and steady myself before getting up and handing Chacey a mirror. She nods her approval and softly whispers, "Thank you."

Peter takes his position in the interviewer chair, and I pull on my producer headset. I glance at my watch. It's almost 7 PM. Time to make TV magic from behind bars.

Our *48 Hours* exclusive interview with Chacey Poynter is the talk of the town, and we got it on camera just in time. Despite her defense attorney's best efforts, Chacey was found guilty of murder and sentenced to life in prison. She was shipped off to prison a few days later, where she would be lost to the inmate intake process for the next two months and unavailable for any media visits.

When NBC found out Chacey had talked to us, *Dateline* producers camped out in the lobby of the defense attorney's office for an entire day. Their secretary finally chased them out onto the curb, where they stood under the awning for another hour, eventually succumbing to the Texas heat and leaving their business cards wedged in the doorframe.

"NBC finally left!" came the text from the defense around 4 PM.

"Wanna grab a celebratory drink?" I replied.

Soon after, we were toasting our success at the wine bar down the street.

Never mind that their client was headed to prison; our on-camera victory still tasted sweet. And as much as I wanted to savor it a bit longer, I knew it was time to move on to the next story.

I had put off Ranger Holland as long as I could on the Samuel Little exclusive, and his August deadline was looming. My success with Chacey Poynter would buy me a few days, reprieve from *48*, and I would need every minute of it.

I spent the next week revising my pitch for *60 Minutes*, and by the end of it, the bluesheet I had written for *48* was almost unrecognizable. Instead of a story on unknown serial killer Samuel Little and his many victims, I was now pitching a profile on an equally elusive figure: Texas Ranger James Holland. Who was this skilled investigator? How did he get a hardened criminal to confess to murder? And why should we believe a career con man like Little? The story was really taking shape, and I could see scenes and sound bites in my head. But I still couldn't get anyone at CBS to pay attention to the story.

I'd sent my revised pitch to Tanya Simon after getting her email address from Hollywood Chuck. But it was like shouting into the void. Days passed and I'd heard nothing. In addition to getting shot down by Judy Tygard at *48*, I'd also been rejected by senior producers at the morning and evening news by way of correspondent Omar Villafranca. He was interested in the story when I pitched it to him, but we couldn't move it up the chain.

I thought maybe if I could get a segment on the daily news about Little, then the pitch to *60* might not seem so far out of left field. Instead, all I had managed to do was strike out with every show at the network. Plus, my boss had come back from vacation. Suffice it to say Kramer was not happy to hear I'd been running around pitching a rejected true crime story virtually nonstop in her absence.

It had been a painful month of trial and error. All signs told me that no one at CBS wanted the story, but I couldn't shake the feeling that it was going to make headlines when it broke. My instinct for news was the only thing keeping me going, but it was enough.

I had a trip to New York for the Poynter story coming up. We were interviewing the victim's family at the CBS Broadcast Center. I've pitched my fair share of stories through email and over the phone, but there's nothing I enjoy more than selling face-to-face. And getting a story greenlit is definitely a sales job.

After the Peace Corps, I spent six months freelance writing before landing a full-time position as a local newspaper reporter. One of my favorite gigs was ghostwriting for a Dallas entrepreneur named Tony Hartl. At the time, he was revising the manuscript for his business book *Selling Sunshine: 75 Tips, Tools, and Tactics for Becoming a Wildly Successful Entrepreneur.*

When we met, he'd just gotten first-draft notes from his publisher and was starting on the revisions. I dove into the process with him, reading his manuscript cover to cover multiple times and coming away with newfound knowledge in sales to complement my writing degree. A deadly combination, as it turns out, for a true crime producer.

It's July 2019, and I'm sitting on a metal stadium seat. It's a small row, only three chairs, and I have it all to myself. I'm not at a baseball game. I'm in Midtown Manhattan, waiting outside CBS News president Susan Zirinsky's office.

The green stadium seats are one of the many pieces of history that she accumulated during her legendary news career. Siding from an FDNY truck that responded to 9/11. Memorabilia from the uprising in Tiananmen Square. Photos with presidents Carter, Reagan, Bush, and Clinton. Rumor has it this particular stretch of seats was salvaged from a remodel at Yankee Stadium, and now they welcome visitors to Z's home base. Batter up.

As soon as I knew my dates for the Poynter interview, I called Z's assistant to see if she could squeeze me in on the calendar. Even though Z had been my boss for five years, I realized that getting face time now that she was president was asking a lot. But I wasn't just stopping by to say hello. I had a story to pitch, a big one, and I needed her advice now more than ever.

Twenty minutes later, I'm called on deck. Z's still on the phone, but she waves me in, and I trade my metal stadium seat for a plush upholstered one opposite her desk. She's talking fast and has her headset on. She winks at me as she continues the conversation.

It's been a whirlwind month for Z, but that's the only way she knows how to live. She recently moved Norah O'Donnell into the CBS *Evening News* anchor chair, replacing Jeff Glor. Glor had been Scott Pelley's unconventional replacement under former CBS News president David Rhodes. Glor had spent less than two years as the top anchor when Z made the switch. It was a bold move but not entirely unexpected. Glor was in his early forties and underperforming. There was buzz around the network that Rhodes moved him into prime time before he was ready.

In many ways, Norah O'Donnell was Glor's contemporary but with a more impressive resume. She'd been chief White House correspondent and was the co-anchor of *CBS This Morning* when she was tapped for the coveted evening time slot. But Z wasn't done shaking things up. She was trying to find a way to keep Glor, a rising talent in the prime of his career, at CBS. He'd recently joined the Saturday morning co-anchor team, alongside Dana Jacobson and Michelle Miller, and was rating well.

The move was a true testament to Z's people skills. She could fire the guy one day, rehire him the next, and somehow still keep the CBS News family together. I glanced down at her desk. It was the same one she'd had at *48 Hours*, and my eyes were drawn to a glass globe on a small pedestal. The engraving read "Z's Beat." Highest praise for the hardest-working journalist in the game. There was never a story outside of Z's reach. Politics, war, terrorism, murder. Nothing was off-limits for Z. And that was exactly what I was counting on.

She takes off her headset and comes around to the other side of the desk to give me a hug.

"Madame President," I say with a deferential bow of my head.

"Please." She laughs. "Can you believe it?"

"Yes," I reply immediately.

Then I go into my pitch. One of the things I love about Z is how there's no need for small talk.

"I have a killer story for the network, and I'm trying to find the right home for it."

I give her my latest version of the pitch with Texas Ranger James Holland at the forefront.

She listens intently, and her eyes get big when I mentioned Holland's television exclusive would be coordinated with the FBI, Department of Justice, and Texas Rangers naming Samuel Little as the country's most prolific serial killer to date.

Seeing my opening, I go for broke.

"If CBS doesn't bite, somebody else will, and I know Holland's already talking to NBC."

Z is pensive for a moment, and then she asks why I thought Judy Tygard passed on it for *48*.

I tell her it was a combination of concerns, likely stemming from the fact that most of Little's victims were prostitutes, and the story was thirty-plus years in the making.

"It's a lot of ground to cover in an hour if you tell the story as a traditional 48," I say. "But if it's a profile of Holland, suddenly it takes a different shape. I know it sounds crazy, but I think it should be on 60 Minutes."

I explain that I tried pitching it to Tanya Simon, and that I also ran it through the senior producers at the morning and evening news, but no one seemed interested. Z smiles. She respects the hustle.

"Sometimes, people don't see the light until it's too late," she says sympathetically.

60 Minutes was virtually the only place at CBS that Z had never worked. Before she was tapped for the presidency, there were rumors she might replace embattled executive producer Jeff Fager, but it never came to pass.

Until he was ousted in late 2018, Fager had been a legend at 60, known for a brash personality of his own as well as his ability to manage the program's notoriously difficult on-air talent. Ronan Farrow's scathing reporting for the New Yorker on allegations of sexual misconduct and harassment at CBS blew the lid off the boys' club.[11] Farrow quoted over a dozen company sources who named Fager, along with former CBS CEO Les Moonves, as complicit in the behavior. Still, Fager might have survived the scandal if not for what happened next.

He sent a thinly veiled threat in a text to CBS correspondent Jericka Duncan, who was reporting on the New Yorker story for the Evening News.[12] Duncan boldly read his words live on the air, holding her cell phone.

"Be careful, there are people who lost their jobs trying to harm me, and if you pass on these damaging claims without your own reporting to back them up, that will become a serious problem."

Fager lost his job, and Duncan became a legend of her own that night.

---

11 Ronan Farrow, "From Aggressive Overtures to Sexual Assault: Harvey Weinstein's accusers tell their stories," New Yorker, October 10, 2017, https://www.newyorker.com/news/news-desk/from-aggressive-overtures-to-sexual-assault-harvey-weinsteins-accusers-tell-their-stories.

12 CBS Evening News, "Fired '60 Minutes' boss Jeff Fager warned CBS News reporter: 'There are people who've lost their jobs trying to harm me,'" aired September 12, 2018, , CBS, https://www.cbsnews.com/news/fired-60-minutes-boss-jeff-fager-warned-cbs-news-reporter-there-are-people-whove-lost-their-jobs-trying-to-harm-me/.

The shake-up at *60* meant the executive producer slot was open for only the second time in the show's history. Bill Owens, Fager's number two, was immediately named interim EP to allow the show to go on as scheduled. Still, most people believed a bigger change was on the horizon, and Z's name was publicly floated as a potential replacement. But just three months later, Z was named CBS News president, ending the *60* rumors once and for all.

Now the job was Z's to fill, and she didn't take the task lightly. She agonized over it for weeks, and the staff at *60* started to get restless. Word got back to Z, and she decided on a whim to head across the street and reassure the troops in person. It was a total Z move. And in typical fashion, she hadn't stopped to look in the mirror first. As it turned out, she was wearing a sweater that said "Time's Up." It had been a gift from a colleague that morning, and Z had put it on as a show of solidarity.

But as Z now recalls to me, it was probably not the most comforting sight for the staff at *60 Minutes*.

"They're not so big on change over there."

In the end, sweater notwithstanding, Z left Bill Owens at the helm, officially naming him as executive producer in February 2019. And that was the last time she'd stepped foot on *60* soil. She was the president of the network, but her sway wasn't on the editorial side of things. Still, she liked my pitch and told me she thought it had a chance at *60*. But it would be up to me to find my own way in the door.

August is a brutal time to live in Texas. The summer usually starts out innocently enough, with leftover spring rain spilling into June, leaving the ground green and dewy. But by August, the sun is baked into every surface of the state. From tree bark to concrete, heat radiates outward and zaps the life out of you. Anyone who can afford to flee Texas in July and August does, but I'm not one of them.

I'd spent my summer pitching the hell out of the Samuel Little story and getting rejected at every turn. Ranger Holland was growing impatient, and his self-imposed deadline to release the news with the FBI in August was weighing heavy on me. I worked at a top true crime show. I knew the president of the network, and yet I couldn't get an exclusive story on the air. I had taken my pitch to anyone at CBS who would listen—and several people who wouldn't. And I'd gotten nowhere. I was finally taking a break.

My son and I both have August birthdays, and it's my tradition to take the week off to celebrate enough for two. He was turning four and obsessed with Spider-Man, so our house was covered in streamers, webs, and lots of red and blue balloons. My family was in town, and we had a full house. Normally, I wouldn't take a work call in a situation like this. But I saw Susan Zirinsky's name coming across the screen, and I couldn't resist.

I stepped away from the living room and tiptoed into the first empty space I saw: my son's playroom. I don't know if you've ever been chewed out on your birthday by one of your personal heroes in front of an audience of stuffed animals, but I wouldn't recommend it.

To this day, I'm not exactly sure why the story tide turned against me, but it was clear Z was no longer on Team Serial Killer. I'm no stranger to getting reamed out by bosses for going rogue in pursuit of a story. It's basically how I've built my whole career. But this one really stung. If I had to guess, I think Z's about-face on the whole story was likely influenced by Kramer coming back from vacation and going on the warpath against me. I knew it was a risk when I pitched the story behind her back, but I didn't really have a choice. The story wasn't going to wait around for Kramer to get back to the office.

I'd gone all out that summer, using my weekends and holidays to search for a way into the story. And I still had nothing to show for it. Worst of all, I was now apparently in the doghouse over it with the president of the network, who had definitely been talking to my boss. Was I about to get fired over a story that wouldn't even run?

With the onslaught in full swing, I'd crumpled down to the floor and realized I was sitting in the corner. Fitting. I was tempted to pull the phone away from my ear and let the criticism rain down on someone else, but I was worried my party guests would hear it. So I kept the receiver glued to my head and waited for it to end. It felt like forever. "Do you not have enough work to do at 48 that you need to go looking elsewhere for stories?" she asked rhetorically, and I wondered if Kramer was in her office, listening in on the call. The last thing Z said to me was "Remember who you work for."

I wanted to hang up the phone right then, but I figured it was as good a time as any to turn on my Texas manners. "Yes, ma'am," I said, wincing.

The rest of birthday week hardly felt like a celebration, and I spent more time worriedly checking job listings than doing anything that resembled a vacation. When I returned to work the following Monday, I knew I was under a microscope, and Kramer was lowering the magnifying glass.

If I had all this time to pitch a serial killer story no one wanted, then I must be slacking off at my actual job. In truth, I'd been burning the candle at both ends once again to keep up with my regular duties and my newfound passion project, and now I was just burned out. But the way Kramer saw it, I had months of work to make up for, and she was going to get back every minute.

For whatever reason, she fixated on sending me to San Antonio to develop a murder case that was set for trial in October. I couldn't have been less interested in this idea. I saw it as a punitive assignment, banishing me to sweltering San Antonio, months ahead of the actual trial, just to keep me busy and out of reach on the Texas Ranger story.

To get Kramer off my back, I called and sent emails to the attorneys on the case and wrote up a half-hearted update to my original bluesheet. Ironically, this had been one of my favorite story pitches years ago, when the case was still classified as an undetermined death.

In the fall of 2017, Cayley Mandadi was a college cheerleader at Trinity University in San Antonio. Her boyfriend, Mark Howerton, had brought her unconscious to a rural hospital and claimed she'd fallen asleep after sex on a road trip, and he couldn't wake her up. But an X-ray showed a brain injury, and her low body temperature indicated a much different timeline of events than Mark was telling authorities.

I'd been tipped off to the case by my brother-in-law, a Trinity University alum who told me the details over Thanksgiving dinner. The life of a true crime producer. You're always gathering intel.

The case had worked its way through the court system for two years, and now Mark was facing trial for Cayley's murder and kidnapping. It was a sensational story, but I didn't have anything pressing to do about it in the middle of August, two months before the trial was set to begin. Still, I knew better than to tell Kramer that. I kept my head down, sent in plenty of notes about the story, answered my phone every time she called, and generally tried to sound very enthusiastic about relocating to San Antonio.

After a week of this charade, I knew I couldn't avoid a trip to the Alamo much longer without arousing suspicion. I still hadn't told Ranger Holland that I was in deep trouble with the story and closer to getting fired over it than I was to getting it on the air. I was sending his calls to voicemail and trying to buy more time with every text. I knew he sensed something was up, and I finally had to confess.

"I've tried everything I can to pitch this story, and nothing is working. In fact, a lot of it is backfiring. I feel like I'm banging my head into a wall, and I don't know what else to do. I'm really sorry. I know it's a great story, and for the life of me I can't understand why CBS doesn't want it. But they've made it very clear to me that they do not."

Holland was kind and understanding.

"You have nothing to be sorry for. Sometimes bosses are just like that. I'm sure you tried everything you could."

As I hung up the phone, those words were ringing in my ears. Had I really tried everything? Was there any play left on the board? Even though it was one hundred degrees outside, I laced up my running shoes and took off down the street. If I couldn't come up with a final move by the end of my five-mile loop, I'd accept defeat and head to San Antonio.

I'm pacing in front of my computer, going back over the email I've crafted line by line. It's a bold move to continue pitching a story that no one wants after getting chewed out by the president of CBS News, but I'm hoping it's the right one. Z had told me to remember who I worked for, and I couldn't forget it. I worked for CBS News. One of the biggest media companies in the country. A place where an exclusive story with national appeal should trump any office politics. It shouldn't matter that I was a field producer from Texas. I had a scoop on a story the whole world would want to hear. I wasn't letting it go without giving it one last play. And it was a Hail Mary.

After my run, I realized there was exactly one person who could still save the day. One person who conceivably hadn't heard my pitch yet, and who actually had the power to greenlight the story: *60 Minutes* executive producer Bill Owens. I didn't have an introduction to him, so I looked up his email in the company directory. I'm nothing if not resourceful. I'd have to remember that line when updating my resume after my inevitable firing.

I type in his email address and delete it at least three times before hitting send with my eyes closed. If he hates the story and tells Z or anyone at *48* that I pitched it to him at this stage, I'm toast. And everyone else I sent the pitch to has either rejected it or ignored it completely. Some would say the odds are against me, but I actually convince myself that all this adversity has made the story stronger. It's now the best possible pitch I could have written, having been revised a half dozen times due to unilateral rejection.

I'm still pacing in front of my desk, giving myself this pep talk when I notice I have a new email. Bill Owens wrote me back in ten minutes flat. Like a swift jury verdict for the prosecution, I'm convinced it's going to be good news. But the reply is ominous. He's given me his direct line and instructed me to call him.

I'm sweating bullets, and it has nothing to do with the Texas heat. I take a deep breath and dial. It's all come down to this: Someone I've never even met will make or break me. *Why did I put myself in this position? Why can't I just have a normal career and do the stories my bosses want me to?*

A woman answers on the second ring, and I introduce myself.

"Bill Owens told me to call him at this number."

She patches me right through. The first words out of Owens's mouth aren't hello or any other pleasantries.

"Judy Tygard is going to kill you."

I laugh out loud because it's too true. At least I did everything I could for the story. And when it ends up making headlines for NBC, everyone at CBS will know they had their chance and passed on it. I'm so lost in my own thoughts that I don't realize that Owens is still talking. And he's not mad.

"This pitch reads like a Sunday feature in the *Times*. It's an incredible story."

I allow myself a few moments of silent, pantomimed celebration before I thank him.

Owens is particularly taken with Little's portraits of his victims, which were sketched in colored pencil.

Compliments aside, Owens now asks the million-dollar question: "Why aren't you doing this story for *48?*"

I hadn't anticipated this, and I'm kicking myself because it's so obvious. I know I can't tell him the truth: that *48* had passed on the story, along with every other news program on CBS. I improvise an explanation, a white lie I'm praying he'll believe. "It's too good for *48.* I had to bring it to *60.*"

I can practically hear him grinning over the phone, and the next words out of his mouth seal the deal: "Do you want to tell your boss at *48* or do you want me to call her?"

I tell Owens I'll talk to *48* and thank him for the offer.

The rest of the conversation is a bit of a blur, but I know Owens wants the story. Before we hang up, he tells me he's going to loop in executive editor Tanya Simon and find a producer and correspondent who I can work with at *60.*

It's a surreal moment, and I know just how to celebrate it. I open my sliding glass door and cannonball into the pool.

17

GETTING AWAY WITH MURDER

It's been a little over twenty-four hours since I apologized to Holland for failing to get his story greenlit at CBS. And I can't wait to call him back and rescind it.

"Remember how I told you I'd done everything I could think of for the story? Well, I thought of something else."

I tell him how I'd pitched the story directly to the top, and because he didn't need anyone else's approval, Bill Owens had greenlit production on the spot. We were officially on the schedule for *60 Minutes*.

Holland is ecstatic—and a bit in disbelief himself.

"This probably isn't the right expression, but I'm just gonna say it anyway. That took some pretty big balls."

I laugh at the absurdity of the phrase but appreciated the sentiment nonetheless. Dudes.

I was elated, and I felt I'd earned a little time to celebrate after everything I'd been through. But I knew I couldn't sit around and bask in my victory just

The *60 Minutes* team sets up Texas Ranger Jim Holland's camera for his interview with serial killer Samuel Little.

yet. Now that I got the pitch approved, I had to deliver the story for *60*. And somehow still do my job at *48*.

I couldn't imagine how I was supposed to break the latest news to Kramer, and my stomach hurt just thinking about it. So I did the next best thing and booked a flight to San Antonio. Sometimes, all you can do is buy a little time to figure out your next move.

I'm sitting barefoot in a cubicle at a security checkpoint in the Dallas Fort Worth International Airport. Because of the amount of traveling I do for CBS, I invested in TSA PreCheck as soon as it became available. I usually fly through security in a matter of minutes, but not this time. At first, I thought it was a random selection, standard search. And maybe that's how it started, but when they confiscated my shoes, things got serious. Then they ushered me into a makeshift interrogation room and closed the door.

A few minutes later, they return with my luggage and the offending shoes. Italian leather flats. My most expensive—and only—real pair of work shoes. I bought them after I got my first CBS paycheck. All my other "nice" shoes gave me blisters when I wore them for ten-plus hours, which is basically part of the job description for a field producer.

I'd never spent more than fifty dollars on shoes before, and these cost three hundred. But I slid into them like butter, and they were worth every hard-earned penny. They were a combination of black and navy, and I wore them with literally everything. I'd had them resoled twice in five years. The TSA agent probably thinks they looked like any old pair of shoes, not one of my most valued possessions. I eye them longingly across the table.

"Where are you traveling to today?"

"San Antonio."

"What's the nature of your visit?"

He's clearly following a script, but we were way past a "random" search in the TSA handbook. I try to stay calm and answer exactly the question that was asked. I know my rights, and I'm fully prepared to invoke my need to speak to an attorney. But I'm also curious where he's going with this interrogation. So I keep talking.

"Business."

"What kind of work do you do?"

Just as I tell him I'm a producer for the true crime television show *48 Hours* on CBS, another agent appears, wearing rubber gloves, and holding promotional DVDs from my suitcase.

"Story checks out," she says as she peeks into the cubicle.

Now I'm really intrigued, and I can't help asking my own questions.

"What's going on? Why am I here?"

The agent levels with me and says they'd run a chemical reaction test on my shoes, and the results were positive for bomb-making materials.

"Any idea why that would happen?"

I rack my brain for a reasonable explanation. I tell him these are my work shoes, and that I'd worn them in courthouses, police stations, and on film sets for years.

"Any of those film sets involve fireworks or explosives?" He's baiting me, and I know it.

In truth, I don't remember blowing anything up for CBS, but I do know someone who had: Hollywood Chuck. I decide to take a little creative license and co-opt his story to get the TSA off my back. I choose my language carefully.

"Actually, we blew up a car for an episode recently. Think that could be it?"

He jots down a few notes and hands back my shoes and luggage. I'm officially cleared to fly again.

"Quick question: Do you know how I can get that off my shoes?" I ask him.

He laughs and says he wouldn't suggest Googling that, unless I want to end up on another kind of watch list.

Perspective is a funny thing. Twenty-four hours ago, I saw San Antonio as a punishment. But when I arrived there it felt like my playground. I had successfully pitched the Samuel Little story to 60 *Minutes,* and now my biggest problem was figuring out how to break the news to my bosses at 48, Judy Tygard and Nancy Kramer. I honestly thought Judy would be happy for me, but Kramer was a different story.

Our relationship was complicated. She'd been my boss for five years, and in that time, she'd seen me grow up from a local newspaper reporter to one of the most productive field producers at the show. It seemed like, as her subordinate, my success was not entirely welcomed.

Because I was always coming up with new story ideas and original ways to tell them, I often had catch-up calls on the calendar with Susan Zirinsky. These so-called "Z chats" were a coveted calendar booking, and lately Kramer had started appropriating my time slots. When Kramer got wind of an upcoming appointment, she'd pull rank and tell Z's assistant she was taking my meeting. Then she'd casually drop the news to me.

"Oh by the way, I took your Z chat," she'd say as we were wrapping up a call. "Hope you don't mind."

And if I thought standing out was hazardous at 48, I knew getting a story on 60 would put an even bigger target on my back. Kramer had once worked at *60 Minutes*, but her tenure had only lasted a year. I don't know why she left, because nobody will talk about it, especially her.

I couldn't have picked a more politically charged assignment if I'd tried. I knew I needed a soft landing, and that meant plenty of conversational padding before I dropped the bomb.

I'd spent days running all over San Antonio, finding voices for the upcoming trial of Mark Howerton for the murder of Cayley Mandadi. I'd worked like a woman possessed, going from office buildings to neighborhoods and setting up coffee and lunch dates with potential characters. By the end of the week, I had a local reporter, the defense attorney, and Cayley's parents out in Houston on board. No one was willing to go on camera right now, with the trial still two months away, but at least I had verbal commitments. I kept Kramer up to speed with that story—and at arm's length from the rest of my schedule. I kept looking for a window to bring up the *60* news in my conversations with her, but nothing felt right.

I had devoted all my daytime hours to the Mandadi story, but when I got back to my hotel in the evenings, I was clocking in to my second job at *60*. And because Ranger Holland worked nights, it was the perfect schedule to check in with him on the Samuel Little story. Kramer had sent me to San Antonio to keep me busy, but she didn't realize that meant I actually had more time to moonlight for *60* than if I'd been home with my family.

On a conference call from my hotel room, I met the rest of the team I'd be working with for the Samuel Little piece. When Bill Owens introduced me to Tanya Simon, I divulged nothing about my prior attempts at contacting her. But she knew; she brought it up when we were alone in person together months later. The way I looked at it, there was no harm, no foul. I was just happy to be doing the story, period.

The lead producer on the story was Draggan Mihailovich, a well-respected and prodigious producer. He'd cut his teeth reporting on the Olympics and had been at *60* since 2004. He had just hired a new associate producer away from the *New York Times*, Jacqueline Williams, and the Little story would be her television debut.

Austin-based Sharyn Alfonsi was the correspondent and one of the show's youngest on-air contributors, still in her forties. I loved the energy and enthusiasm everyone had for the story. I felt like I had hit the jackpot with the chemistry on the team, especially considering everything I had heard about the cutthroat culture at *60*. I wondered if the show's reputation was one big exaggeration meant to keep the riffraff out.

I'm walking through the yard at the California State Prison for Los Angeles County. It's easily one hundred degrees out, but I regret my wardrobe choice of a sleeveless dress. Amid the catcalls and whistles, I'm trying to keep my eyes fixed on the building in front of me, lest I draw any more specific attention by meeting an inmate's gaze. I cannot believe I ended up in the prison yard wearing a summer dress. It certainly wasn't my plan.

How did I end up here? There's not a straight line of logic to trace back, because no one in their right mind would orchestrate this series of events. But now I'm in the land of psychopaths and serial killers. It's a whole new ball game. So let's jump back a few days, and I'll try to retrace my steps.

I got to Los Angeles traveling with Ranger Holland. And that's been an experience in itself. Imagine taking a lone ranger who has spent his entire career avoiding the media and putting him on the same itinerary as a TV producer. He eyed me suspiciously at every turn. I can't blame him. I was holding a camera on him most of the time.

It was just too tempting to grab shots of this Texas cowboy sauntering through California. The boots and hat with a backdrop of palm trees. What kind of TV producer would I be if I let that shot slip through my fingers?

I still can't believe I made it on this trip. When Holland told me he was going to California to interview Samuel Little again, I jumped into action, getting *60* to approve the trip first and then finally telling *48* about everything. Well, almost everything. I may have fudged the timeline just a little.

The thing is, I still had a full-time job at *48*, and that meant I was juggling a handful of true crime stories in addition to my newfound side hustle at *60*. Because we are in reruns over the summer, the senior staff is able to knock off for a few weeks or months without anyone bothering them. But field producers like me work overtime in the summers, finding and developing the stories that will carry the show through the upcoming season. A producer in Manhattan can't write a script from their corner office without a field producer first locking down characters and setting up interviews. The initial legwork is what makes an episode possible, even though it's the final-stretch producers who get the most credit.

In the end, I chickened out on telling Kramer and went straight to Judy, who I saw as a mentor and ally. Following Peter Van Sant's sage advice about death islands, I knew I had to go around Kramer if I wanted any chance of making it to California. The conversation went a little like this:

"So, remember that story about Samuel Little? You were right. It's not a fit for 48, and I understand that now. But I did find a home for it. Bill Owens wants it for the season premiere of 60, and he's asked me to travel with the Texas Ranger next week to Los Angeles."

Judy was definitely surprised by the news, but she also seemed genuinely happy for me. Of course, she was still my boss, and she pointed out that traveling to California for another show wasn't part of my job description. I had anticipated this argument, and I told her I was prepared to use my vacation days to take the trip. Although I'd later negotiate a side contract at 60, at this point I wasn't getting paid any extra for the Samuel Little story.

It was unconventional, but if I wanted to spend my PTO stringing for 60 at California State Prison, Judy wasn't going to stand in my way. She approved my vacation request and graciously told me that she'd update Kramer for me. A huge weight had been lifted from my shoulders, and I thanked Judy for her support.

Once I got to LA, I made it my goal to spend as much time with Holland as possible. You never know where the TV magic might reveal itself. The more comfortable characters are with you, the more they let their guard down and give you authentic moments on camera. Holland's walls were prison grade, and I knew I wasn't getting through them without putting in some overtime. As we headed to the rental car facility, I realized that the LA traffic from the airport would be an excellent opportunity for some quality time together. I clicked cancel on my own rental agreement. Surely he wouldn't leave me stranded in the parking lot.

From the look on his face, I think he wanted to. We spent the next hour trading stories, and I tried to keep my camera use to a minimum, only grabbing the essential shots when we hit iconic streets. Despite looking every bit the native Texan, I learned Holland was actually from Chicago. He moved to

Texas for a job after college, his first and only stint in the private sector before catching the law enforcement bug and entering the police academy.

All of these details would be useful for my reporting, but I had my eye on a bigger prize. Although Holland was letting me tag along on the trip, I didn't have permission to actually go into the prison with him. He said we were taking it "one day at a time," and that his first priority was getting another interview with Little to introduce him to additional detectives with open cases that matched his victim descriptions. I knew I was lucky to be on this trip at all, so I was willing to play the long game and sit tight until my number was hopefully called. Or that's how I wanted it to appear, anyway.

Truthfully, I was already working back channels to smooth my path into the prison. I'd looked up all the available information online for media visits at California State Prison, and I had a local camera crew on a soft hold for the rest of the week. I like to underpromise and overdeliver, so I hadn't told anyone at 60 that I was angling to get a crew into the prison by the end of the week. As far as they knew, I was just getting shots of Holland with my field camera and gathering information for our reporting. Glorified research trip.

We were staying in different hotels but still sharing a rental car, so we'd trade off on driving. I couldn't pass up the opportunity to mess with a cop in the passenger seat. I picked him up and peeled out of the hotel entrance. I didn't even make it out of the parking lot before he made me pull over and switch seats with him.

We were headed to the grocery store to select treats for a serial killer. Holland knew exactly what Little liked, and we whipped through the produce and bakery sections in a matter of minutes, snagging a coconut cream pie and a bunch of bananas. Holland placed the coconut cream pie in the back seat, unbuckled, and told me to drive very carefully. I was beginning to understand how good Holland was at manipulating people and situations.

I made it through the next day without causing any more trouble, lying low at the hotel and doing research on my laptop while Holland went to the prison with a couple of detectives. I didn't want to appear too pushy from the jump, but after two days in LA, I was getting restless for results.

I had booked a separate hotel from Holland because it felt like the safe choice. I wanted to maintain my independence while I let Holland grow to trust me a bit more. But as the days ticked by, I realized my hotel across town was probably doing more harm than good. Traffic aside, I knew I was missing out on evening drinks with all the cops, and you can't put a price on that.

I booked into the same hotel as Holland and the other detectives, and it paid off almost immediately. That evening, I wandered into the lobby and found all the guys crowded around a table, drinking beer. They were clearly flustered about something, and it didn't take long to realize it was a tech issue.

Holland had used a digital camera to record the interviews with Little, and now he wanted to put that file on a thumb drive for one of the detectives to take back to the district attorney. But Holland's laptop didn't have an input for the camera's memory card. They were looking sideways at all the equipment on the table, trying to will it to be compatible. I'm not a computer whiz in most circumstances, but in this crowd, I was the techie one.

Happy to have a reason to join in on the conversation, I took a sip from my beer and told them I knew of two ways to solve this problem: they could go to Best Buy and purchase a USB card reader, or they could use my laptop to transfer the file because I had a built-in one.

Holland quickly dismissed the idea of using my laptop. "No way. We're going to Best Buy." He was gathering his things to head out when one of the detectives piped up. It was after 9 PM, and Best Buy was already closed. The detective was flying out first thing in the morning.

Grinning, I repeated my offer to let them use my laptop to transfer the file. They all guffawed, except for the detective who was hoping to leave in the morning.

"I'll go get my laptop and then you can decide," I said as I headed for the elevator.

When I returned, it was clear two camps had formed. Holland and another detective were sitting, arms crossed, on one side of the table. The early-bird flier was sitting on the other side, waiting for me. I showed them the card reader slot and explained how my laptop would serve as a transfer mechanism, getting the file from the camera to the USB drive.

"I won't have a copy of the file. It will just pass through my laptop en route to its final destination."

Holland narrowed his gaze. "Yeah, I know how computers work, but we aren't doing that. This is evidence in a criminal investigation. A murder case. We aren't putting it on a journalist's computer, even for a transfer. Too many things could go wrong."

I could tell the sympathetic detective was trying to find a way to win Holland over. He really wanted to be on that morning flight.

"What if we deputize her? Then her laptop would be like police property."

Now I was really intrigued. I'd never had this option floated before, and I appreciated the novelty of it. But I knew CBS would kill me if I let the police commandeer my laptop. I remained silent and let it play out among law enforcement. Holland waved his arms and issued a ruling.

"If we put anything on her laptop, then you are taking it back with you as evidence."

Well, that settled it. There would be no deputizing tonight. The detective was all set to change his flight to the afternoon when the other detective put his badge to use and found a Walmart nearby that was open twenty-four hours.

Crisis averted.

I'm in California for three days before Holland agrees to let me follow him to the prison. And that's all I'm allowed to do. *60* wants video of Holland driving out to the prison and of his car going through the gates. Since I have a camera with me, they ask me to do it rather than hiring a whole crew. There's just a small snag in this genius, cost-saving plan: How am I supposed to drive a car and work a camera?

I have a rental car on hold, and I'm trying to think my way through hiring a driver when the solution dawns on me. Instead of renting a car, I'll order an Uber. The only issue is inputting the prison address as a drop-off location. California prisons don't allow drop-offs or pickups. You have to drive your own vehicle on and off the premises for security reasons. I pull up the route from the hotel to the prison and find the nearest business to use as a decoy drop-off. It's an animal shelter, which is an odd place to visit when you are staying at a hotel, but it is less problematic than prison.

Arms crossed, Holland is shaking his head as we wait for the Uber.

"This is not going to work."

I do my best to assure him it will, promising we won't get close enough to the prison to set off any alarm bells. The plan is for me to ride with Holland until we got to the animal shelter, where I'll hop in the Uber and film him driving into the prison gates. Now I just have to convince my Uber driver to go along with my master plan. He pulls up in a minivan, and I go to work.

"So I actually have an unusual request," I say as I whip out my camera and explain the whole operation.

Being LA, this isn't that far-fetched of a scenario, and luckily my driver is on board. We make our way down the desert highway and knock out the shots in short order, kicking up dust that looks as good as anything Hollywood Chuck could have concocted.

I had been to the prison gates, now I just needed to get inside them. The day after the Uber adventure, I'd finally rented my own car, plus I'd passed a background check with the visitors' department of the prison. Two hurdles down, an unknown number to go. Holland vouched for me with the media relations office, and I set up a meeting.

As I went over the visitor requirements, I did a double take on the dress code. No blue jeans allowed. The inmates wore jeans as part of their uniform, and no one else could be in denim for security reasons. But jeans were the only pants I had packed. So guess what the other option was?

I was already nervous about being on prison grounds, and my unintentionally bold wardrobe selection did not help. It was one thing when I was in a conference room with the media relations team, but after we finished talking, they asked me if I wanted a tour. Our meeting had gone well, and I felt like they were leaning toward letting me come back with a camera crew. As much as I didn't want to be paraded around the prison, I didn't feel like I could say no to the tour.

And that's how I ended up walking through California State Prison in a sleeveless dress.

The next day, I'm standing inside the interview room where Ranger Holland first got Samuel Little to spill his darkest secrets. It's a small, windowless room with a table and two chairs. It may not look like much, but this is all Holland needs to make the confession magic happen. And now we just need to capture it on camera.

When I tell the team at *60* that I got permission to film inside the prison, they spring into action. Producer Draggan Mihailovich jumps on the red-eye from New York to LA, and we meet the crew for coffee early the next morning to get acquainted.

We have clearance to bring our camera into the prison, but there are conditions. Namely, we can't actually interview Samuel Little ourselves. He won't even know that we are in the building. Our camera crew is allowed to film Holland and other prison staff, and we can set up Holland's camera for his interview with Little. Holland likes to have a backup recording of his interviews, just in case one method fails. So while he has a digital recorder going, he also brings in a small camcorder to sit on the table. I'd seen his footage from previous interviews, and it wasn't exactly ready for prime time. The angles were off, the shot was blown out, and Little was usually eating while he was talking.

Thankfully, we have the pros with us. In short order, we coach Holland, and the crew formats his camera. When Little gets in the room, the camera looks the same as it always had to him, but now it's operating in *60* style.

Once we have Little's shot ready to go, we can focus on Holland. We need images of him walking around the prison. You know the ones: metal bars clanging open and closed, tough guy with a badge striding through them. It is clear Holland has made an impression on the prison staff, and they are bending over backward to let us have the run of the place. It's not every day that a cop gets a hardened murderer to confess to his crimes and share so many details of his victims that the cases can be closed outright. (The Little confessions are a wild ride—worthy of their own book— but that's a story for another day.)

Holland was already a law enforcement celebrity, and thanks to the *60 Minutes* cameras, he is well on his way to becoming a household name.

Filming Ranger James Holland in his office, surrounded by the drawings of serial killer Samuel Little.

Three of the haunting drawings that Little made of his victims.

We make our way through the grounds, getting shots of the razor-wire fence and armed guard towers before crossing the yard to Little's cell block. At least this time I have a group of people with me. Little had already been removed from his cell, along with everyone else from the floor. The door to his cell is open, and they let us walk right in.

Letters from "fans" are tacked to the wall, along with pictures he'd drawn of victims. His pantry is overflowing with instant noodles, snack cakes, and bags of chips. There is a local Ohio newspaper on his bed and a small TV in the corner. Except for the bars, it could pass for a spartan summer camp cabin. Considering Little was arrested at a homeless shelter, this is probably something of an upgrade to his living quarters. Less freedom, sure, but also more amenities.

After four hours, we have everything we need out of California State Prison, LA County, and I'm itching to rejoin the free world. There's nothing like time behind bars to make you appreciate the simple things in life, like doors that don't lock behind you and access to your cell phone.

Our success in California had the *60 Minutes* team in New York working overtime to put the piece together as part of the season premiere lineup. I couldn't believe how much had changed over the summer. I'd gone from a pariah pushing a story no one wanted to a jet-setting producer with a coveted time slot. But the news gods are fickle, and I was still a ball of nerves, wondering how everything would play out.

The editors were getting ready to cut the first draft of our piece, and I desperately wanted to be there for it. I knew I was already pushing the limits of this unique working arrangement between *48* and *60*. Considering my bosses had already acquiesced to several outlandish requests, I needed backup on this one. Ranger Holland was nonnegotiable for the trip. He had custody of the interview footage with Little and wasn't going to let it out of his sight. It would be a lot harder for them to say no to a Texas Ranger than to me. I pleaded with Holland to tell *60* that he wanted me to travel to New York with him. He begrudgingly agreed, under one condition.

"If I do this, you owe me. And I always collect."

I'm walking down Fifty-Seventh Street in New York, heading to the CBS Broadcast Center. I'm planning to stop by *48* first, before going into the *60 Minutes* building across the street.

"Gosh, Claire, are you nervous?" Holland asks, clearly bemused.

I hadn't said a word. How did he know I was nervous? I squint curiously at him and stay silent.

Laughing, Holland says my "tell" is actually refusing to speak.

"Most people get really chatty when they are nervous. They can't shut up. But you are the opposite. You talk a million miles per hour when you're comfortable, and you clam up when you're not."

It didn't take a human lie detector to predict that I'd be nervous heading into *60 Minutes* for the first time, but I still hated that he was right.

My phone starts ringing, and I see it's my boss, Nancy Kramer, calling. This can't be good.

I scowl at the screen and compose myself before answering, channeling my cheeriest self. She cuts right to the chase.

"I know we were planning to meet in the morning, but something's come up, and I need to push it to two PM."

Of course she does. That's the exact time that we're doing a team screening of our piece at *60*. But how did she know that?

I tell her I can't do 2 PM, but she won't let it go. I finally have to admit that's our screening time.

"Oh, just ask them to move it for you. They do stuff like that all the time," Kramer says casually.

I stifle a laugh. This belongs under the "Comically Terrible Career Advice" heading. And I'm not falling for it. It seemed like my boss was deliberately trying to sabotage me. But how to play it?

"Okay great, I'll do that," I lie. "Thanks for the tip."

We get to the *60 Minutes* building and have to be buzzed in at the security desk. I can tell Holland is amused by the rent-a-cop routine, but he's a good sport about it. Once we're inside, the office looks like any other CBS floor. The executives have big corner offices with window banks. Correspondents and capital-P Producers are in the next-best digs, and the rest of the team is either in a bullpen of desks or small, windowless offices in interior hallways. The pecking order is familiar and comforting, but soon something else takes center stage: paranoia.

We're told not to introduce Holland to anyone as a Texas Ranger, lest they get curious and start poking around to see what story we're working on. Also, about that, the story now has a code name: "Cat Litter." All story files will be saved under variations of Cat Litter on the show's hard drive. Holland looks at me to see if this is normal procedure. I shoot him the expression for batshit crazy.

At 48, we enjoyed sharing the details of our upcoming stories with our colleagues. There's plenty of murder to go around. But at 60, every story is in competition for airtime. And the season premiere is even more cutthroat. I hadn't set out to get a piece of such prized TV real estate. The FBI and DOJ had sealed that fate when they named their target deadline for the news embargo as August. 60 Minutes didn't go on the air until late September, so the season premiere was offered up first. The feds agreed, and we were all racing to the finish line.

The team at 60 had plenty of tasks to knock out, but Holland had some of his own. Specifically, he needed videos cut of Samuel Little describing unknown victims so the FBI could post them after our story aired. Holland had hours of footage with Little, but he wanted five bite-sized videos with only the key descriptions that would help the public identify the victims. We had all been so caught up in the 60 profile of Holland that this item had slipped our minds. But Holland wasn't really asking.

The 60 editors and producers balk at his command. They're in the middle of a breakneck production schedule as it was. Most 60 stories had months or years in the making. Ours had a few weeks. But Holland wouldn't budge. No victim videos, no story. Everyone looks down the line until they get to me.

Holland puts his hand on my shoulder.

"Remember that favor you owe me?"

At this point, the number of bosses I have to answer to is growing at an alarming pace. I remember I'm still on the hook to meet with Kramer, and I groan as I look at the clock and see 2 PM is approaching. The 60 team all turns from the edit bay screens to face me. I figure it's as good a time as any to come clean about this particular predicament, and I spill my guts about my boss setting a meeting at the same time as our screening. "Who is your boss?" asks one of the veteran *60 Minutes* staff editors. "Nancy Kramer," I answer, and he laughs.

"Kramer? You don't even need a good excuse to ignore her. She can't hurt you here," he tells me.

Yeah, but she can hurt me there.

I swallow the lump in my throat and call Kramer.

"Hey, they won't move the two PM screening for me, sorry. Can I come by after instead?"

"Yeah, that works," she says. "See you then."

When I make it to the 48 offices later that afternoon, Kramer greets me with a hug, and I half expect to feel a knife in my back. But she's always been more subtle than that. We discuss the Mandadi case and where I left the story when I was in San Antonio. I'm trying to keep my mind from wandering when senior producer Patti Aronofsky pops in the doorway. "It's the *60 Minutes* producer!" she says with a tinge of sarcasm. I smile demurely and say nothing, counting the seconds in my head until I can steal away across the street and back to my other job.

It's approaching midnight, and I'm still up at the 60 offices. The shine of my first morning in the building has officially worn off as I comb through over a hundred hours of footage to create five time-coded scripts for our editor to piece together as part of our deal with the FBI.

My eyes are starting to cross when my cell phone rings. It's Holland.

"What are you doing?" he asks gamely.

"Working for the FBI, apparently," I reply, exhausted.

The next morning I'm up at 7 AM, heading out the door in my running shoes to work out the insanity of the last twenty-four hours. It's drizzling, but Central

Park is just a few blocks away, and I have to clear my head before another day of Cat Litter. I'm rounding the corner in the lobby when I see Holland, sipping coffee and surveying the room.

"Are you about to go for a run?" he asks incredulously.

I nod and pop in my headphones as I make my way through the crowd, breaking into a jog the moment I hit the street.

The rest of the week is a blur of editing bays, script rewrites, and voice-over recording sessions. The story is really taking shape, but we are missing a key element: Samuel Little's answers to our own questions. While the piece is a profile of Ranger Holland, he wouldn't be on 60 without Little, and we need to try one more time to get an interview with him.

California State Prison rules dictate no media interviews on the grounds, but we're not in California anymore. What if we placed a call to Little through the prison and recorded it on speakerphone? Holland helps us cut through the red tape, and in a matter of minutes, we're on the line with the most prolific serial killer in America.

Correspondent Sharyn Alfonsi has a list of questions to run through, and Little seems happy to answer them.

"They were broke and homeless, and they walked right into my spider-web," Little says of his victims.

His responses range from bizarre to disturbing, but he's not mincing words, and we know we'll find something usable.

"I don't think there was another person that did what I liked to do. I think I'm the only one in the world. That's not an honor. That's a curse," Little tells us.

This was the final element our reporting was missing, and we practically cheer when she hangs up the phone.

At this point, it felt like nothing could stop our piece from making deadline. But there were bigger forces at play, ones that would send our killer story into no-man's-land.

Spending all day at the office in New York is a grind. I've been running every morning to dull my nerves, and today, Holland says he's joining me. I give him a quizzical look. Does he really think he can hang with me for five miles? But he has no intention of working out my way. He's stacking the deck in his favor, like always.

"Coffee before you puke?" he texts me at 8 AM.

I meet him in the hotel restaurant, and he's all bright-eyed and bushy-tailed. I can see he's written out a CrossFit-style workout plan on a sheet of hotel stationery. My eyes are scanning a long, numbered list as he folds the paper up and sticks it in his pocket. My stomach flips, and I wonder what I've gotten myself into.

"Lead the way," he says as we exit the hotel lobby.

It's a sunny, clear day, and we're just a few blocks away from Central Park. I spy the crosswalk signal change and pick up the pace to catch it. Holland follows close behind. I'm hoping the novelty of running in Central Park will be enough to hold his attention for a mile or two, but he stops me as soon as we come to a grassy clearing.

It's fenced in low and has a sign saying "Keep off." Undeterred, we step over the fence line, and he pulls out his sheet of paper. He reads off a couple items and watches my reaction before settling on push-ups. The nerve of this guy.

"How many?" I ask.

"Ten," he says.

I make short work of the assignment and pop back up. A little too quickly. Holland has his hands on his hips.

"Actually, make that twenty-three."

I eye him sideways and quip back, "Why twenty-three?"

"Michael Jordan," says the Chicago native.

Back at the office, I'm trying to play it cool as we go over rewrites to the script. Producer Draggan Mihailovich asks me to hand him a stapler and my arms shake as I pass it over. Holland can't resist ribbing me. "Hey, Claire, stick out your arms again."

The first twenty-three push-ups weren't that bad. It was the second and third rounds that really got me. And now I have Jell-O for my upper appendages. But Holland isn't satisfied.

"Do you know Claire's nickname?" he asks the room, which includes correspondent Sharyn Alfonsi and associate producer Jacqui Williams.

No one replies, and I cross my arms and wonder where he's going with this one.

Then he uses a private nickname known only to my husband and son. It's a two-letter abbreviation and an inside joke.

How did he come up with that?

I'm searching my brain for a time he could have overheard it but drawing a blank. I snap back to the current conversation.

"But what does it stand for?" he asks the confused group rhetorically. No one responds, and Sharyn and Jacqui look at me for a sign that I'm in on the joke. I shake them off as Holland laughs.

He ventures a few guesses but can tell by my reaction that he hasn't hit a winner.

"I guess it'll just stay a mystery for now," he says. "Unless she wants to tell us."

"I do not," I say, narrowing my gaze.

Jacqui rescues me by jumping back into the script, and I make a mental note to thank her later.

I need to focus on the task in front of me, and I try to push all the distractions out of my mind.

Holland's comment might be harmless—maybe he saw me answer a text message and spied the nickname inadvertently. If so, he's messing with me like a mischievous friend. But considering he's buddies with the FBI and a relentless investigator, I can't help but wonder if he got the information by other means.

What kind of head games is Holland playing?

18

PUNISHMENT FITS
THE CRIME

It's Thursday, September 26, 2019. I remember the date because it's my ninth wedding anniver-
sary, and Riley is flying up to New York for the weekend so we can celebrate.
I spend a few hours blissfully unaware that anything has changed. And then
I get to the office.

Associate producer Jacqueline Williams pulls me aside and turns around
her monitor. It's displaying a story from the *Los Angeles Times*—"A Texas
Ranger got a prolific serial killer to talk: This is how. "[13] Holland's face is staring back at us, flanked by Little's artwork. I feel like I got the wind knocked
out of me. We'd been scooped, two days before the season premiere.

We knew the *LA Times* was working on a piece about Holland and Little,
but the ranger had assured us it was going to publish on Sunday, the same

---

13 Del Quentin Wilbur, "A Texas Ranger got a prolific serial killer to talk. This is how," *Los Angeles Times*, September
26, 2019, https://www.latimes.com/world-nation/story/2019-09-25/texas-ranger-got-one-of-the-nations
-worst-serial-killers-to-talk-this-is-how.

day as *60 Minutes*. My head is spinning, but I force myself to read every line in the article. I'm frantically searching for any mention of the FBI-embargoed information about Samuel Little being named the most prolific serial killer in US history. I get to the end and realize it's not in there. We've been cut down to size, but there's still a sliver of our exclusive left. Holland had already flown back to Texas. I place a call to tell him his *60* profile is on life support.

"*60 Minutes* will take a hundred-thousand-dollar bath rather than be embarrassed. They won't even think twice about killing the story if the FBI releases the news today."

He's unconvinced, and I'm apoplectic.

I explain that the whole timing of the story; the main reason it was green-lit was the promise of an exclusive TV interview with Holland, coordinated ahead of the FBI's release. If the order flips, it will look like we were chasing a press release, which is the opposite of everything that *60 Minutes* stands for.

We don't follow the news cycle, we dictate it.

"What do you want me to do? The *LA Times* isn't television. We didn't break the agreement," Holland says.

"You have to get the FBI to hold the release until our story airs, or it will never see the light of day," I tell him. "It will be like the last three months never happened."

I'm in a windowless interview room somewhere deep inside California State Prison. My hands are gripping the sides of the metal chair as I try to figure out my next move.

Serial killer Samuel Little is sitting across from me, licking his lips and laughing maniacally.

I see him lunge toward me, his outstretched hands as big as saucers. I leap from my chair and into the corner of the room. "I've got you now," he says as he closes in on me.

I'm trying to climb the walls like Spider-Man when I wake up in a cold sweat. It takes me a minute to realize I'm not in California at all. I'm at the Parker Hotel in Midtown Manhattan. I pull off the covers and stare out the window at the view of Central Park. I take deep breaths until I feel my heart rate slow down.

The Samuel Little story and my life are inextricably linked somewhere deep in my psyche. I need to find a way to separate them. But for now, all I care about is getting the story on the air. Maybe that's what would get it out of my head.

I'm still reeling from the *LA Times* article when another event takes over the news cycle. There's a new impeachment inquiry for President Donald Trump. Rumor has it that *60 Minutes* has obtained exclusive documentation about the source of the inquiry, and Scott Pelley is already en route to DC to shoot interviews with Nancy Pelosi and Kevin McCarthy. There are three slots for the season premiere, and we're the only story that just got scooped by the *LA Times*. Guess who's first up on the chopping block?

It takes a few hours before the official word comes down and our profile on Holland is taken out of the Sunday lineup. We're told it will air October 6, provided the FBI doesn't jump the gun before then. It was one thing when we had to stop the feds for two days, but now it's a whole week?

The *LA Times* had all but served the story up on a silver platter. And thanks to *60 Minutes*, the FBI had five shiny new videos of Samuel Little describing his victims. It was hard to believe how fast everything had gone south on us. I commiserate with correspondent Sharyn Alfonsi.

"This is the worst feeling I've ever had about a story," I tell her.

"Welcome to *60 Minutes*," she replies.

Riley arrives a few hours later, and I try my best not to ruin our anniversary weekend in New York. We have dinner reservations and tickets to a Broadway show. In my heart, I know the story getting shelved is not the worst thing that could have happened. But to be so close to the end and then have the finish line extended is something I'd never experienced.

I'm in the theater lobby during intermission when my phone rings with an unknown 212 number. I should be off the clock, but that's not a real thing in journalism, so I pick it up. Nancy Kramer is on the line.

"I heard about your story getting cut from the premiere. I'm so sorry," she says gleefully.

I do a double take at my phone before I realize she must have deliberately called me from a different number. Classic.

It's Sunday morning, and Riley and I aren't flying back to Texas for hours. I should be relaxing, but I can't stay still. I give Riley a kiss, lace up my shoes, and head out the door for Central Park, now a familiar backdrop for my runs. It's a beautiful day, and I'm trying to will myself to enjoy it. But I feel like I don't deserve a nice morning in the park after failing on the story.

I finish my standard five-mile palate cleanser and punish myself with sprints. My lungs are on fire and my legs are screaming, but I keep going until I can't feel them anymore. After God knows how long, my phone buzzes with a text from Riley. "Are you ever coming back?"

Where would I be without him? Stories come and go. Careers rise and fall. And no matter how much you think you love your job, it will never love you back.

"I'm on my way," I write, then I jog back to the hotel and into his arms, as fast as my weary legs will carry me.

The next week was agony. Every day, I checked with Holland about the FBI and held my breath for what felt like the inevitable press release. I couldn't imagine one Texas Ranger could control the entire FBI, but I shouldn't have sold Holland short. He kept his word, and the FBI held their fire.

On October 6, 2019, "The Ranger and the Serial Killer" premiered on *60 Minutes*. It opened with these words:

"Tonight, you're going to hear about the man the FBI is calling the most prolific serial killer in the history of the United States. His name is Samuel Little, and over the course of a year and a half he confessed to ninety-three murders. That's more than were committed by Ted Bundy and Jeffrey Dahmer combined. No one would have known the scale of Little's crimes if not for a Texas Ranger, who had a hunch."

Five minutes after our story aired, the FBI published their release.[14] The combination sent the true crime world into a fervor over Samuel Little

---

14 "FBI Seeking Assistance Connecting Victims to Samuel Little's Confessions," FBI press release, posted October 6, 2019, https://www.fbi.gov/news/stories/samuel-little-most-prolific-serial-killer-in-us-history-100619.

60 Minutes finally airs the story that no one wanted . . . until they did.

and Ranger Holland, one that continues to this day. *60 Minutes'* coverage spawned hundreds of articles, along with a smattering of podcasts and books about the subject. For its part, *48 Hours* never covered the story of Samuel Little, though the show did go on to do two serial killer hours in 2020, one on Ted Bundy and another on Israel Keyes.[15]

Later on, when I was producing a *60 Minutes* piece with Scott Pelley, he wanted to know how we'd ended up with the exclusive on Samuel Little before the FBI had named him the country's most prolific serial killer.

"How in the world did we get that story?" he asked me.

"Well," I said. "It all started at a murder trial in Texas."

15 *48 Hours*, season 33, episode 26, "Live To Tell: Surviving Ted Bundy," aired April 11, 2020, CBS, https://www.cbsnews.com/news/ted-bundy-serial-killer-survivor-stories/.

48 Hours, season 33, episode 30, "Tracking the Murders of Israel Keyes," aired May 9, 2020, CBS, https://www.cbsnews.com/news/israel-keyes-serial-killer-skulls-blood-48-hours/.

19

GOING ROGUE

After my *60 Minutes* piece ran, Kramer started calling me "superstar." It felt less like a compliment and more like a target on my back. I'm not prone to paranoia, but my experience across the street had left a mark. It's one thing to deal with sabotage from the competition—at this level of journalism, I've come to expect it. But when the danger seems to be coming from inside the building, it's unsettling in a different way. The kind of work environment that makes you slowly go crazy.

When "The Ranger and The Serial Killer" aired, I was already working on another murder trial for *48*. Sitting in court, day in and day out, in a small Texas town where the local police had bungled a murder investigation.[16] It was a familiar atmosphere, and I worked the trial on autopilot. Lunch with the lead investigator, check. Access to the evidence through the court reporter, check. It was a little too easy, and I started to feel restless. I could do this job in my sleep, but did I even want to anymore?

.16 *48 Hours*, season 33, episode 8, "The Case Against Sandra Garner," aired March 7, 2020, CBS, https://www
  .youtube.com/watch?v=kJzWo7a_XUQ.

My story sense has always been my guiding principle as a journalist. Above all else and against the odds, I fight for the stories that I believe in. What is the point of being a journalist if you aren't telling the stories that no one else will?

. I thought back to everything I'd risked for the sake of a story: sneaking into jail with wily defense attorneys, putting myself in harm's way with suspected killers, being detained over false accusations, and most recently, the threat of being fired for my relentless pursuit of a story that nobody seemed to want. I had done it all willingly, eagerly even. Because I saw those stories as *my stories*. Only they weren't. By definition, they were the property of CBS News, then ViacomCBS, and as I sit writing this today, Paramount Global.

Every story I ever produced for an episode on CBS is theirs, worldwide, in perpetuity. I'd been all too happy to sign on the dotted line and give all my intellectual property rights away back when the contract was my lifeline to buying a house and paying off student loans. But nearly a decade later, I was wondering if it had really been worth it. The stories I had fought for with everything I had belonged to someone else. And through licensing deals with cable networks, CBS was reselling, repackaging, and redistributing those stories across the world for an enormous profit. One that I had no share in. It was perfectly legal, but that didn't make it right.

I knew I'd never have a chance at owning a piece of *48 Hours*. But maybe I could strike out on my own with the right story, in the right way, and actually have ownership for once. My experience fighting for the Ranger Holland story and ultimately getting it on *60 Minutes* had given me a newfound level of confidence in my story judgment. And there was one case in particular that I felt had a deep reservoir of untapped potential. Not necessarily for television, but for a different medium with an endless supply of airtime: podcasts.

I'd been an early adopter of the podcast craze, and I started by listening to *This American Life* in the early 2000s. I later gravitated toward true crime shows like *Serial*, *Dirty John*, and *Up and Vanished*. By the time I was working at *48*, I was a full-blown podcast junkie, loyally listening to a half dozen shows each week.

Back then, I never saw myself as a potential podcaster. I was happy just to be a fan and consume the content. But I know a good idea when I hear one, even in a cold pitch on LinkedIn. A media recruiter reached out, and it didn't take me long to jump on the phone and entertain the novel proposal to host my own true crime podcast. The fact that there was very little money involved was of no consequence to me. I was making plenty of that on television. Actual ownership, however, was in short supply.

The recruiter was looking for a host for a specific, unsolved case out of New York City in the 1960s. I tried to feign interest at first but quickly came clean. I had zero connection to a case twenty-five years older than me, and in NYC of all places. But while that particular plotline was a dead end, the podcast idea had started to grow on me. And I knew just the story I wanted to tell. It was one I'd pitched—unsuccessfully—to 48 Hours almost immediately after joining CBS in 2014. Back then, I was still working at CultureMap Dallas. And my first bylines on the story appear there.

It was one of my stories that I'd stayed close to for years; at this point, it even outdated Judge Kocurek's attempted assassination. Sticking with compelling stories, long after everyone else moved on to chase the news cycle, was a favorite tactic of mine. And this case in particular had so many twists and turns that it had kept me on the hook for years.

Dammion Heard was a Texas state champion wrestler who'd gone to college in Colorado on an athletic scholarship. But the freshman had gone missing after a team party, and his lifeless body was found days later in a remote location. After a bungling small-town police investigation, the case had been ruled noncriminal and closed for good. But his family and friends had never believed the official narrative of self-harm. And five years later, they were all still willing to talk to me, on the record, about Dammion.

There was widespread media coverage of Dammion's disappearance and the resulting investigation into his death, from local outlets in Colorado to Good Morning America. But once his case was ruled a suicide, it dropped off the headlines. I was struck by the fact that none of the initial questions in the investigation had ever been answered.

After the case was closed, I submitted a public records request with the Gunnison Police Department. They granted it in full, and I had forty-seven interview recordings and hundreds of pages of documents at my fingertips.

When 48 passed on the story, I'd turned all my research into a three-part investigative series for CBS News online. Producer Alec Sirken had helped shepherd the project as my mentor, and both our bylines appeared on the

2015 story "What Happened to Dammion Heard?"[17] While I was glad I had gotten something on the record about Dammion's mysterious death, I couldn't shake the feeling that there was still so much more to learn.

For years, all the evidence sat in a manila folder in my desk drawer. But once a story grabs me, I never let go. It had taken longer than I'd ever expected, but the light bulb had finally appeared. I knew just what I wanted to do with Dammion's story: make a podcast.

I'm sitting across from *48 Hours* executive producer Judy Tygard in her corner office. It's the first time I've seen her since my *60 Minutes* coup. We're in Midtown Manhattan at the CBS Broadcast Center, and for the second time in as many years, I'm pitching an original story in an unusual format.

I tell her that *Final Days on Earth* is an investigative podcast series that will cover mysterious deaths. Each season will dive deep on a single case and follow the story wherever it goes. To bolster my pitch, I created a video trailer for the series. I knew speaking the language of television was my best chance at getting the green light.

Intriguingly, my boss, Nancy Kramer, is actually supporting me in this new endeavor. The uncharacteristic move has me on high alert for sabotage, but so far, Kramer appears to genuinely be on my side. She even composes a glowing email introduction to CBS News Radio Network vice president Craig Swagler. Calling me "superstar" again, Kramer gives me credit for developing "all our programming and content in the great state of Texas." It's a level of praise and acknowledgment that I've never experienced with her before. I'm convincing myself that it's a good thing, not a setup.

Back in Judy's office, I'm on the edge of my seat, and I lean in and put my elbows on her desk. I believe in the story, and I want her to see my dream of building a new true crime podcast franchise for *48 Hours* and CBS News. Considering Judy had once created her own *Live to Tell* miniseries, I'm hoping she'll see the merit in expanding the brand again.

---

17 Claire St. Amant and Alec Sirken, "What Happened to Dammion Heard?" CBS News, August 17, 2015, https://www.cbsnews.com/news/what-happened-to-dammion-heard-part-1/.

Back then, the only *48 Hours* podcast was a radio cut of our weekly epi-sodes. The scripts weren't tailored for an audio-only audience. Meanwhile, NBC's *Dateline* and *20/20* on ABC had original podcast programming that complemented and expanded their television brand. I told Judy we could capi-talize on the popularity of true crime podcasts by using the *48 Hours* platform to promote my new investigative audio project, one that I'd already spent years researching and reporting for CBS.

At this point, I guess I shouldn't have been surprised that Judy was telling me no. But her reasoning for this particular rejection was hard to hear.

"If I let you have a podcast, I'll have to give every producer their own podcast," she said.

I'm biting my tongue to keep from pointing out that no one else had pre-sented their own concept for a true crime podcast. And wouldn't it be great if my show inspired a surge of enterprising activity among producers? But I sense Judy isn't going to be swayed, and pushing back doesn't seem prudent. Plus, I'd learned so much from the last time she'd told me no. To think, if *48 Hours* had actually produced the Samuel Little story, I never would have ended up at *60 Minutes*. The biggest blessings often come in disguise.

I take a deep breath to center myself and thank Judy for her consideration. Then I let her know I'll still be pursuing my podcast outside the CBS walls.

"I always find a home for my stories, one way or another," I say, and we both laugh.

20

LOCKDOWN

We all have a last moment in 2020 before we realized the magnitude of the Covid-19 pan-
demic. For me, it was a carefree selfie in downtown Tulsa. My face smashed
up against a dear friend's, smiling from ear to ear, without a mask in sight.
The date was March 11, 2020.

I'd arrived in Tulsa to speak at a business luncheon on "The Art of Storytelling." Fresh from New York, and with only a handful of confirmed corona-
virus cases in the state, I hadn't taken any precautions. I flew into LaGuardia
and did a double take when I saw a woman in a full hazmat suit methodically
washing her hands in the bathroom. I chalked it up to big-city oddities and
went on my way.

When I got to the CBS Broadcast Center, it appeared to be business as
usual. A dozen or so of us crammed into the screening room and shared a
bowl of popcorn. I took the subway uptown for dinner, and I didn't even own
a bottle of hand sanitizer.

When I was saying my goodbyes, senior producer Patti Aronofsky was
the only person who wouldn't give me a hug or shake my hand, which seemed

about right. She waved from across the room as she blurted out something about a virus.

But everything changed on March 12, 2020. Broadway announced it was suspending all shows. The NCAA basketball tournament was canceled. The following day, President Trump declared a national emergency in the United States, and the world came to an abrupt stop. But when you work in news, events that send everyone else running away are the ones that draw you in like a magnet.

There wasn't a clear crime nexus to the health crisis, so I pivoted. Ranger Holland told me he had family members on a Princess Cruise ship that wasn't being allowed to dock in San Francisco. I pitched the story to the *CBS Evening News* through Omar Villafranca and his producer Rodney Hawkins, and it made the air. They even repackaged it for a story on the morning show.

Next thing I knew, *60 Minutes* called, asking me to produce stories on the pandemic response in Texas. CBS had grounded all personnel, and we couldn't fly to other cities without getting special approval and following strict health protocols. Because my home base was already in Texas, I could drive across the state without triggering any quarantine restrictions, provided I didn't have any symptoms of infection. I went into the CBS Dallas Bureau and was issued two pairs of latex gloves, two N95 masks, and a full bodysuit. Considering everything I was risking to work for *60* on the side, I was no longer interested in doing it for free. Of course, I didn't realize at that time that getting paid would mean they'd no longer give me on-screen credit for my stories.

On a whim, a *60 Minutes* producer said he wanted footage inside DFW Airport, where law enforcement was recording contact-tracing information from all incoming passengers. I tried to go through the traditional media channels for filming at the airport, but they were giving me the runaround. Short staffed and on high alert for potential problems, a press agent helpfully told me, "Unless you are on a flight, you aren't getting past security."

I hung up and booked the cheapest flight I could find. Half an hour later, I passed breezily through TSA before breaking out my field camera and filming in the terminal.

There are a lot of factors that contribute to a story making it on the air at *60 Minutes*, but I'd be lying if I didn't tell you that convenience is often one of them. While most of *60*'s correspondents live in New York, two have houses in Texas: Sharyn Alfonsi and Scott Pelley. At the height of the pandemic, *60* had built-in field operations in Austin and San Antonio. Can you guess where their Texas coverage kicked off?

Our piece, "The State of Texas," premiered May 3, 2020, and tackled rural healthcare in the wake of the pandemic. To get everything we needed for the story, I crisscrossed Texas with Sharyn, going from the capital in Austin to tiny towns like Bedias, outside Houston. From there, *60* sent us to the border town of Laredo to cover the controversial practice of antibody testing. Our next story, "The Wild West of Testing," aired in June. From the border, I hit the road to San Antonio and produced a story with Scott Pelley called "The Long Siege." It was about Covid's impact on the economy and joblessness, and we used San Antonio as a test case.

While every industry was reeling from the pandemic, CBS News had its own complicated internal issues to deal with. Namely, *60 Minutes* had partnered with a new streaming company called Quibi and had promised to deliver a brand-new version of the show called *60 in 6*. Billed as the next generation of *60 Minutes*, the abbreviated version of the show had all-new, young correspondents and was being produced with the same high standards as the flagship program.

There was a lot of excitement about the latest extension of the *60* brand, and the company flew in correspondents from Rome and Seattle for a launch party in early March 2020. Like Quibi itself, this event would go down in infamy. It is largely believed to be the source of "Patient Zero" at CBS News, causing the first of many outbreaks at the network and shutting down access to the broadcast center.

No one knew it at the time, but Quibi was doomed from the start. Led by Jeffrey Katzenberg and Meg Whitman, Quibi launched on April 6, 2020, with $1.75 billion from big-name investors, including Disney, NBCUniversal, Warner Media, Viacom, and MGM Studios. It wouldn't even make it nine months, officially ending its flash-in-the-pan run in December. The service was only able to generate half a million paid subscribers, seven million below its own projections.

When CBS News announced it was partnering with Quibi in January 2020, I had actually applied to be a producer at *60 in 6*. I was feeling unsettled, like a change was in the air. But this move would have been the wrong one. Thank God they didn't want me.

I had plenty of stories to keep me busy, but I was looking for something more than my next news fix. Everything in me was shouting that it was time to make a change. To what, exactly, I didn't know, and I was reaching out for any shiny new thing I could find. If I wasn't satisfied working for *60 Minutes* and *48 Hours*, what was I even doing at the network anymore?

While *60 Minutes* had taken the lead on pandemic coverage, *48 Hours* was about to enter the fray with a tantalizing new murder case. The virus itself was taking center stage in a missing person's investigation down in Florida. The case was breaking new ground at *48*, because we were producing the entire show remotely to comply with pandemic protocols.

While novel in some regards, the basic premise of the crime remained the same: a jilted husband had killed his estranged wife and tried to cover it up using the events du jour. So instead of a Texas woman allegedly lost in a hurricane, it was a Florida woman supposedly quarantined in a hospital ward.

By the time authorities caught up to the victim's husband in New Mexico, he'd pawned all her jewelry. "'Til death do us part" has a different meaning for some people. He cut a deal to reveal the location of the body in exchange for a reduced sentence, and the whole thing was over without even going to trial. Our production schedule had been hamstrung by pandemic woes, and this awful murder was really saving our skin. Man, I needed a new job.

From my desk in Dallas, I zoomed into interview feeds in Florida. Correspondent Peter Van Sant was in New York, interviewing via a Zoom call with his own camera crew on the East Coast to make the shot seamless.

You might think making television this way would be cheaper, but the way CBS did it, it was actually more expensive. We had to pay for two crews on the ground in two different cities, and to pull off all the logistics, there were ten assigned producers. A normal show might have two or three.

But the biggest headline belonged to Alec Sirken. You won't see his name on the credits, however, because he was fired in the middle of production.[18] Despite all the inappropriate things that Alec said and did during his career, it took the words of a Florida Man to finally get him fired.

---

18 *48 Hours*, season 34, episode 31, "The Covid Cover-Up: Searching for Gretchen Anthony," aired May 8, 2021, CBS, https://www.youtube.com/watch?v=X4C4cCtS88s.

One of the hardest roles for a true crime producer is finding people willing to speak on behalf of an admitted murderer. It's a thankless job, but somebody's gotta do it. And back in 2020, that somebody was me. I scoured social media for former friends of the killer and cast a wide net with my direct messages. Eventually, I got a few bites.

Most people were conflicted about participating, which was understandable. But there was one guy who had zero qualms about going on camera in defense of a murderer. His comments about women were deeply disturbing, and after a couple of wildly misogynistic conversations, I told my colleagues in New York that I was done talking to that guy. If they wanted to book him for the show, that was their business, but I didn't think 90 percent of what he said was fit for air.

Meanwhile, I kept at it and found several other people who'd known the couple. Including investigators and attorneys, it seemed like we had more than enough characters to fill the hour. I was as surprised as anyone when I saw we'd kept the Florida Man on the interview schedule. But nothing could have prepared me for what happened when he actually showed up to the venue.

Although he'd never been shy about sharing his opinions before, Florida Man now insisted that we shoot him in shadow, obscuring his identity and altering his voice. This was an absurd request because his safety was not at risk. He simply didn't have the guts to put his face with his beliefs, and he'd prefer to hide in the dark than censor his own comments.

I still can't believe we filmed with this guy. It was a vanity interview with no upside. When it mercifully ended, we all agreed that he didn't have a usable line in the interview. That should have been the last we ever heard of Florida Man.

But Alec just couldn't leave a joke unsaid.

And so, the next week, when we were selecting sound bites to use in our script, Alec sent in the most offensive paragraph he could find in Florida Man's transcript. The lead producer either hadn't worked with Alec much, or he'd just had enough of his antics. Either way, it escalated to HR. I'd tell you more, but the rest is sealed in a private settlement that ended Alec's employment with CBS News once and for all.

Even before Alec's sudden departure from *48 Hours*, the pandemic had caused me to reevaluate my career path. It wasn't that I hadn't enjoyed my time running and gunning for CBS. Beating the competition, winning over characters, and scoring exclusive access were some of my greatest joys in life. But I'd started to realize that as long as I worked for CBS, they would always reap an outsized benefit for my hard work. As much as I was risking to get the story, as long as they owned the show, I'd never truly have any skin in the game. I spent a lot of sleepless nights agonizing over my next move. Had I come this far in my media career only to quit? And was it really quitting—or changing the game?

One night, I was tucking my son into bed and trying to soothe both of our anxieties with a story. I'd developed a tradition of getting my son a book on every work trip and writing the name of the city I was visiting on the inside cover. Now, I scanned an overflowing bookshelf. Dozens upon dozens of titles, ranging from board books to graphic novels, his latest obsession.

I flipped through the covers: Los Angeles, New York, Denver, Miami, Austin, San Antonio, Fort Lauderdale, Oklahoma City. I had basically become the *Where's Waldo?* of murder. Staring at that bookshelf, my eyes glossed over, and I imagined a future where I could tell new stories on my own terms.

In 2019, Viacom had once again merged with CBS, bringing the Paramount brand along with it. For years, CBS had toyed with the idea of a powerhouse streaming service, with CBS All Access serving as the interim solution. In 2020, Viacom-CBS announced it was rebranding CBS All Access as Paramount+, and the service would include original content alongside all the Viacom-CBS-owned properties that weren't currently licensed to other streaming platforms. Like every existing show at CBS, *48 Hours* was tasked with coming up with pitches for a spin-off series.

Executive producer Judy Tygard sent an email to the entire staff, asking for original content in the *48 Hours* wheelhouse. I had been searching for a new chapter in my career, and this call for pitches landed in my inbox like a lifeline. Had my boss really just given me license to create my own concept for a true crime show? She wouldn't have to wait long.

It wasn't public knowledge who all sent in their ideas, but I knew of one other producer who had a bottom-drawer life as active as mine: Hollywood

Chuck. He told me his pitch was on the Black Dahlia murder, an infamous unsolved case out of Los Angeles. The gruesome crime has stymied investigators from LAPD, the FBI, and everywhere else since 1947.

It was a compelling choice, and I was sure Chuck made a strong case as to why it should be a series. But I was hoping I'd have an advantage working with more recent headlines. I pitched a show on Texas Ranger James Holland, and I used the latest coverage of Samuel Little on *60 Minutes* as my hook. There was a big catch, though. Holland wasn't actually available to start filming right away. He was in the middle of several active murder investigations but planned to retire by the end of 2021. I was using all the best journalism bait: an exclusive character with an inside angle who wasn't even on the market yet.

Still, I figured my pitch's chances of getting picked off the pile were slim. There was nothing similar to my proposal on network television at the time, and at a place as steeped in tradition and conformity as CBS, that wasn't usually a good thing.

When I saw Judy's name on my caller ID, I wondered what kind of trouble I was in this time. No one was more surprised than me to learn that a corporate exec had hand selected my series as the *48 Hours* spinoff. In fact, the president and CEO of CBS Entertainment, George Cheeks, was so enthusiastic about the Texas Ranger–focused series that he wanted to do a presentation on it for the first-ever Paramount+ upfronts in February 2021. The network upfronts are an annual industry event where new and returning shows are announced to advertisers. It's a star-studded, black-tie affair, and only executives and on-air talent are invited. And Judy had called to ask *my permission* to make the announcement.

As much as I wanted to immediately agree, I knew we couldn't include Holland's name on any public-facing materials. Minor detail: He hadn't actually agreed to do the series. Because Holland wasn't retired yet, he couldn't engage in any discussions about projects on his career in law enforcement. Every time I'd tried to bring it up post–*60 Minutes*, he'd immediately cut me off. "Cart before the horse, Claire," he'd say. "I got too much shit to do before I can even start thinking about retiring and doing a TV show."

But now I had CBS convinced we did have the green light from the reclusive ranger. In the next few days, I'd have to figure out a way to walk back the idea of using Holland's name in the upfronts, while also avoiding any suspicion about the state of the series. I hoped my one-liner about Holland's tentative 2021 retirement date would cover my ass with George Cheeks.

When I spoke to Judy, I tempered my excitement with ground rules.

"We can't use Holland's name until after he retires, and he won't be on any calls, review any documents, or otherwise engage in the process until then."

The funny thing is, when you're speaking for a Texas Ranger, people tend to take your word for it. Cheeks had no issues toeing the line. He wouldn't use Holland's name, but he did need something in the meantime. A new name for the series.

In my pitch documents, I had called it "*Holland, Texas Ranger,*" a nod to the long-running CBS drama *Walker, Texas Ranger.* It was always a place-holder title. But now I needed to come up with the real one, in the span of a weekend, to be announced live alongside the launch of Paramount+. It was absurd, but the whole pitch had been a wild shot in the dark anyway. I didn't have time to stress out about it. I just laced up my running shoes and headed out the door.

I pounded the pavement, letting my footfalls be the only sound in my head. No playlist this time. I needed the quiet rhythm of feet and breath to work out an idea as big as this one.

My mind wandered back to the beginning: The story that no one at CBS wanted had now become its first choice. If I'd listened to my bosses back then, I'd never be where I am right now. They would have killed the story before it ever had a chance to live.

My legs were flying down neighborhood streets. This was the best kind of problem to have. I needed to come up with a title that captured Holland's unique brand of interrogation method while obscuring his identity. There could be no mention of his name, and I was leaning toward leaving Texas Ranger out of the title altogether. I wanted the appeal for the show to be bigger than Texas. The best titles were short, one to three words. Too bad *Cops* was already taken.

I played *Tetris* with word combinations in my head. *The Interview Room. Inside the Interview Room. Truth or Lies. Reading the Room.*

The Lie Detector.

I stopped running. It just felt so right. In one of our recent interviews with Holland for *48 Hours*, he'd likened himself to a human lie detector, reading people's reactions and indications of deception without any instrumentation.

If you boiled it down, that was the essence of Holland's interrogation method. Honed over twenty-five years, Holland had developed his own brand of interview techniques for psychopathic killers, and he was getting unprecedented results. Closing cold cases not only with confessions, but with physical corroboration that only the real killer would know.

An hour had passed since Judy tasked me with finding the perfect title for my series. I didn't want to come off as rash, so I took the rest of the weekend to mull it over and try alternatives. In the end, I still had *The Lie Detector* at the top of the page. On Monday morning, I shared it with Judy. She liked it instantly and sent it up the chain. A few weeks later, George Cheeks made it official from the main stage.

The new 48 Hours *true crime docuseries, exclusive for Paramount+, is called* The Lie Detector. *A Texas Ranger has spent twenty-five years getting into the minds of killers in high-profile, twisted murder cases.*

He will take viewers behind the scenes into some of the most infamous cases he's handled. You'll find the same style and quality of true crime reporting you've come to expect from the producers of the Emmy- and Peabody-award-winning 48 Hours, *but this time in a new and compelling original format.*

As soon as Cheeks finished his presentation, I started Googling entertainment attorneys. The whole concept for the show was still just a Word document on my laptop in Texas. As much as I tried to always believe in myself, this was a stretch, even for me. I'd often thought I was the only one faking it 'til I made it. But if the highest-ranking executive at CBS was using smoke and mirrors, maybe we all were.

I'd seen what happened to other *48 Hours* producers who came up with original ideas for new shows, and it was a cautionary tale. There were two *48* spinoffs on CBS already: *The FBI Declassified* and *48 Hours: NCIS*. If I was lucky, they'd keep me on as a producer-writer, but there were no guarantees. Except, of course, that they'd never let a field producer from Texas be credited as an executive producer. I knew that to hold on to my rights with *The Lie Detector*, I'd have to be willing to leave CBS. The only question was: Did I have the guts to do it?

I'm sitting on a black leather couch, with my arms crossed over my chest. There's a table in front of me with tissues and a candy dish, and I consider taking one of each.

"What brings you here today?" a man with a kind face asks me.

I've stared down murderers, kidnappers, and rapists, yet this is the hardest conversation of my life.

It's my first time in a therapist's office, and I feel like bolting. Instead, I steel myself in place with a deep breath as I cross my arms tighter.

The truth is: The final blow that brought me to therapy wasn't my job in true crime television. It was a far more personal tragedy. It feels wrong to write a memoir and then leave a piece of myself out of it. But for once, it's really not my story to tell. Because the reason I finally walked through the therapy door was because of something I witnessed happening to someone I loved, and it changed me forever.

In 2021, events in my personal life caused the trauma dam I'd carefully constructed to finally give way, and I've been riding the currents ever since. It took me years before I ever admitted to my husband, or even myself, that I'd been deeply affected by working in true crime television. The things I'd seen and done to get stories on the air before the competition were not normal workplace experiences. Once, after I'd gotten a law enforcement official to copy over evidence in a murder trial, he told me there was a "price of admission." Then he opened a file on his laptop of the defendant masturbating in the shower and made me watch it.

By entering therapy, I've slowly started to unpack the darkness that still haunts me from being intimately involved with dozens of murder cases. The nightmares. The intrusive images. The hyperalertness in crowds when I start to visualize a mass shooting.

It's not normal to have this many disturbing memories at the ready. But my job is to memorize every detail of these horrific cases and spit them back out during interviews and edit sessions. Where am I supposed to file it all when the story ends? I finally decided to figure that part out.

It was 2021 when I started slaying my demons for the first time. I began regular therapy sessions and was taking most of the advice my therapist suggested to heart.

It was an interesting year for a host of reasons. We were post-pandemic but still in the middle of a global health crisis, and no one's job looked the same as it did in 2019. Mine included.

I was still working at CBS, juggling stories for *48 Hours* and *60 Minutes*. But after three years of dreaming and scheming, I had finally made a deal for my podcast: *Final Days on Earth with Claire St. Amant*. I felt a little self-conscious putting my name in the title, but I knew I needed to own it in every sense of the word. For my first season, I partnered with the recruiter who'd originally contacted me on LinkedIn, and we set out to pitch the podcast far and wide.

After countless rejections, I got my first real offer. PodcastOne, an LA-based network with over two hundred podcasts, wanted to partner with me on *Final Days*. My introduction to this West Coast company came from a savvy Dallas entrepreneur—and my former boss—Tony Hartl. He vouched for me with radio execs, who passed along my trailer and pilot episode to the director of programming. A few days later, they were drawing up the paperwork.

I was elated, and everyone was telling me to take the offer and run with it. But once I got over the initial excitement that someone actually wanted my podcast, I realized it was a pretty raw deal. They were offering a fifty-fifty split, and nothing else.

I solicited advice from Tony and others, who confirmed that I'd be selling myself short to accept this deal outright. I told PodcastOne that I appreciated their offer very much and that I really wanted to work with them, but I needed a higher percentage of the revenue and a guarantee per season.

Even after three years of bootstrapping it, I was prepared to walk away. Thankfully, I didn't have to. They agreed to my counteroffer and tacked on a second season. Confidence pays.

My first season of *Final Days with Claire St. Amant: The Life and Death of Dammion Heard*, debuted in April 2021, marking the seventh anniversary of the young wrestler's untimely death. The experience of creating, reporting, producing, and hosting my own investigative crime show was a thrill like no other. The first time I got a revenue check, and actually shared in the profits of my labor, was a moment I'll never forget. It was less than what I was making in television, but it had a whole different feel to it.

I was telling a new story, one that network television had deemed too messy and complicated. Because of the nature of podcasts, I was able to let the story really breathe, and it was taking on a life of its own. By detailing every facet of the case, I was getting more information out on the investigation than ever before. As a result, I started hearing from new witnesses who'd never spoken to police or other authorities. Experts from around the globe volunteered their services to weigh in on the forensics and crime scene dynamics. The result was a deeper, more nuanced conversation about the case than I ever could have gotten on television. My podcast has opened doors and avenues for further investigation of Dammion's death that I truly hope authorities will pursue one day.

Around the same time as my podcast came out, I was watching another drama unfold in the music world. Taylor Swift announced she was re-recording all of her songs so that she would own the rights to them. It was a headline-making, ball-busting move, and it gave me a crazy idea of my own.

Ever since I'd started working at *48 Hours*, it was a conversation magnet. From moms I met in the carpool line to dads I ran into at the dog park, everyone who asked what I did for a living seemed to light up when I talked about *48*. And they didn't just want to know about my latest story. They were endlessly curious about what it was like, day-to-day, as a true crime television producer. A killer story that had never been told, this could be a way to take back every story I'd ever worked on for CBS News and own the IP for once. Because I'd write about it all from a new perspective: mine.

I can't remember exactly how I first heard about the latest *48 Hours* licensing deal, but when you're based over a thousand miles from HQ, that tends to happen. When I started out at the show in 2014, I knew reruns aired on Investigation Discovery, OWN, and TLC. But by 2021, our archive of episodes could also be found on Paramount+, the streaming service CBS News 24/7, and the latest addition to the Viacom family, Pluto TV.

The deal had been in the works for years, with Viacom acquiring the former start-up streamer in 2019. By 2021, Pluto TV was dedicating an entire channel to our reruns, which would air around the clock. Since then, nearly all CBS shows have joined Team Pluto, and the free, ad-supported streaming service has publicly credited CBS as the "No. 1 driver of audience engagement and revenue." In case you're wondering, Pluto TV became a $1 billion annual business in 2021.[19]

In conversations with colleagues, this number was shared with excitement and pride, as if we, the producers of this mountain of entertainment, actually got a piece of it. To me, it felt like the corporate execs essentially wanted to throw a party over the news, pay us in cake, and hope nobody noticed. But it didn't feel like a cause for celebration in my book.

I'd been in the media game long enough to know that despite shrinking salaries and ever-present layoffs, there was actually plenty of money floating around if you knew where to look. The problem is: I was on the wrong side of the table.

19 Dade Hayes, "Pluto TV to add 6,300-plus episodes from CBS vault to its free streaming service as Paramount Global divisions harmonize," Deadline, October 31, 2022, https://deadline.com/2022/10/pluto-tv-cbs-episodes-free-streaming-service-paramount-global-1235159033/.

21

HELD IN CONTEMPT

It's the summer of 2021, and I'm sitting in a hotel lobby in Beaufort, South Carolina, waiting for a man I've never met. Like the rest of the true crime world, I've been living out of a suitcase for weeks thanks to the machinations of Alex Murdaugh. Once a prominent attorney with a well-connected family, Alex's fall from grace has overshadowed everything else in his life.

For over a hundred years, the Murdaugh family's star burned brightly in South Carolina legal circles, with generations serving as high-profile lawyers and prosecutors. But the light started to dim in February 2019 when Alex's son, Paul, was arrested in connection with the boating death of his classmate Mallory Beach. Paul was caught on camera using his older brother's ID and purchasing alcohol the night of the crash. The Beach family had filed a series of lawsuits in connection with the tragic death.

It was a local scandal, and it might have stayed that way if not for what happened two years later.

In June 2021, Paul and his mother, Maggie, were gunned down at the family's remote hunting lodge. Nothing was stolen from the scene, and authorities quickly established it was a targeted attack. But who would want a mother and son dead? The cold-blooded, contract-style killings spawned theories of a possible connection to other mysterious deaths in the tight-knit community—or even an inside job. At least one of the guns used in the murders belonged to the Murdaugh family. There were whispers about a housekeeper who'd died mysteriously years ago, and citing evidence recovered at the scene, authorities revealed they were reopening a seemingly unrelated homicide: the 2015 "hit and run" death of Stephen Smith.

It was all incredibly sensational and the kind of story that no one in true crime television could pass up. That meant every outlet in the country was looking for an exclusive angle, and if I didn't find one soon, we'd be interviewing the janitor at Murdaugh's law firm.

The man I'm waiting for is a former Beaufort County Sheriff's deputy. He says he lost his job for standing up to the Murdaughs after the 2019 boat crash. The deputy was the first person to question the surviving boat passengers about who was driving, and he wrote the name Paul Murdaugh in his report. Despite pressure from the family, he never backed down. He says they harassed him for over a year to change his report, and when that didn't work, they discredited him with allegations of prescription drug use. He lost his job and is now working in the private sector.

We'd repeatedly tried to find sources within the Murdaugh family but couldn't get anyone to go on camera. The story was too big to fail, so here I am, waiting on the former deputy and working the phones and social media for any other willing characters. Ironically, I have a great character sitting right next to me, a young woman who was a Beaufort local and had known the Murdaughs for years.

Julianna Love Dunphy was the newest broadcast associate at 48. She was twenty-three years old, and this was her first story. A few weeks earlier, senior producer Patti Aronofsky had plucked young Julianna's resume off a massive pile based on her unique middle name. I couldn't believe the luck. We needed an insider perspective, and we had one served up on a company platter. Lovely Julianna couldn't turn us down, even if she wanted to, but there was one little problem: She really wanted to be on TV. And in the cutthroat world of national television, they don't just put pretty young things on camera the minute they walk in the door from South Carolina.

I tried to coach her.

"Don't go in there all smiley. You are not excited about this," I said emphatically. "You don't even want to go on camera. But you are a team player. You'll do whatever you're told."

Looking at Julianna's eager smile and thin resume, I knew Kramer would never let her on the air. It was a damn shame too, because Julianna was perfect for the role in every way except office politics. And I could have booked my flight home in record time.

I glance back at my phone and see the three dots hovering in my latest message to the former deputy. I hold my breath and wait for the verdict.

"I'm so sorry. I overslept. I have to be at work in an hour. I can't make the interview."

I want to throw the phone across the room. But I compose myself and give him a call instead.

He picks up, sounding groggy, and I go straight for the kill.

"Hey man, I'm so sorry you overslept. I hate when that happens to me. Look, it's no problem at all. We don't have to do your interview today. But the whole crew is already set up and waiting, and honestly, they just really want to meet you and shake your hand. Do you think you could come by and say hello on your way to work? It would mean the world to them."

It was a wild line, and one I'd actually never used before. But I'd been through every page in my own playbook on this story already, and nothing had worked. I was imitating a strategy I'd seen Ranger Holland employ with Samuel Little. Play to his ego in the extreme by treating him like a celebrity. It had worked with a serial killer, why not try it with a former cop?

An hour later, I had to stop myself from smirking when the would-be star of the show sheepishly walked into the hotel lobby. He was wearing a stained undershirt and a pair of cargo shorts. Smart guy. He knows I'd never put him on camera looking like that. But I still have a few tricks up my sleeve.

Correspondent Nikki Battiste and I greet him warmly and guide him into the waiting interview room. I've told the crew to treat him like a celebrity, and they play the role perfectly, glad-handing him and slapping him on the back.

Nikki, a former booking producer turned on-air talent, knows just how to coax reluctant characters into the chair. And once we got him in the room, he never really had a chance.

The interview that almost wasn't. He's wearing a shirt loaned by our sound technician.

We ask him to take a seat, so we'll know how to frame his shot when he does eventually do an interview with us. He sits down in a daze, and the crew starts to mic him.

"I can't go on TV looking like this," he says, pulling on his stained shirt.

"You're right," I tell him. "What size shirt are you?"

The sound tech is a perfect match, and he'd worn a clean button-down to work that day. Presto chango, and our man is camera ready. I was signaling to roll, but he had other ideas.

"I only have about fifteen minutes before I have to be at work," he says.

"No problem," I lie. "That's all the time we need."

We filmed with him for the next hour, and he called his boss during a break to say he was coming in late. That didn't seem like a tough conversation for the ex-deputy, despite his initial hesitancy to change his schedule. People are usually pretty accommodating when you mention you're doing a national television interview on an unsolved murder case.

It's Friday afternoon, and I'm meeting Julianna for lunch on the water at one of her favorite restaurants. It's a beautiful day, and I'm soaking up the scene. It had been a very successful shoot, and Julianna was going to stay put in Beaufort to handle any additional characters that came up over the weekend. I booked my flight home yesterday, and I was double-checking my gate information when I saw a call coming through.

Kramer. On a Friday afternoon. This can't be good.

I pick up, and she's in a tizzy. She didn't realize I was planning to go home over the weekend. I think the word "permission" was bandied about.

"Julianna is too inexperienced to be left alone in the field, booking characters on her own," Kramer tells me.

I try to reason with her: "But this isn't 'the field.' It's her hometown. She is literally in her own backyard. I think it's okay for her to be unsupervised."

Kramer isn't having it, and she goes off on me. But I'm in no mood for a lecture. I put the call on speaker, mute my audio, and place my phone on the table in between our ceviche and guacamole. I crunch on a chip as Kramer prattles on, and Julianna's eyes get as big as our lunch plates.

I don't remember exactly what was said, but it's clear Kramer doesn't approve of me flying home. In the past, I would have apologized, canceled my flight, and yes ma'amed the hell out of her. But I wasn't going to do that anymore.

I finish my chip and dust off my hands before unmuting the line. Kramer is still giving me an earful. I cut her off.

"Nancy—hey, Nancy—my cell phone battery is about to die. I don't know—" Click.

I hang up the phone midsentence and promptly turn on airplane mode.

Julianna stares at me in disbelief.

"What looks good for lunch?" I ask her. "CBS is paying."

In December 2021, I started working on what would become my last story for *48 Hours*. It was a local Dallas case that had made headlines the world over: the murder of Jamie Faith. A mild-mannered IT executive, he had been shot seven times while walking his dog during the pandemic as his wife, Jennifer, looked on in horror.

As I parsed through the facts of the Faith case, I was struck by a macabre déjà vu. It didn't take long to find a cheating spouse, a life insurance plot, and a lover turned assassin at the center of it all. Kramer was thrilled with the predictable nature of the spousal murder story. It was the bread and butter of our show. My stomach was turning, but they wanted additional helpings.

I'd known of the case since its inception and had flagged Kramer on the developments, including when Jennifer Faith was charged for the federal murder-for-hire conspiracy and the killer was revealed as her high school boyfriend. While the story was sensational true crime fare, it was still early days. No evidence had been released, and a trial was years away. I figured we'd eventually do an episode, but the timeline changed overnight when *People* magazine ran with the Faith story in late November 2021.[20]

Nothing gets a new *48 Hours* episode greenlit faster than a splashy story in *People*, the quintessential reading material of soccer moms ages twenty-five to fifty-five, aka our key demographic. When the Faith story hit newsstands, I'd just gotten back to Dallas after covering a cold case murder trial in Colorado that had ended in a hung jury.[21]

I'd actually left before the verdict, on Friday afternoon in the middle of the defendant's testimony, to switch stories. It was a call I'd made on my own, and I was still catching heat from it. I'd given senior producer Patti Aronofsky a heads-up on my plans while en route to the airport. To say she was displeased was an understatement. I think her exact words were: "You can't leave in the middle of testimony without telling me!"

"That's why I'm telling you now," I said calmly, baiting her.

20 Marc Peyser, "After a Husband Is Shot on His Own Street, Police Arrest His Wife—and Her High School Boyfriend," *People*, November 26, 2021, https://people.com/crime/jennifer-faith-alleged-murder-for-hire-plot-high-school -boyfriend/.

21 *48 Hours*, season 34, episode 26, "The Kidnapping of Jonelle Matthews," aired March 27, 2021, CBS, https://www .cbsnews.com/news/jonelle-matthews-murder-kidnapping-steve-pankey-trial-48-hours/.

If I'm gonna get yelled at, I might as well have a little fun with it. I waited for her to take a breath, and then I tried a new tack.

"I'm already at the airport. But I can fly back to Colorado on Monday if that's what you want."

Patti exploded. "What I want? I want you to stay in Denver! Monday is too late! You'd have to fly Sunday night, which means you might as well just stay put this weekend."

I knew she had a point, but I'd been gone all week, and I was at my limit. Some might even call it acting out. But all I really cared about now was getting Patti off my back, fast. I figured the best strategy was to give her another target. And I had the perfect person for the job.

"I can't be in two places at once, and Kramer needs me in Dallas for the Faith story. Take it up with her."

I chuckled to myself at the believability of my story. By the time Patti figured out that Kramer hadn't ordered me back to Dallas, I'd be thirty thousand feet in the air.

Considering the fact that Patti didn't call me on the carpet for my stunt in Colorado, I'm guessing she never confronted Kramer about it. (Well, now you know, Patti.)

When I got back to Dallas, Kramer quickly assigned a production team to the Faith story, and in short order, we had characters lined up for interviews in Phoenix, where the victim had lived most of his life. In a cost-saving measure, I was told I'd be conducting the interviews instead of a correspondent. In the past, this news would have thrilled me, but now it felt like an additional burden.

I typed up interview questions for the victim's friends, and I couldn't believe how quickly the document came together. I'd done this so many times before that I'd developed something akin to muscle memory for the aftermath of a murder.

Scheduling interviews in December is always a crapshoot, and before long we'd marked through every available date except for December 23. A pit formed in my stomach. In all my years at CBS, I had only ever said no to traveling on a story once. That was July 23, 2015, and I was nine months pregnant. *CBS This Morning* had asked if I could go to the scene of a mass shooting at a movie theater in Lafayette, Louisiana. I told them I wasn't supposed to fly this late in my pregnancy, and they offered to rent me a car for the eight-hour drive from Dallas. I had politely declined.

This time around, I didn't have a medical reason to refuse the trip. But I had a six-year-old son, and they were asking me to travel on Christmas Eve. Images of canceled flights and lonely hotel rooms danced in my head, and I just couldn't bring myself to do it. I told Kramer I wasn't available for the December 23 interview unless it was in Dallas. Another producer, who was unmarried and childless, volunteered to go instead. Everything was set, when the character called to cancel at the last minute. Very glad I stood my ground. To this day, my son repeats the story proudly. "Remember that time your boss wanted you to work on Christmas Eve?" he says, shaking his head. I wonder where he gets his flair for storytelling.

I celebrated the holidays with the usual fanfare, taking only a brief break from the festivities to book my travel itinerary for January.

Before I knew it, it was New Year's Day 2022. I remember seeing "Texas Ranger James Holland" come across my caller ID. But why was he calling me now? He'd already told me he was spending the winter break with his family skiing, a ritual I gathered was sacred. Intrigued, I picked up the call in my pajamas.

"Today is my first official day of retirement," Holland said.

I was too stunned to reply. After years of hemming and hawing about the decision, he'd finally pulled the trigger. Holland was a free agent. I found my voice and congratulated him. And in the next breath, I brought up that television show I'd been trying to talk to him about since 2019. For once, he didn't cut me off.

A week later, I was packing my suitcase for Phoenix. While most people would love to visit Arizona in January, I wasn't one of them. I tried to put my feelings into words with my husband. I'd been on a hundred trips like this before. Why was this one bugging me so much? The Faith case wasn't really that different from any other murder story I'd covered.

And maybe that was the problem.

"I feel like we're trafficking in tragedy, and there's no redeemable quality to the story," I said. "I don't even know why we're telling it, other than the fact that everyone else is. I have no interest in being part of this business model."

He was sympathetic. He'd never really been a true crime fan to begin with. Still, it was hard to believe I was the one who wanted to pull the plug.

When I first started working at CBS, I never could have imagined walking away. But almost a decade later, I was starting to realize that I'd hit my limit of what network television could do for me. In the time I'd spent at *48 Hours*, I'd seen budgets shrink and story quotas rise. The result was an even greater demand for murder stories, but with fewer resources and staff to pull them off, which led to the same old story, on repeat.

On some level, I was conflicted, because I still had a soft spot for murder. Just not the mass-entertainment variety. I wanted to tell stories that made a difference. I wanted to fight for victims the justice system had failed and to bring light to the darkest corners of true crime. I'd found a way to do that through my podcast, but I was looking for more than a side hustle.

I realized that unless I made a big change, I'd be stuck telling the same stories as everybody else. It seemed rash to quit on the spot, so I finished packing and set my alarm for a morning flight.

We'd set up a series of interviews in Phoenix. There was a married couple who had been close friends with the victim, and then the big prize, one of Jennifer's surviving ex-husbands. At this point, I knew Jennifer had been married three times. From scouring online databases, I could see that she'd had a daughter with her first husband, filed bankruptcy with her second, and had more than likely killed her third. Considering all the publicity surrounding Jennifer Faith, I was pleasantly surprised when her second husband, Rick, agreed to an on-camera interview.

He'd presented us with only one request: Could he bring his dog?

The complication was twofold: the noise and distraction of an animal on set, and the logistics of it going down in a hotel. Although unusual, it wasn't entirely unprecedented. In an interview for the Houston hit man case, one of the characters was interviewed with a terrier sitting on her lap.

While my first canine caveat had been under twenty-five pounds, Rick's was a large breed, a boxer mix and pushing one hundred pounds. He called it his "emotional support animal," though based on the dog's behavior, I doubt it had received any formal training.

After a hefty deposit and a pile of paperwork, the hotel agrees to let us bring the behemoth boxer inside, setting up one of the most bizarre interviews of my life.

In the first five minutes, Rick reveals he'd started seeing Jennifer while she was still married to her first husband.

"I guess I should have known it was trouble in the beginning," he tells me. "I wish I had."

Nearby, the dog shakes its collar and the whole set groans. We pause so Rick can remove the collar, then help the dog onto a velvet couch. I notice its fingernails are painted.

The interview resumes and Rick tells me that just a few weeks into their affair, Jennifer wanted to take a trip together. It was an unusual location for a romantic getaway.

"She wanted to go to Disneyland."

This made sense, in a way, because Jennifer had a three-year-old daughter. But strangely, she didn't bring her along.

"That seemed odd," Rick admits. "Every child's dream is to go to Disneyland, and we're doing it on the sly."

The trip got even weirder when Jennifer pulled Rick aside to have a serious talk. Right there in the middle of the happiest place on earth, Jennifer made graphic claims of suffering sexual abuse, torture, and mutilation dating back to her childhood and continuing with her current husband.

"It was unbelievable, and a lot to process, especially at Disneyland," Rick says, clearly still affected. For a moment, I'm actually grateful the guy's emotional support dog is here.

I quickly learn this appalling aside is just the tip of the iceberg of Jennifer's deceit. And in a wide-ranging conversation that lasted nearly four hours, Rick shares a number of deeply personal stories. They all had one thing in common: Jennifer's keen ability to use shock as a manipulation tactic. For whatever reason, Jennifer got off on convincing people that she had been through horrific experiences, though there was never any evidence it was actually true.

In fact, once authorities examined Jennifer's computer after Jamie's murder, they found numerous forged documents and proof of staged injuries. In one case, she'd used photos of her face after a car wreck as false evidence that her husband had hit her. Through the years, there were diabolical and intricate cons, complete with fake identities, dummy email accounts, and even staged deaths.

Rick also details a debilitating series of health battles, all related to his digestion, during a period when he was unemployed and still married to Jennifer. I asked him who usually prepared his meals. Surprise, surprise, it was Jennifer.

It's hard to keep up with all the lies he's presenting and even harder to believe that one person could be responsible for so much pain. As one particularly bold and outlandish example, Jennifer created a fake romantic interest for herself as a way to make Rick jealous. Once she'd gotten all the mileage she could out of that situation, she'd killed off her pretend boyfriend in a fiery car crash. Jennifer even left Rick to babysit her daughter while she allegedly attended her lover's funeral.

"Did you ever see an obituary or a program from the memorial service?" I prod Rick, willing him to connect the dots that this person had never existed, let alone died.

"I don't think so, and I certainly can't find one now. Believe me, I've looked," he says, flabbergasted.

Was this my job now? Telling hapless men about the depths of their partner's depravity?

I knew most of this interview would never air on 48 Hours. It was too strange and complicated. The part we'd use would be about Rick's shock upon learning that Jennifer's third husband had been murdered, and how he'd come to see his own marriage in a whole new light—one that left him thankful he'd gotten out alive.

By the time we finish the interview, it's nearly midnight. And I'm wrung out. I thank Rick for his time as his dog zooms around the hotel suite. Then I eat dinner out of a vending machine and crawl into bed.

It's the morning after the weirdest interview of my life, and I switch on the hotel TV to CBS. Gayle King, Tony Dokoupil, and Nate Burleson are on the screen, chatting with a career expert from LinkedIn.[22] The topic? "Quitting Gracefully." I laugh as I brew a cup of terrible instant coffee. I'm the kind of person who listens when the universe speaks, and I wasn't going to ignore yet another God nod telling me it was time to exit stage left.

And while the Jennifer Faith story was driving me crazy, another Jennifer was calling my name. I had finally landed on a cold case for the second season of my podcast, *Final Days on Earth*: the unsolved murder of Jennifer Harris, with a family who had been searching for justice for almost twenty years. It was the polar opposite of the Faith story, and I couldn't wait to dive back into it.

I'd first covered the Harris murder for *48 Hours* in 2018, and the whole experience had left a bad taste in my mouth. The impetus for our episode had been the shocking tragedy of it all. Jennifer was just twenty-eight years old when she disappeared on Mother's Day 2002 in her hometown of Bonham, Texas. The last thing Jennifer told her best friend was that she was pregnant and had decided to keep the baby, against the wishes of the father. Her naked body was found four days later in a river. There'd never been an arrest or indictment, despite a strong circumstantial case that overwhelmingly pointed in one direction.

For reasons I'll never fully understand, *48 Hours* focused on a private investigator from the East Coast who believed the case was unsolvable. Our episode basically concluded that the case was a dead end, and Jennifer's killer was beyond the reach of justice. It was a gut punch for everyone involved in the investigation, except the actual murderer, who was effectively given a pass on national television. The victim's family told me that the day our episode aired was the second worst day of their lives, the first being when Jennifer's body was found. Talk about nightmare feedback.

I'd stayed in touch with Jennifer's family and had never stopped believing her case could be solved. During a conversation with the family in 2021,

22 *CBS Mornings*, "Quitting Gracefully," aired January 20, 2022, CBS, https://www.cbsnews.com/video/linkedin-career-expert-on-great-resignation-changing-workforce/.

REWARD $10,000
Leading to the **Arrest and Conviction** in the Death of
Jennifer Lynette Harris

Jennifer was last seen on Mother's Day Sunday May 12, 2002 at approximately 8:00 p.m. driving a 2000 forest green Wrangler Jeep which was found by Lake Bonham near the Hoe-Down Hall on CR 2610. Jennifer's body was found Saturday May 18, 2002 in the Red River two miles east of Highway 78 River Bridge.

If you know anything or even THINK you know or may have seen something related to this case, Please contact the agencies listed below.

Fannin County Sheriff's Department
Lt. David Perkins   903-583-2143

Texas Attorney General's Office Austin, Texas.
Major Offender Unit
Captain Jeff Bishop 512-463-0272
E-MAIL: JEFF.BISHOP@OAG.STATE.TX.US
OR
Louie Laurel 512-463-2257
LAUREL@OAG.STATE.TX.US

The unsolved murder of Jennifer Harris would be the second-season focus of *Final Days on Earth*.

we discussed the upcoming twentieth anniversary of Jennifer's murder. I had started *Final Days on Earth* to dive deep into cold cases where victim's families had nowhere else to turn.

From my hotel room in Phoenix, I outline the second season of *Final Days*. My fingers fly across the keyboard as I punch out a treatment for twelve episodes on "The Life and Death of Jennifer Harris." I email it to the senior staff at PodcastOne with the proposed timing as May 2022. Before I even head to the airport, PodcastOne is on board with my plan. And a few hours later, my plane home takes off, and I'm calculating my exit strategy from CBS as we climb into the clouds.

I'm not the type to put all my eggs in one basket, and so my second season of *Final Days* was just one component of why I felt ready to leave *48 Hours*. As much as I loved my podcast, I had other production plans that I wanted to see through as well, ones that would use my television talents in a fresh format as an executive producer of *The Lie Detector*. It had been over two years since I'd first met Ranger Holland at a murder trial in Galveston. And in that time, we'd practically become coworkers. After securing his story on *60 Minutes*, I hadn't let a second go to waste. The following season, Holland appeared on *48 Hours* to discuss a twisted murder case where he'd once again elicited a shocking confession from the killer.

Ranger Holland has become the toast of the true crime world, and he's only talking to CBS. It is starting to make the rest of the media a little crazy. Everyone from print, television, and even Hollywood is trying to get a piece of this guy. He'd play the desperate voicemails for me, laughing. Everyone loves to be wanted.

With Holland finally retired as a Texas Ranger, I know I need to find a way to keep him occupied and in the TV fold, fast. Developing his own docuseries would take time, and even though I had a running start with Paramount+ announcing *The Lie Detector* as coming soon, shows aren't made overnight. And Holland isn't the type to sit idly by, hands in his lap, while executives hash out contracts.

I'm on another tightrope walk on this one, balancing my new golden talent, my exit strategy, and my still-current job. Thankfully, they all converge with a request from senior *48 Hours* producer Peter Schweitzer. He's asking for more voices on Jennifer Faith and has even suggested we hire a consultant to weigh in on the uniqueness of the case. And I have just the man for the job.

I dial up Schweitzer and pitch him on hiring Holland as a CBS News consultant. It's an easy sell, and I'm all too happy to interrupt the end of Holland's ski trip to give him the news of his first post-retirement gig. We set up an interview for when he returns to Dallas, and I get to work compiling a research packet for him to review about the case.

There's still one ball in the air, though. No one at CBS knows that I'm eyeing the door, and that this episode could be my last.

It's February 2022, and I'm at a hotel in downtown Dallas to film Holland's interview. As I walk on set, I'm hit with feelings akin to senioritis, both nostalgic for the *48 Hours* process and totally sick of it. It might have something to do with the fact that the heater has failed in the ballroom that we're filming in, and it's hovering around fifty degrees on set. Winter in Dallas almost always means ice and freezing temperatures. I'm reminded of the frigid scene of my first *48* shoot as a field producer, in 2015, at a feed store in Kaufman, Texas. Back then, I was thrilled to be freezing to death for CBS News. And today, even though I can't feel my toes, I still have a modicum of appreciation for the privilege of working on national television. Am I really ready to give up my safety net and strike out on my own?

The crew is still setting up, so I slip out of the room to try to warm up in the lobby. I'm scrolling through my phone when I remember I bookmarked the *CBS Mornings* story on "Quitting Gracefully." I read through the recommended resources and a "Burnout Inventory" catches my eye.

"I feel run down and drained of physical or emotional energy." Check.

"I have negative thoughts about my job." Double check.

"I feel that I am not getting what I want out of my job." Triple check.

I flash back to a recent conversation with my boss, Nancy Kramer. She had called to find out why I wasn't in Oklahoma City, chasing down leads on a crazy murder conspiracy case involving a local attorney in a love triangle.[23] It was all over the news, and I was just three hours down the road. Before, I would have jumped at the chance to work the story out of my car and beat back reporters from the rest of the country. But now, I was frozen with anxiety at the thought of leaving my family indefinitely to chase down suspected murderers for an interview.

In the middle of getting reamed out, I did something I'd never done in front of a boss in my entire career. I broke down. Embarrassed, I muted the call and tried to compose myself. Realizing it was hopeless, I hung up and stared at the screen. Figuring Kramer would try to call me back, I fired off an honest text.

"I'm sorry. I just need a minute."

Instantly, three dots hovered in response. I braced myself for impact. But all Kramer unloaded on me was compassion.

23 Nolan Clay, "New Evidence links OKC attorney to triple homicide," *Oklahoman*, April 9, 2020, https://www.oklahoman.com/story/news/columns/2020/04/09/new-evidence-links-okc-attorney-to-triple-homicide/60406815007/.

"You can take more than a minute. Why don't you take a couple days off?"

I thanked her and did just that. But it was a Band-Aid on a broken bone.

I finish taking the quiz and add up my results. No surprise, my numbers are off the charts.

I see Holland's truck pull into the valet stand, and I get up to greet him. I calculate this will be the third time I've gotten the reclusive Texas Ranger on national television. So much for that no-media policy, eh? I smile to myself, imagining how the rest of the true crime world will react when Holland once again graces a CBS time slot.

It's fun making the other media heads explode with these appearances, but I have my eye on a bigger prize. Sure, I could keep having Holland appear on CBS, but there'd be no guarantee as to how many episodes they'd want him to consult on. And I'd still be running around the country, working on a dozen murder stories at once, because that's my job at *48 Hours*. Unless I leave, I'll never have the creative freedom to work on the stories that matter most to me. I'll be stuck chasing all the same sensational murder cases as everyone else, with precious little time to devote to stories I actually care about, which I'll have to fight tooth and nail to get on the air.

All these thoughts are swimming in my head as Holland makes his way out of the cold and into the toasty hotel lobby. He rubs his hands together and points toward the hallway. "Lead the way, Claire," he says.

"Yes, sir," I say with a smirk.

22

BREAKING FREE

Two months have gone by, and I'm flying with Holland to New York to meet with Susan Zirinsky about the future of *The Lie Detector*. In the past year, Z has exchanged one president's office for another. No longer the head of the network, Z is now running See It Now Studios, the brand-new home for all CBS-made unscripted projects. "Unscripted" is a bit of a misnomer, because there are indeed scripts; the term means that the show does not employ actors or tell interviewees what to say on camera. See It Now will also buy outside documentaries for Paramount+ and other company extensions like Showtime, MTV, and BET.

After his announcement at the Paramount+ upfronts a year ago, CBS Entertainment president and CEO George Cheeks put *The Lie Detector* on Z's plate, and now, theoretically, all that's left to do is seal the deal with Ranger Holland. Everyone has treated his involvement like a forgone conclusion, but Holland doesn't actually work for CBS and is under no obligation to agree to their terms. Considering the entire concept for the show revolves around his career, Holland holds all the cards. What else is new?

The trip coincides with the screening for my latest *48* episode—and Holland's—"The Plot to Kill Jamie Faith." All the stars seem to be aligning for this to be my farewell tour at CBS, but I'm still keeping that under wraps for now. I don't want to lose the element of surprise.

In addition to meeting Z at See It Now and Judy Tygard at *48*, I've set up a few other appointments to make the most of my time with Holland in the City That Never Sleeps. We have a meeting in Brooklyn with an outside production company, breakfast with an entertainment attorney, and a couple of other confabs with potential writers, editors, and agents. It's a whirlwind schedule, and I'm stressing about how to juggle all my commitments.

After dinner with Holland on our first night in New York, I go back to the hotel and pretend to tuck in for the evening. Then I text producer Ryan Smith. "Are you in town? Wanna meet up?" Ryan knows all the best places in the city, and he directs me to a multistory bar near my hotel. It's 10 PM on a Monday, and there's plenty of space to sit and chat.

Considering everything I've been through with Ryan at CBS, I trust him not to blow my cover. Ryan was my ticket into *48*, and it's only fitting that he's the first person I tell I am leaving. I take a sip of my drink and reveal that I'm planning to quit and pursue independent projects. He's shocked but supportive, and I dive into the short version of why I'm joining the Great Resignation. I tell him about my dreams for *The Lie Detector* and my podcast, and he listens intently. But I'm still holding something back.

Not only do I have my podcast and the original series with Holland, but I also have this crazy idea to write a book about true crime television. It's something I've been kicking around in my head for a while, but I've never actually said it out loud before. And I won't cross that bridge tonight.

"You're really going to quit, aren't you?" Ryan says to me.

"I think I really am," I reply with a nervous laugh, because I still can't fully believe it myself.

My whirlwind week in New York with Ranger Holland is underway. First, we meet with Z and her team at See It Now to discuss the path forward for *The Lie Detector*. Before we could do anything else, they'd have to draw up a contract with Holland. I bite my lip and hope no one is as good at reading me as the ranger. I'm betting they don't realize that I've barely said a word this whole meeting, and that's highly unusual for me. They don't know that I'm planning to join Holland's side of the table for negotiations.

In my experience with CBS, I know they will cut me out of the process if they can. But if I change teams, they won't have that power anymore. I'll be aligning with Holland, a retired cop and shrewd interrogator. Out of the frying pan into the fire. But from what I've seen of Holland, he's a man of his word, and he gets results. On the other hand, I'm pretty sure he's carried out his own investigation of me on the sly, and he gets a big kick out of making me do push-ups. Gotta take the good with the bad.

We finish the meeting with Z without divulging anything about our intentions, and I breathe a big sigh of relief. Our next stop is *48 Hours*, and I pretend to be disappointed when Kramer tells me she's not coming into the office today.

Judy Tygard greets us warmly and gives Holland the nickel tour. He's turning heads all over the building and loving the attention. After we make the rounds, we return to Judy's corner office and take a seat on the couch. We talk about the Jennifer Faith episode and all the twists and turns of the wild case. Then the conversation turns to *The Lie Detector* and what that means for my future at *48*.

"I don't want to hold you back," Judy tells me, and I believe her. "I want you to be able to follow your dreams."

She seems genuinely happy for me, and in that moment, it pains me that the only way forward I can see is to quit. As we go to leave, I give Judy a hug and hold on a beat longer than I normally would. Then I walk out of the building and wonder if I'll need a visitor's pass the next time I come to town.

Even though we're in New York, our screening for "The Plot to Kill Jamie Faith" is still a virtual one. The pandemic workflow showed how much was possible remotely, and the return to the office is piecemeal at best. I log into Zoom in the hotel lobby and pull up an extra chair for Holland.

We watch each act and pause to discuss any outstanding concerns. I usually pick up on little things and weigh in on the conversation, but I'm too distracted this time around to contribute.

My stomach twists as I do the obligatory Zoom wave and sign off the call.

It's April 2022, and I've been invited to speak to business journalism students at my alma mater, Baylor University. I'm one of those weird people who actually enjoys public speaking, so it's usually a delight for me to do these talks to students. But this year was different. My career was in total flux, and I wasn't sure what my path forward as a journalist looked like anymore.

I laughed out loud at the thought of delivering advice when I was walking away from a six-figure salary.

"If you work really hard, kids, one day you, too, can quit your job in network television!"

Writing has always been a refuge for me, a way to work out my inner conflict and see my way through real-world problems. As crazy as everything was in my professional life, I recognized these were great problems to have. I had created a concept for an original true crime show that a media giant like Paramount wanted to make, and my biggest concern was them stealing it from me. I had a popular true crime podcast, a unique idea for a memoir, and the media contacts to make it all happen. Plenty of producers would kill for problems like that. And as Susan Zirinsky is fond of saying, "A crisis is a terrible thing to waste."

Late one night, after tossing and turning for hours, I crawl out of bed and tiptoe down the stairs into my office. I fire up the computer, crack my knuckles, and write this speech to the next generation of journalists—and to myself:

My best career advice can be distilled down to two basic journalistic principles: follow the story and own the story.

With the exception of my very first job in journalism, I have never job hunted. But I've story hunted every day of my life. And I've often found inventive ways to own a piece of my stories.

For tax purposes, I've been working full time as a journalist for twelve years, but my true journalistic journey dates back to grade school, when I started a neighborhood paper called *Kid's News* with a friend down the street. Side note: we both ended up working at the *Baylor Lariat*.

I've always loved getting hooked on a good story. And every turn of my career has been story driven. Because when I find a really good story, I follow it wherever it takes me. And while the journey can get long, it has never been a fool's errand. The adventure I find along the way, and the twists and turns the narrative takes, keeps me coming back for more.

Allow me to let you in on a little secret: if you build a career story by story, the jobs will find you. And you might even create your own opportunities if you keep an entrepreneurial eye open.

Because I have always been a story-first journalist, it took me a while to realize journalism is in fact a business. And a very profitable one for many people. But the people who profit the most off of journalism are not usually the ones creating it— they are the people running media companies.

The way most employment contracts are written, once you are hired by a media company, or signed by a label or studio, they own your stories. Forever. You get paid once, and they get paid "in perpetuity, throughout the universe."

And if you're good at what you do, you will make lots of money for these companies, for many years, in many different forms, by telling great stories. But you will never see that money. In many cases, you might not even realize all the places your story has been resold, repackaged, and redistributed for someone else's profit.

In the eight years that I have worked for *48 Hours*, I've made over twenty episodes for them, and I own zero percent of that revenue. They pay me once, and they make money every single time it airs. Including the reruns that they've sold to cable networks: Discovery ID and OWN, the Oprah Winfrey Network.

Because she is one smart cookie. And someone who once had a show on CBS, though she definitely didn't own that one. I can promise you the name of Oprah's network is more than just an acronym.

This probably sounds depressing, but I want you to see it as inspiring. Your stories have incredible value, and knowing your value will allow you to stand up for yourself and get to a place where you have a seat at the table—and a piece of the pie.

Everybody has heard of "the artist formerly known as Prince." And if you're like me, you probably never realized that was a reference to his contract.

Dave Chappelle talks about this in his 2020 Netflix special. Prince didn't even own most of his songs because of the way his contract was written in the early days of his career. It was so hurtful that he didn't even want to be called by his own name anymore.

And Chappelle understood this, because he didn't own his own show. *Chappelle's Show* was actually owned by Viacom, who licensed it to Comedy Central.

Decades after it was over, they resold it to Netflix and were making money hand over fist off of the genius of Dave Chappelle. It took Dave getting his own Netflix special to be able to even address it.

You don't have to be Dave Chappelle or Prince or Oprah to deserve to own your story. You just have to recognize your value and learn how to negotiate your rights.

I recently told CBS that I was taking a step back from *48 Hours*, and I'm still figuring out what exactly that will look like going forward.

My most recent *48 Hours* episode aired this weekend and was called "The Plot to Kill Jamie Faith." It was an extremely unusual case, not lacking in any story value. But what I am most interested in these days are projects where I can not only tell great stories but have actual ownership.

The fact is: *48 Hours* is never going to cut in its producers and talent on the revenue stream of the show. Why would they? CBS News created the show, which is designed to make money for its parent companies, including Viacom and Paramount.

But I started to wonder if I really wanted to spend the majority of my time creating content for other people to make passive income off of in perpetuity throughout the universe. Which I think is a valid question that all content creators should consider. And journalists definitely fit into that category.

The idea that I want to leave you with today is that no matter what else is going on and what opposition you face, nothing is more important than following the story.

So many people and institutions will try to sidetrack you on your reporting journey. You have to choose to follow the story at every single turn.

Finding a home for your story is a great problem to have. Because there are endless outlets for excellent journalism. What is in short supply are great stories.

My hope for you is that you find your own stories and follow them wherever they take you.

It's been two weeks since I gave that speech, and now I'm fidgeting nervously in my home office chair at 8 AM. I'm finally ready for my own reckoning.

Any second now Judy Tygard will call me, and I'm going to deliver the news: I'm quitting. Even though I know I'm making the right decision, going through with it is really hard. I have been practically daring *48 Hours* to fire me for the past six months, but no matter how insubordinate I am, they won't take the bait. I'm going to have to do the deed myself.

Judy's name pops up on my phone, and I pick up immediately. I tell her that I've made the decision to leave *48 Hours* to pursue independent projects. "I'm stunned," Judy says. It's not every day that producers walk away from network television. But as crazy as it sounds, I know it's the right thing to do for my own sanity.

In a surprise twist, Judy pivots to full support. She points out that multiple senior staffers at *48* have left at one time or another before finding their way back into the fold.

"There will be lots of times you'll say to yourself, 'What have I done?' But trust that you've made the right decision; go do what you need to do," Judy says.

Although I'm leaving *48*, my role in developing *The Lie Detector* with Z's studio means CBS hasn't quite seen the last of me yet. "I'll be rooting for you," Judy tells me.

I hang up the call and put my hands behind my head. My new life of crime is about to begin.

ACKNOWLEDGMENTS

It is a privilege to tell stories for a living, and I'm still pinching myself that I get to do it. I don't think anyone in their right mind sets out to pen a memoir in their thirties. But life takes turns you never expect, and I'm along for the ride.

So many people have helped me on this journey to write my first book. I wish I could mention you all.

Riley, none of this would be possible without you believing in me and sacrificing for my dreams. Choosing to spend my life with you is the best decision I have ever made. I am so grateful to have you by my side. Your many, varied talents never cease to amaze me. Thank you for being my uncommonly wonderful husband and a one-of-a-kind dad to our son. We'd be lost without you.

Amber Robinson, my sister and OG BFF. Thank you for being my very first manuscript reader (and podcast listener). You always give thoughtful feedback and heaps of praise, and I cannot thank you enough for all the ways you light up my life. I love you.

Susan Passoni, my writing partner, sister from another mister, and the other half of my brain. How did I ever write without you? True crime podcasts brought us together, and we've been dreaming and scheming of new projects ever since. I can't wait to see what we'll do next.

Carrie Pestritto, agent extraordinaire. Thank you for taking a chance on a first-time author and for plucking my cold query out of the pile. Your enthusiasm for my writing buoys my spirit and inspires me to keep going.

You believed in *Killer Story* before anyone else in the industry, and I'll never forget it.

To everyone at BenBella Books, I am so grateful that you helped me shape and present my memoir to the world. Glenn Yeffeth, thank you for recognizing my vision for *Killer Story* and for jumping on a call with me right away. I respect people who know what they want and go for it. Rick Chillot, you made me feel like I hit the editor lottery! Your notes were so thoughtful and measured, and I always looked forward to hearing from you. High praise in my world. Sarah Avinger and the design team, thank you for a killer cover. You really know how to get a girl's attention. Jennifer Canzoneri and the marketing team, thank you for launching *Killer Story* into the world with a bang.

My parents, who loved me from the start. Thank you for letting me chase my dreams and get lost in a good story. You never put limits on what I believed I could achieve, even when I said I wanted to be a professional basketball player as a child. I love you for humoring me, among many other things.

Lindsey Moorhead, the best attorney in the world. I can't remember a time when I didn't know you. What a gift your friendship has been. I like you so much I might even learn to play golf.

My Tuesday Night Prayer Ninjas, thank you for always being there for me. I am so grateful to know all of you and be part of each other's lives.

The entire Baylor Journalism Department, especially Elizabeth Bates, Cassy Burleson, Sommer Dean, Bruce Gietzen, Mia Moody-Ramirez, Brad Owens, Julie Reed, and Kevin Tankersley. Your friendship and support have been off the charts. Sic 'em forever.

Janice Su and Alise Weber, original gnomes. I could write an entirely different book about our adventures during my time at CBS, but some things are best kept secret. Thank you for always laughing through life with me.

Jim Holland, this book wouldn't exist without you. Thank you for everything.

ABOUT THE AUTHOR

Investigative journalist Claire St. Amant developed and produced crime stories for CBS News for nearly a decade. She is credited on over twenty episodes of *48 Hours*, including murder-for-hire stings, cold case kidnappings, and an assassination attempt. In 2019, St. Amant began contributing to *60 Minutes* with "The Ranger and the Serial Killer."

Photo credit: Norton Fulbum

She built her unconventional career one story at a time, rising up through local media to national television and her own network podcast, *Final Days on Earth with Claire St. Amant*. A returned Peace Corps Volunteer with eclectic tastes, she is always on the hunt for her next adventure.

Follow her online for a link to the companion playlist for *Killer Story* on Apple Music, Spotify, or Amazon Music.

www.clairestamant.com

X: @clairestamant

Instagram: @clairesta

Facebook.com/journalistclairestamant